D1083029

SOCIAL EXCHANGE THEORY

The Two Traditions

SOCIAL
EXCHANGE THEORY
The Two Traditions

PETER P. EKEH

Harvard University Press
Cambridge, Massachusetts
1974

HM
24
.E37

To the Memory of
My
PARENTS

Contents

Preface

For a considerable part of the fifties and the sixties George Caspar Homans was embroiled in a controversy with the French social scientist, Claude Lévi-Strauss. One of the earliest reactions to Lévi-Strauss' *Les Structures élémentaire de la Parenté* was Homans and Schneider's sixty-four-page book, *Marriage, Authority, and Final Causes: A Study in Unilateral Cross-Cousin Marriage*. Many of the ideas in this small but important book have been repeated by Homans in his attacks on functionalism in several writings. The substance of the disagreement between Homans and Lévi-Strauss, with more pointed reference to social exchange theory, will be considered later in this book. However, the nature of the controversy illustrates the intellectual concern of this work. In spite of numerous attempts to clarify the issue[1] neither Lévi-Strauss nor Homans yielded any grounds and each of them claimed victory.[2] When reasonable men, especially men who have made deep impressions on their separate professions, disagree so profoundly, it is sometimes wise to quit asking the question, who is right and who is wrong? Rather it may be fruitful to ask: why do they take the positions they take? That question provides the intellectual context for this book.

Its central thesis is that two distinct traditions in sociology underlie two separate types of theories of social exchange. On the one hand the French 'collectivistic orientation' in sociology informs Lévi-Strauss' social exchange theory; on the other hand, the British 'individualistic orientation' in sociology has shaped the outlines of Homans' exchange theory. For accidental reasons, in part perpetuated by professional and conceptual boundaries

---

[1] See especially Needham [1962], Lane [1961], and Bertling and Philipsen [1960].
[2] See Lévi-Strauss [1963: 317–318; 1969: xxxiii–xxxiv] and Homans [1962: 250–256].

between sociology and anthropology, Homans' exchange theory and its off-shoots are better known to sociologists than Lévi-Strauss' exchange theory. Part of the concern of this work is to promote Lévi-Strauss' exchange theory, or at least a sociological restatement and reformulation of it, in the sociological profession.

Homans' exchange theory is closely, though negatively, related to Lévi-Strauss' exchange theory. I argue that Homans formulated his exchange theory in reaction to Lévi-Strauss' 'collectivistic' theory of social exchange. In *Marriage, Authority, and Final Causes*, Homans' response to Lévi-Strauss' exchange theory is on the whole muted, but he gave enough information in that work to indicate that Lévi-Strauss' key innovation in exchange theory, namely, the concept of *generalized exchange*, is unacceptable to him. Homans' subsequent limitation of exchange behaviors to 'face-to-face' relationships is all the more impressive because it deliberately defied Lévi-Strauss' concept of *generalized exchange* which deals with exchanges mediated by others, in the form of indirect reciprocities.

Even though Lévi-Strauss and Homans are the most important modern theorists of exchange behavior, the contributions of earlier sociologists and anthropologists in this area are significant for a number of reasons. The development of social exchange theory has largely been in the context of a polemical interplay between the British individualistic orientation and the French collectivistic orientation in theory construction. Sir James George Frazer's conception of social exchange provided the polemical context for Lévi-Strauss' work. Moreover, Frazer's strategy in exchange theory, once shorn of its anthropological terminology, closely foreshadows Blau's exchange theory. Two other early scholars in this area are Malinowski and Mauss. Although Malinowski's work is generally cited in sociological discussions, the significance of his analysis of Kula exchange has not been brought into the mainstream of sociological theory. I attempt to do that in this book. Lastly, I argue that the main significance of Marcel Mauss' brief contribution to social exchange theory is his argument that social exchange behaviors and institutions yield for the wider society a morality and a religious spirit that inform and influence all aspects of life. In modern Mertonian functional analysis, one would say that Mauss pointed out the unintended consequences of social exchange behavior for the wider society in promoting a moral code of behavior.

The main characteristic and, I believe, the main weakness, of Homans' exchange theory is the fusion of elementary economics and behavioral psychology. This fusion, by no means successful, accounts for a number of disjunctions in *Social Behavior: Its Elementary Forms*, in which Homans offered his social exchange theory. This is particularly true of the disjunctions, which I attempt to unravel in Chapters Five and Six, between the first four propositions and the distributive justice principle and between the formal exchange propositions and the empirical data invoked to validate the theory. The further development of Homans' exchange theory has followed the two branches of his theory. On the one hand, Blau has sought to develop the theory along its economic lines, with little or no emphasis on its psychological assumptions. On the other hand, Emmerson has spearheaded the move to develop Homans' theory along its Skinnerian psychological lines. This break-up of the theory is a natural consequence, I believe, of the incompatible assumptions in Homans' fusion of elementary economics and behavioral psychology.

*   *   *

I owe so much to so many that I cannot possibly do justice to all here. But a few must be mentioned. My undergraduate studies at the University of Ibadan featured heavily in anthropology and economics, both of which have been of some advantage to me in dealing with social exchange theory. I owe my literacy in anthropology to two remarkable teachers, Dr. Raymond Apthorpe and Dr. Peter C. Lloyd. Professor Ulf Himmelstrand, now of Uppsala University, Sweden, and Professor Joseph Black, now of the Rockefeller Foundation, were instrumental in my choice of sociology for a career. Both of them have continued to benefit me by their encouragement and advice. At Stanford University, Professor Sidney Verba's friendship was of immense benefit in my very first year outside the familiarity of my country.

My experiences at the University of California, Berkeley, deserve special mention because they have decisively shaped my commitments to sociology. In working with them I have gained immensely from my teachers at Berkeley: John A. Clausen,

Wolfram Eberhard, William Kornhauser, Leo Lowenthal, Philip Selznick, and Neil J. Smelser. By leading me through the pathways of their own distinctive styles of thinking, they all have shown me that conventional sociologists hardly ever break new grounds in our discipline. Although the work that led to this book is unrelated to my doctoral dissertation on the sociological study of dreams, Professor Selznick's early interest in my ideas in social exchange theory must be counted as one of the greater benefits I derived from Berkeley. I gained a great deal from that informal fellowship among graduate students that has become an established tradition in Berkeley sociology. The earliest discussions of my ideas in social exchange theory were held in the intimacy of my 'Mock Orals Group'. I want to thank the other members of that fine team: Ayad Al-Qazzaz, Ruth Dixon, Dain Oliver, and James Wood.

I wrote this book in the last two of my three years as a faculty member of the Department of Sociology, University of California, Riverside. Several colleagues were most helpful. In particular, I wish to thank Edgar W. Butler for being so responsive to a variety of requests—not all of them confined to academics. Jonathan H. Turner was the first sociologist to read the first version of this book and his comments were of great help. Noonhour discussions with Sheldon Bockman, John Freeman, Tomas Martinez, John Long, and Charles Starnes were always stimulating in leading to new ideas. Finally at Riverside, I owe a lot to the many undergraduate and graduate students who participated in my courses and seminars on Sociological Theory. Many of the ideas discussed here were first presented to them and their reactions helped me in many ways to clarify my arguments.

Early personal encouragement about the importance of my venture in the comparative study of social exchange theories came from Hugh Cline, President of the Russell Sage Foundation. Of the rather large number of social scientists who reviewed versions of this book in manuscript, Professor Ralph H. Turner's comments were by far the most comprehensive and most provocative of new ideas. Other comments, helpful in various ways, came from Dr. Christopher Badcock, Polytechnic of the South Bank; Professor William E. Henry, University of Chicago; and Professor Robert A. Nisbet, University of Arizona.

As for institutions, I wish to thank the Rockefeller Foundation for supporting my graduate studies at Stanford University and at the University of California, Berkeley. Two University of California, Riverside, Intramural Research Grants for 1971–72 and 1972–73 partially provided the funds paid for typing various versions of this book.

My sojourn in America has been so worthwhile only because my wife was always ready to help with our common problems. This book owes much to Helen's endurance.

Finally, it is with pleasure that I thank Mrs. Clara Dean of Riverside, California, for her remarkable typing and her unfailing sense of humor. Needless to add, neither she nor any other person mentioned herein is responsible for errors of argument or indelicacies of expression in this book. These I will accept.

PETER P. EKEH

Acknowledgements

The author and publishers are grateful to the following for permission to reproduce extracts from the copyright material listed below.

Routledge & Kegan Paul Ltd., and Macmillan Publishing Co., Inc., for George C. Homans *Sentiments and Activities*. Routledge & Kegan Paul Ltd., and Harcourt Brace Jovanovich, for George C. Homans *Social Behavior: Its Elementary Forms*. Macmillan Publishing Co., Inc., for George C. Homans and David M. Schneider *Marriage, Authority and Final Causes*. The Estate of Sir James Frazer for Sir James Frazer *Folklore in the Old Testament*. Routledge & Kegan Paul Ltd., and E. P. Dutton & Co., Inc., for Bronislaw Malinowski *Argonauts of the Western Pacific*. The Berkeley Journal of Sociology for Peter P. Ekeh 'Issues in Social Exchange Theory', *Berkeley Journal of Sociology* Vol 13 (1968). Routledge & Kegan Paul Ltd., and Humanities Press Inc., for Werner Stark *The Sociology of Knowledge: An Essay in Aid of a Deeper Understanding of the History of Ideas*. Sage Publications Inc., for Ralph H. Turner 'Types of Solidarity in the Reconstituting of Groups', *Pacific Sociological Review* Volume 10, No. 2. Hutchinson & Co., Ltd., and Macmillan Publishing Co., Inc., for Arthur Koestler and J. R. Smythies *Beyond Reductionism*. Eyre & Spottiswoode Ltd., and Beacon Press for Claude Lévi-Strauss *Elementary Structures of Kinship*. Heinemann Educational Books Ltd., and Basic Books Inc., for Alvin Gouldner *The Coming Crisis of Western Sociology*. Basic Books Inc., for Jean Piaget *Structuralism*. John Wiley & Sons Inc., for P. M. Blau *Social Exchange and Power in Social Life*. Macmillan Publishing Co., Inc., for P. M. Blau 'Interaction: Social Exchange', *International Encyclopedia of the Social Sciences*, Vol. 7. Prentice Hall Inc., for J. F. Scott *Internalization of Norms*.

Part One

INTELLECTUAL BACKGROUNDS

I
The Two Sociological Traditions

In *The Sociological Tradition*, Robert A. Nisbet [1966] has argued that sociology matured and flowered in the nineteenth century as a conservative reaction to liberal individualism in Europe. 'The fundamental ideas of European sociology,' Nisbet [1966: 21] maintains, 'are best understood as responses to the problem of order created at the beginning of the nineteenth century by the collapse of the old regime under the blows of individualism and revolutionary democracy.' The radicalizing changes instigated by the Industrial Revolution and the French Revolution provided the conservative cast, by way of reaction, for modern sociology. Both Revolutions led to convulsive individualization, the abstraction of individual actors from their concrete traditional bases, and the generalization of individual ties beyond the immediate context of family and community to more idealistic commitments such as socialism and democracy [Nisbet, 1966: 42–44]. Sociology as a discipline emerged at an intellectual level to restore a semblance of order in a chaotic world.

It may be true, as Nisbet has argued, that the two Revolutions have imparted a broad conservative tradition to sociology—an intellectual tradition of thought that might have been less conservative if the two traditions did not take place at the times they did and in the nations in which they occurred. But within the emergent sociological tradition there are significant shades in areas of emphasis. The technological ideals of the Industrial Revolution did spread beyond its home base in the British Isles and the democratic ideals of the French Revolution had appeals all over Europe and even beyond. But each of these Revolutions, and the reactions it instigated, left behind in its home base some

3

characteristic cultural residues. As Veblen [1954: 85–86] said of the spread of the Industrial Revolution to Germany,

> the German people have been enabled to take up the technological heritage of the English without having paid for it in the habits of thought, the use and wont, included in the English community in achieving it. Modern technology has come to Germany ready-made, without the cultural consequences which its gradual development and continued use has entailed upon the people whose experiences initiated it and determined the course of its development.

Similar results are true of the acceptance of the ideals of the French Revolution outside France. The ideals may have spread, but their precipitating causes have a unique character of thought and behavior for French intellectual life.

These cultural residues are by no means identical in their intellectual consequences. After all, the intellectual reactions that Nisbet emphasizes are not against the same type of disorder. 'There are, to be sure,' Nisbet [1966: 10] concedes, 'striking differences between the liberals of Manchester, for whom freedom meant chiefly the release of economic productivity from the fetters of law and custom, and the liberals of Paris in 1830, for whom liberation of thought from clericalism loomed up as the major objective.' The intellectual reactions to the disorders created by the two Revolutions did not lead to a monolithic sociological tradition, but to two different traditions of sociological imagination.[1] There exists the possibility also that the reactions consolidated, rather than simply originated, modes of thought that had been characteristic of the two nations and that might have surfaced at any rate even if the Revolutions had taken other forms of expression and had produced more orderly consequences.

---

[1] Both Morris Janowitz and Talcott Parsons see Nisbet's *The Sociological Tradition* as representing one, and neglecting the other, tradition in sociology. Thus Janowitz [1967: 638] notes: 'There is little concern with national differences . . . The book is really about a small group of classical French and German thinkers . . . Sociology has been built not only by the contributions of the "collectivist", but also by the efforts of the "individualist", who is concerned with the contribution of self-interest to social morality.' And thus Parsons [1967: 642]: 'I would criticize Nisbet's relative neglect of the positive importance of English utilitarianism and the ways it was connected with economics, with biological thought and the beginnings of anthropology as a discipline.'

Individualistic and Collectivistic Traditions in Sociology

These two traditions around British and French intellectual frames of reference are what Talcott Parsons has labelled the 'individualistic' and the 'collectivistic' orientations in sociology:

> The considerably fuller flow of what could now be termed secular general social thought did not begin until the seventeenth century. When it had become established, sociologically the most relevant polarization there was was that between 'individualistic' and 'collectivistic' references [Parsons, 1961b: 86].

Moreover, Parsons [1961b: 86] sees their genesis in separate religious traditions: the British 'individualistic' orientation in Protestantism and the French 'collectivistic' orientation as a legacy of 'the Catholic viewpoint, which sees a collectively organized church, and the other collectivities of a society infused with the collective Christian spirit, interposed between the essential individual and the system of interactive rights and obligations in which he is involved'. Parsons [1961b: 87] believes that 'Modern sociological theory may be described as a result of a special "marriage" between the individualistic and the collectivistic strands'.

Such 'marriages' may have taken place in certain areas of sociological theory and they may have seemed to be stable over a period of time. But as the attacks on Parsons' own work by such theorists as Homans [e.g., 1964a, 1969] and Gouldner [1970] have shown, it is not always a happy marriage. Indeed at many times the 'marriages' face dissolutions and the partners go their separate ways. In many other subfields of sociological theory no marriages were ever contemplated. Such is the case with social exchange theory, the main concern of this book. Two distinct traditions of social exchange theory, the 'collectivistic' one by Lévi-Strauss [1949, 1969] and the 'individualistic' one by Homans [1958, 1961, 1967a], exist in non-marriagable terms—only joined by the virulence of the polemics against each other's tradition of thought. In analyzing them one comes to see sociology in its two separate traditions in their purities.

These two traditions, it must be stressed, are not exhaustive of the scope of sociological theory. As a matter of fact Talcott Parsons [1961b, 1967, 1968] has recognized in the 'collectivistic' orientation in sociology a subset of German idealism. What is of significance in the distinction between the British individualistic and the French collectivistic traditions does not lie in their separate existences, but rather in the polemical relationship between the two. The growth of modern sociological theory was largely a result of the polemical interplay between these two traditions. The much recognized German idealism in sociology developed in relative isolation from other traditions of sociological imagination; not so the French and the British traditions. Rarely has any major French sociologist formulated a theory without opposing it to a British individualistic tradition of thought. Similarly, most individualistically oriented sociologists, beginning with Spencer and including their modern day descendants in America, have formulated their theories as pointed contra-conceptions of the collectivistic tradition. This polemical interplay between the two traditions is most apparent in the development of social exchange theory. Lévi-Strauss' [1949] collectivistic social exchange theory was developed in pointed reaction to Frazer's (1919) individualistic exchange theory of cross-cousin marriage. And Homans' [1958, 1961, 1967a] exchange theory was preceded, if not provoked, by Homans and Schneider's [1955] rejection of Lévi-Strauss' social exchange theory on the grounds of its collectivistic assumptions.

Many sociologists may doubt that British social thought, at least as reflected in sociology, can be so completely differentiated from French collectivistic sociology in view of the fact that Radcliffe-Brown, a British social anthropologist, perfected for many English-reading sociologists and anthropologists Durkheim's collectivism. It is here indeed that one comes to a paradox in British intellectual life. As Gouldner [1970: 125] has noted, Durkheimian 'Functionalism has been incorporated primarily in English anthropology rather than sociology'. In effect, the British have had two sociologies: one was based on individualistic social thought and was presumed to be operative in Britain. The other was predicated on Durkheimian collectivistic sociology and was assumed to apply to colonized peoples—outside Britain. The two sociologies never crossed in their paths—a fact that partly accounts for the poverty of British sociology. The massive influence of British social anthropology in British colonization in Africa left Britain itself untouched. The most urgent need for colonial administrators concerned the mechanisms for controlling the colonized.[1] From an intellectual point of view, nothing could be handier in achieving social control than through the instrument of Durkheimian functionalism. And yet, the 'metropolitan' values, the predominant emphasis on utilitarian values in Britain, remained intact on the understanding that 'primitive' colonized peoples were different from the English.

Furthermore, it ought to be pointed out that in seeking to adapt Durkheim's collectivistic sociology to British intellectual pursuits, Radcliffe-Brown unwittingly changed a great deal of what was unique to the French tradition from which Durkheim's sociology emerged. In talking about society as reality *sui generis*, Durkheim did not limit himself to facts that are only amenable to sensory observation. Society was for Durkheim something of a theoretical construct, in much the same way as the superego is a theoretical construct for Freudian psychology. As such its validity was to be determined by the results it helps the sociologist to achieve in research. But in interpreting, or at least in adapting, Durkheim's work to Anglo-Saxon scholarship, Radcliffe-Brown [1940] insisted that 'In the study of social structure the concrete reality with which we are concerned is the set of actually existing relations, at a given moment of time, which link together certain human beings' [p. 192], and that 'We cannot study persons except in terms of social structure, nor can we study social structure except in terms of the persons who are the units of which it is composed' [pp. 193–194]. Radcliffe-Brown's main criterion for differentiating 'social structure' from 'culture' is that

> We do not observe 'culture', since that word denotes, not any concrete reality, but an abstraction, and as it is commonly used a vague abstraction. But direct observation does reveal to us that these human beings are connected by a complex network of social relations. I use the term 'social structure' to denote this network of actually existing relations [Radcliffe-Brown, 1940: 190].

Although Durkheim's original meaning of society, for which

---

[1] British social anthropologists were most active in areas of the colonized nations in which social organization and hence the means of social control were weakest. This can be seen in the greater emphasis on 'stateless' societies—on the Tiv, the Tallensi, the Nuer, the Ibo—than on well organized polities.

term Radcliffe-Brown uses 'social structure', includes the factual emphasis on content, the French sociologist's meaning of the term is more of an abstraction of the order of culture than of Radcliffe-Brown's 'social structure'. One must conclude for Radcliffe-Brown that he sees society as being no more than the sum of the individuals who compose it. As such his concern may be said to be more with societies as 'aggregates' than societies as 'structures'. As Piaget [1968: 6–7] has argued, it is important to understand

> [the] fundamental contrast between *structures* and *aggregates*, the former being wholes, the latter composites formed of elements that are independent of the complexes into which they enter. To insist on this distinction is not to deny that structures have elements, but the elements of a structure are subordinated to laws, and it is in terms of these laws that the structure *qua* whole or system is defined. Moreover, the laws governing a structure's composition are not reducible to cumulative one-by-one associa-tion of its elements [as in the case of an aggregate]: they confer on the whole as such over-all properties distinct from the properties of its elements.

This meaning of structure, to which Durkheim's use of society belongs, is a far cry from Radcliffe-Brown's [1940] insistence that 'Social structures are just as real as are individual organisms' [p. 190] in such a way as to enable us to make 'direct observations' on them [p. 192]. It is only in the historical light of being the first social scientist to sensitize British intellectuals to Durkheim's sociology and only in terms relative to the individualistic tradition of British sociology, can we claim that Radcliffe-Brown was Durkheimian. There is a great deal of justice in Lévi-Strauss' [e.g., 1966: 52] objection to Radcliffe-Brown's use of social structure as being too factual in representation if indeed the latter was, as is usually the case, understood to translate the collectivistic features of Durkheim's sociology into British social science.[1]

---

[1] On this point concerning fundamental changes in Radcliffe-Brown's inter-pretation of the meaning of Durkheim's assumptions in sociology see Chapter Four. Also cf. Gardner [1973: 36–37]: 'seeking to fuse the strengths of the Anglo-Saxon and Gallic traditions was Alfred Reginald Radcliffe-Brown, a distinguished British anthropologist who sponsored and conducted field work while also promoting Durkheimian views of society and social phenomena. Almost alone in his generation, Radcliffe-Brown did not hesitate to view society as a biological organism and to deal with such relatively abstract notions as social structure and social relations.

To point to another area of difference, the relationship between British sociology and British social anthropologists' interests in non-Western societies is different from that in France. Durkheim, Mauss, Lévi-Strauss, etc., studied 'primitive' cultures in order to shed light on the working of complex civilizations. On the other hand, Radcliffe-Brown and even Malinowski, and their students who now dominate social anthropology in Britain, studied 'primitive' cultures as a type apart. Sometimes British social anthropologists have bent over backwards to emphasize that different mental principles govern 'advanced' cultures and 'primitive' cultures. In this connection it is noteworthy that evolutionary thinking—the drawing of a direct line of progress linking 'primitive' and 'advanced' cultures—has persisted longer in French sociologists than in British sociologists or social anthropologists. For Durkheim, Mauss, or Lévi-Strauss, the collectivistic attributes in non-Western cultures were elementary forms of their more complex representations in advanced Western societies. For the British the collectivistic characteristics they attributed to non-Western cultures were totally inapplicable to their island civilization.

American Sociology as Individualistic Sociology

How is this distinction between individualistic and collectivistic trends in social thought related to the dominant mode of sociological imagination in the U.S., the home of modern sociology? If one can characterize the relatively monolithic sociological climates in France and Britain, is it not hazardous to seek to identify the tremendous output of sociology in the U.S. with one but not the other of these two traditions?

He construed society as a system of interdependent parts, searched for analogous structures among diverse groups, and attempted to make those general comparisons which would illuminate the nature of social institutions. Unwilling (or unable), however, to divorce himself entirely from the British empiricist tradition, Radcliffe-Brown looked for revelations of social structure and relations in the overt daily interactions among individuals. He thought of society as the mere sum of individual social relations at a given moment, structure as "this network of actually existing relations". This view was sharply criticized by the Durkheimians, who, anticipating a fundamental tenet of structuralism, preferred to posit a model remote from surface phenomena, one which captured the underlying reality, of which the naïve observer or participant might be unaware.'

There is clearly a greater variety to American sociology than to the character of sociology in any other nation. And yet, the predominant mould of American sociology is individualistic. There are sociologists in the U.S., mostly trained in European universities, who defy classification. Nevertheless, there is a notable strain toward an individualistic mode of sociological imagination: collectivistic models in U.S. sociology tend to be unstable. Even when adopted, they are usually changed in the direction of individualistic models. At least, American sociology is still more compatible with traditional English assumptions concerning the relationship between the individual and society than it is with the French assumption on this relationship. That is the import of the perceptive view of a modern French sociologist: 'it seems that very often, in the United States, the emphasis given from the start to the idea that society is a body of individuals and that it has no existence of its own contrasts to a certain extent with the French conception that first considers society taken as a whole' [Lauwe, 1966: 248].[1]

---

[1] Professor Ralph H. Turner commented on my characterization of American sociology as individualistic as follows: 'That U.S. sociology has been more individualistic, which is in the British tradition, is agreed. But this summary seems to over-simplify both the opposing currents in American sociology and the other foreign streams in our tradition. First, in the U.S., it seems important to note the University of Chicago as the historical fountainhead of authoritative sociology, and the particular European currents to which Small, Park, Thomas, Wirth, and other key theorists exposed themselves. These influences were more German than either French or English. I have the impression that sociologists who emphasized social psychology (Ross, Faris, etc.) were the ones that looked principally to France, and secondarily to England (Herd Psychology, etc.). But in looking to France they found the lines drawn in the choice between two French scholars, Tarde (individualist) and Durkheim (collectivist). Fay Karpf [1932] in her book, *American Social Psychology: Its Origins, Development, and European Backgrounds*, presents this as the major controversy. But for the more structural sociologists, the German lines of influence seem more crucial. With Chicago as the center, dissident centers also grew up around key figures. Long before Parsons was heard from, Sorokin was a challenger of Chicago hegemony: I suppose he represented a more collectivist orientation in opposition to Chicago individualism. Even earlier, Lester Ward's biological models certainly lacked the simple individualistic assumptions of a Tardean such as E. A. Ross.

'The simple opposition between individualism and collectivism also seems not to do justice to what was a major preoccupation of a key body of intellectuals, whether within sociology or widely read by sociologists. This was the reconciliation of maximum individualism with the irreducible minimum of consensus and control. John Dewey, Walter Lippman, Robert Park, and Louis Wirth were among the key people here, and George Mead's philosophy was of so much current interest in part because it seemed to effect one sort of synthesis.'

Doubts may arise in the minds of many sociologists largely because influential sociologists like Parsons and Blau have not only been characterized by others as 'collectivistic' or 'Durkheimian' sociologists, but have in fact sometimes seen themselves in such terms. We shall have time to see later how individualistic Blau's social exchange theory is. But what about Parsons? He has indeed dissociated himself from 'individualistic social theory':

> Social systems are those constituted by states and processes of social interaction among acting units. If the properties of interaction were derivable from properties of the acting units, social systems would be epiphenomenal, as much 'individualistic' social theory has contended. Our position is sharply in disagreement: it derives particularly from Durkheim's statement that society—and other social systems—is a 'reality *sui generis*' [Parsons, 1971: 7].

It is all the more remarkable then that Gouldner has detected in Parsons' sociology a transformation of Durkheim's functionalism in the direction of individualism. In spite of the apparently collectivistic and conservative appearance of Parsons' *The Structure of Social Action*, written amidst the crisis of the Great Depression, it nevertheless represents

> a very American form of conservatism, which tempers loyalty to established institutions with individualism. If its responses to the vast crisis seems insufficient because it still stresses individual effort rather than collective solutions, and if it neglects the *needs* of individuals, nonetheless it also retains a sensitivity to their potency. Conservative though it was in comparison with the changes upon which the nation was then irretrievably launched, it was, by comparison with Durkheim's social theory, a step

---

This historical package, apparently borne out of Professor Turner's close acquaintance with American sociology over the years, is an important one. More than anything else, however, it conveys to me an idea of the stability and staying power of individualistic social thought in the U.S. There is little doubt that if modern-day American sociology is seen as the result of the historical 'opposing currents' in American sociology, the stream has been diverted in the direction of individualistic sociology. Moreover, it should not be forgotten that even men like Sorokin can be deemed to have shared in a collectivistic orientation only in terms relative to American sociology. In other words, a good many American sociologists who wear the collectivistic label would sound rather individualistic were they to practise their profession in France or Germany. My personal impression is that American sociologists do not sufficiently grasp the fact that their sociological orientation is significantly different from continental European sociological commitments in matters of assumptions regarding the relationship between society and the individual.

toward liberalism. Unlike the latter, it does not obliterate individuals in its concern for social order and solidarity; it does not see them as tools and embodiments of the collective conscience and exoteric social currents; it does not exhort them to be suspicious of industry and of man's greedy insatiable appetites, to bow dependently before society, to like the idea of circumscribed tasks and limited horizons, to curtail ambitions, or to be docile to authority. With the shift from Durkheim's to Parsons' Functionalism, the values embedded in Functional theory have appreciably shifted [Gouldner, 1970: 196].

Gouldner [1970: 182] seems to trace the differences between Durkheim and Parsons to different religious influences. He sees

a visible difference between the early Parsons' cautious Protestant perfectionism and Durkheim's more Catholic organicism . . . Although Parsons fully shares Durkheim's concern for social order and equilibrium, he in principle, envisions a somewhat more dynamic equilibrium, more susceptible to influence by men's active efforts in pursuit of their moral ideals.

Since Durkheim was not a Catholic one must assume that Gouldner was referring to the French Catholic influence on sociology and that Parsons' 'Protestantism' must be seen in broader terms as referring to American cultural influence.

The potency and relative autonomy of the individual are matters of central concern to even the least of individualistic sociologists in the U.S. Even though Parsons may be less individualistic than Homans, his sociology is not as Durkheimian as appearances make it seem. In the area of social exchange theory, at the very least, the American mode of sociology has stamped its individualistic characteristics on the works of Homans, Blau, and Emmerson. There are, of course, shades of individualism in the social exchange perspective: but they represent differences of degree, not of fundamental kind between individualistic and collectivistic sociologists.

The Elements of the Two Traditions

There has always existed in utilitarianism, the body of theories that place individual desires and wants in the center of their concern, an inherent tension between two incompatible trends:

between exclusive concern with intrapersonal matters *and* matters of relative interpersonal relations; between here-and-now pleasure-seeking hedonism with the avoidance of all forms of pain *and* the inclusion and control of costs in the maximization of benefits; between a consumption orientation *and* a production orientation. With particular reference to the social sciences these incompatible trends led to a natural bifurcation of utilitarianism into elementary economics and psychology. As Halévy put it:

> The Philosophical Radicals wished to make social science a rational science; they held that all social phenomena are reducible to laws, and that all the laws of the social world are in their turn explicable by 'the laws of human nature'. But the laws of human nature are themselves of two kinds: physical laws, the definition of which the *economist* and the jurist borrow from the physician, from the geologist and from the biologist; and *psychological* laws (Halévy, 1928: 433, italics added].

The development of utilitarianism in social science along these two lines of economics and psychology was well under way before sociology came of age. In the process of the development of the individualistic tradition in sociology, it became clear that the physical laws of economics and the psychological laws of the human mind have equal but separate places in sociology. In fact they rarely converge in any one sociologist—at least any given theorist has tended to emphasize one but not the other of the two. Even in Spencer, the sire of utilitarian sociology, the separation of the two is noticeable, with economic assumptions gaining ascendance. It is Homans, the most prominent individualistic sociologist of modern times, who has consciously sought to weave the two separated strands of elementary economics and psychology into his exchange theory. As I shall show later, that attempt at the fusion of the two pose some important problems that Homans has not resolved.

On both these faces of individualistic sociology, the French collectivistic orientation is opposed to the centrality and autonomy of individual self-interests, wishes, and desires as a motive force in social action. Rather, the collectivistic tradition in sociology postulates that social processes gain relevance according to the degree to which they contribute to a definition of the corporate existence of society or of particular groups. Its opposition is based on its distaste for lack of distinction between social processes on the one hand and psychological and economic processes on the other.

Beginning with Comte and Spencer, much of the sociology that developed under these two banners of individualistic orientation and collectivistic orientation did so in constant polemical confrontation with each other.[1] These polemics have been focused on the nature of the relationship between the individual and society. The intervention of society in individual life is the credo of the collectivistic orientation in sociology; it is on the other hand the anathema of individualistic sociology.

Durkheim has brought many of these points of contention into modern sociology with his double attack on utilitarian economic assumptions in sociology and on the introduction of psychological variables into sociological explanation. His famous statement, 'sociology is not a corollary of psychology', has become the whipping boy for Homans' counterattacks on collectivistic assumptions in sociology. In a world of fashionable quantitative sociology, of popular appeals and shallow attachments to individual prominent sociologists rather than to traditions of social thought, sociologists are apt to forget that the points of view they espouse were nurtured in polemical confrontations. Lest the adherents of Homans' exchange theory and of the so-called behavioral sociology forget this point, this monograph seeks to remind sociologists that even Homans' exchange theory is connected with this on-going polemic.

The Two Traditions and Theory Construction

The basic assumptions of the two traditions have also influenced the style of theory construction advocated or practised by those

---

[1] The differences between Spencer and Comte are in particular noteworthy because of the erroneous impression that the two pioneer sociologists are alike in their sociology. It is such 'wrong impressions' that led Spencer [1864] to document the differences between him and Comte. When these differences are examined, one is left with the impression that Spencer is right in seeking to be differentiated from Comte. Comte [1848: 400], for instance, saw one of the highlights of his 'religion of humanity' as follows: 'The most important object of this regenerated polity will be the substitution of Duties for Rights; thus subordinating personal to social considerations.' Spencer [1864] specifically distinguishes himself from Comte by advocating, for instance, a society 'in which social life will have no other end than to maintain the completest sphere for individual life' [Spencer, 1864 [1968]: 17].

who share them. The founders of utilitarian thought modelled the social sciences on the physical sciences: 'Bentham and James Mill were rationalists in the sense that they held all the social sciences, and . . . the science of mind [i.e. psychology] on which they are based, were deductive sciences analogous to rational mechanics and celestial mechanics' [Halévy, 1928: 436]. The logico-deductive tradition in theory construction is still being pursued relentlessly, indeed with new vigor in the seventies, by individualistic sociologists. It leads directly to logico-deductive reasoning in social theory and to the belief that a theory with a logical consistency can be constructed in abstraction and that from it actual human behavior can be deduced. Such a strategy in theory construction has come to be predicated on the 'behavioral sociological' assumption, especially advanced by Homans [1961, 1969], that the differences between animal behavior and human behavior are quantitative, not qualitative; differences of degree, not of kind. Accordingly, behavioral psychology offers the most inclusive generalizations to which to reduce other social science propositions; in other words, behavioral psychology and the social sciences are interlinked by a chain of deductive reasoning.

In sharp contrast, the French collectivistic orientation has usually encouraged theory construction based on the assumption of the autonomy of society and the irreducibility of social processes to psychological ones. Durkheim has offered the best justification for this strategy in theory construction: 'In a word, there is between psychology and sociology the same break in continuity as between biology and the physico-chemical sciences. Consequently, every time a social phenomenon is explained directly by a psychological phenomenon, we may be sure that the explanation is false' [Durkheim, 1938: 104]. The assumption here is that the differences between psychology and sociology are *qualitative*, not *quantitative*. The collectivistic orientation has thus discouraged theories constructed in the abstraction of what Frankl [1969: 402] has called 'sub-humanism' to which to reduce less general human principles of behavior. Rather, it has encouraged grounded theory construction. The theorist does not attempt to construct a set of logically interrelated propositions ungrounded in data; he sets out on the contrary to explain some social phenomenon and in the process of research with data he constructs a theory. For example, Durkheim set out to explain variations in the rates of suicide. In the process of this research on suicide, he advanced a theory of integration, which not only explained his data but which also has turned out to be useful in the explanation of a variety of other social phenomena. It is not by accident that Glaser and Strauss' [1966: 4, 11] examples of classical grounded theories are those of Durkheim and Weber— both of them prominent sociologists with collectivistic orientations, although with considerable national variations—while their primary example of ungrounded logico-deductive theory is Blau's individualistic social exchange theory.

The basis of such differences between the two traditions with respect to theory construction has been traced by Werner Stark to underlying religious world views. Catholicism tends to be characterized by certain types of intellectual organization while Calvinism leads to a different mode of intellectual pursuit:

> We are asserting that this power wells up from below, not that it comes down from above—that it is an influence welling up from the deeper forces and drifts of social life. Just as a society usually contains a satisfied and a dissatisfied social class, so every society embraces tendencies towards community and tendencies towards association (in the terminology of Ferdinand Tönnies), tendencies towards a close integration of social life and tendencies towards individual freedom. Catholicism and Calvinism are representatives of these very real forces. Catholicism is essentially the community-type of religious life and ecclesiastical organization, Calvinism, with its emphasis on the supremacy of private judgment and its congregationalism, the associational type. It would not be too difficult to work out a paradigm for religious communities . . . Let us mention only a few items that would have to appear in it.

	Catholicism	*Calvinism*
1.	Tendency towards an organic world-view	Tendency towards an atomistic world-view
2.	Realism	Nominalism
3.	Society conceived as prior to the individual	Society conceived as posterior to the individual
4.	The community the carrier of all truth	The individual the carrier of all truth
5.	Symbolism, Artistic creativeness	Realism, Sobriety
6.	Emotionalism, Mysticism	Rationalism

7. Cloistered contemplation as   Innerworldly observation as the
   the ideal way to truth   ideal way to truth
                                             [Stark, 1958: 81]

These two orientations also influence the time frame of reference
in social analysis in different ways. The time frame in collectivistic
sociology tends to be much broader than that in individualistic
sociology; while the former has usually concerned itself with social
processes that span an individual's life, individualistic sociology
is more likely to focus on processes that form only part of
the individual's life experience. It is in this differentiated sense
that Stinchcombe's [1968: 11] contention, that the 'most useful
concepts of sociology have no men in them', gains maximum
meaning. When, for instance, suicide is considered in terms of a
large time frame of reference it can be established that society
imposes its own laws of self-destruction irrespective of variations
among particular individuals in society. On the other hand, when
suicide acts are considered in individuals, what they do does
matter—because the time frame is narrow. One may also react
to Homans' persistent complaint that Durkheimian functionalism
wrongly treats consequences as causes in the explanation of social
phenomena in these terms. Within a large time frame, it is possible
to treat evaluated consequences of some past action as con-
stituting the cause of some future action. With Homans' narrowed
time span, for instance in a small group experiment, such an
approach to causality would understandably appear to be
untenable.

It is in the light of the influence of these two traditions in
theory construction that the exiguous results of the perennial
attempts by sociologists to forge syntheses between differing
perspectives should be viewed. This is especially the case with
the type of synthesis intended to achieve uniformity and thus
silence controversy.[1] 'Syntheses' that ignore underlying philo-

---

[1] Modern examples of uniformitarian synthesis, designed to silence controversy
and thus achieve a uniform perspective in sociological theory, may be seen in van
den Berghe [1963], Denzin [1969], and Singleman [1972]. Such uniformitarian
syntheses emerge primarily from uneasiness in the face of contending paradigms in
sociological reasoning. It would seem that one attitude to such plurality of theoretical
models would be in the direction of attempting to indicate how much one gains
by using them in different contexts. But there appears to be some discomfort over
plural models in sociology and it does appear that synthesis for synthesis sake has
a special appeal to the present generation of sociologists, particularly in the U.S.,

sophical assumptions of the authors of the differing perspectives, especially with regard to the differences in their conceptions of the nature of the relationship between society and the individual, are inherently unstable. This matter may be discussed profitably by referring to Talcott Parsons' views on the subject. As I have previously indicated, Parsons [1961b: 86] believed that modern sociological theory was the result of a synthesis between the individualistic and collectivistic currents in social thought. In his more recent pronouncements on the subject, apparently based on the resurgence of self-conscious individualistic sociologists, Talcott Parsons [1968: 235] now concedes that there is a 'dialectic tension' between utilitarian individualistic trends in social thought and the more 'holistic trends deriving from Durkheim, Weber, Mead, and their forebears'. Parsons is, however, convinced that pure utilitarianism, the modern version of which he identifies with Homans' work, will not be viable. Rather, 'a synthesis of the utilitarian contribution and those contributions deriving above all from German idealism and from French collectivistic positivism will prove to shape the theoretical future of the sciences of human behavior, society, and culture more than any one of these traditions taken alone' [Parsons, 1968: 235].

Parsons' position here urging a synthesis between the two traditions may well have its merits. There appears to be an alternative way of looking at this matter, however. It seems to me that insofar as syntheses have been achieved and are achievable in sociology, they are not between the two traditions, but rather within each of these traditions. Differing views on a common theme or theory within each of the traditions may be successfully reconciled precisely because they share an underlying philo-

---

who tend to be more affected by fads than older sociologists. As Mannheim [1952: 225] once remarked, 'Syntheses do not float in abstract space, uninfluenced by social gravitation; it is the structural configuration of the social situation which makes it possible for them to emerge and develop'. But uniformitarian synthesis, especially sensitized to silence controversy rather than to enhance our explanation of a phenomenon, is bound to be unstable. As Mannheim [1952: 225] also indicates, syntheses are in general difficult to achieve: 'The instability and relativity of any synthesis is shown by the emergence in place of the homogeneous Hegelian system itself, of right and left Hegelianisms'.

My own personal preference in synthesis is in favor of combining the strengths of various perspectives in order to enhance the level of explanation of a phenomenon. This is different from what I now call uniformitarian synthesis in that the original perspectives are not thereby abolished, as it is intended in uniformitarian synthesis.

sophical position. But when the relationships between the two traditions are considered, progress may be registered more by considering the ways in which each serves as a gadfly for the other. The polemical confrontations involved in such a relationship have led to progress in theory building—but that is not by way of synthesis. Later in this book, I shall attempt to achieve a synthesis between the views of Durkheim and Lévi-Strauss regarding social solidarity. However, I will not, as many a sociologist may hasten to demand, attempt to forge a synthesis between individualistic social exchange theory and collectivistic social exchange theory. Rather, I shall demonstrate that these two separate traditions in social exchange theory are related to each other in a continuing polemical confrontation which has led to the formulation and the enrichment of the two types of social exchange theory—to the benefit and growth of sociological theory.

2
Interpretations of Non-Western Social Exchange Behaviors

The influence of the European encounter with the non-Western world, especially in the nineteenth and the early twentieth centuries, has not been assigned a weight in the history of the development of sociological theory and thought. It does seem, though, that the rich comparative data available from these encounters were used more to justify philosophical positions already held by various theorists than to reorient their former positions. Even in modern times the reluctance of American and European sociologists to assign equal weights to Western and non-Western behaviors and experiences in their theory construction is apparent. The early interpretations of the behaviors of non-Western peoples were in the final analysis reflections of the sociological suasions of the theorists who attempted them.

It is only with non-Western exchange behaviors as seen by some three theorists that I shall be principally concerned in this chapter. Their interpretations of these behaviors not only reflect the individualistic and the collectivistic traditions of sociology; they have also influenced later social exchange theorists a great deal. Beyond the significance of their work for later developments in social exchange theory, their thoughts on social exchange behaviors are worth careful study for the important fact that some of their insights have been independently rediscovered by some modern social exchange theorists who apparently had no acquaintance whatsoever with these earlier works. Such, for example, is the parallel between Frazer's [1919] social exchange theory and Blau's [1964] social exchange theory.

But the proper point at which to introduce Western interpretations of non-Western social exchange behaviors is Spencer's [1896: 388–391] brief attempt at a definition of social exchange behavior. It is notable for the light it sheds on Homans' theory of social exchange. The nearest Spencer came to such a definition is 'the barter of assistances' as distinct from the more tangible 'barter of commodities'. But, perhaps more importantly, he attributed a primitive religious character to non-utilitarian exchange behaviors: 'Thus,' he concludes, 'the very idea of exchange, without which there cannot begin commercial intercourse and industrial organization, has itself to grow out of certain ceremonial actions originated by the desire to propriate' [1896: 388]. This position is of significance for Homans' exchange theory in two ways. First, there is the similar assumption made by Homans [1961: 387–391] that economic activities are the outgrowth of more elementary social exchange behaviors. Secondly, the non-utilitarian behaviors to which Spencer had assigned a religious non-utilitarian character have been brought by Homans into modern social exchange theory by simply defining them as 'activities' and 'sentiments' with a utilitarian value amenable to measurement. This utilitarian valuation of 'activities' and 'sentiments' releases modern utilitarian social exchange theory from the embarrassment which Spencer's [1896: 391] conception of social exchange was exposed to:

> Even in the drinking of men in a public-house, there are usages curiously simulating primitive usages. The pots of beer presented by one to another are by and by to be balanced by equivalent pots[1] ... We have here, indeed, a curious case, in which no material convenience is gained, but in which there is a reversion to a form of propriation from which the idea of exchange is nominally, but not actually, excluded [Spencer, 1896: 390–391].

It's too bad Spencer did not have Homans and Blau at his side to advise him to watch out for the sentiments—the smiles, the

---

[1] This custom of exchange of wine has also been described by Lévi-Strauss [1969: 58–59] for the French. But his conclusion is invested with a typically French sociological assumption: 'The two bottles are identical in volume, and their contents are similar in quality. Each person . . . received no more than if he had consumed his own wine. From an economic viewpoint, no one has gained and no one has lost. But the point is that there is much more in the exchange itself than in the things exchanged' [Lévi-Strauss, 1969: 59].

handshakes, etc.—that accompanied the exchange of the equivalent pots of wine. But Spencer might have wondered why serious scholars should be interested in such matters.

Sir James George Frazer's Social Exchange Theory

In the second volume of *Folklore in the Old Testament*, Frazer [1919: 94–371] carried out a study of kinship and marriage behaviors, which is of great relevance for social exchange theory. The institutions of cross-cousin marriage; the prohibition of parallel cousin marriage; the practice of sororate and levirate; the practice of marriage exchange; and the performance of services as bridewealth payments for wife: all these received detailed attention. The first two of these—cross-cousin marriages and the rarity or, as Frazer then understood it, the prohibition of parallel-cousin marriage—became twenty years later the fertile ground for a full-fledged theory of social exchange by Lévi-Strauss [1949]. Of course Lévi-Strauss took to a path of explanation opposite that of Frazer's. It is one of those consistencies in social thought that Homans and Schneider [1955] were to challenge Lévi-Strauss on the very grounds of cross-cousin marriage which provided the reasons why the French anthropologist had earlier challenged Frazer. Indeed, Homans and Schneider's [1955] alternative theory of cross-cousin marriage has all the individualistic trappings of Frazer's [1919] earlier theory on the same subject.

Frazer's query was: 'Why is the marriage of cross-cousins so often favored? Why is the marriage of ortho-cousins [i.e., parallel cousins] so uniformly prohibited?' [Frazer, 1919: 194]. Frazer thought the answer was to be found in the most elementary conditions of life among native Australians and he came out with the following answer: economic motives explained it all. 'Having no equivalent in property to give for a wife, an Australian aboriginal is generally obliged to get her in exchange for a female relative, usually a sister or daughter' [1919: 195]. But once the institution of marriage exchange of sisters and daughters was established, other forms of behavior could be derived from it— all governed by the iron law of economic motives. The institutions of society tend to be so arranged as to subserve this primitive law of economic motives. Hence dual organizations arise: 'Thus the exchange of sisters, whether sisters in the full or in the group sense of the word, appears to have been the very pivot on which turned the great reformation initiated by the dual organization of society' [Frazer, 1919: 234].

Thus dual organizations are a derivative phenomenon. Once established, the institutions of society that are congruent with these first derivatives—in this case dual organizations—tend to be encouraged while those that are incongruent with them are discouraged. Such is the origin of the preference for cross-cousin marriage and the prohibition of parallel cousin marriage:

The preference [for cross-cousin marriage] may well date from . . . the remote time when the custom of exchange was first systematized as the fundamental base of the new organization of society into two exogamous classes . . . it was only the marriage of cross-cousins which the new system permitted; the marriage of ortho-cousins was barred from the very foundation of that system by the rule which placed the children of brothers in the same exogamous class [Frazer, 1919: 234–235].

The validity of Frazer's theory is not in question here, although the matter seems to be of topical interest to social science. It is his strategy that I seek to highlight. That strategy is not different from the emphasis in Blau's [1964] exchange theory; only their contents differ. Social exchange processes derive from the economic motives of individuals in society. Once they become stable other institutions emerge from them. These emergent institutions can then be used to explain the existence or non-existence of other phenomena in society.

The basic nature of economic motives in Frazer's theory led him to emphasize a matter of enormous importance in exchange theory, namely, the exploitation of social exchange for power and status differentiations. The system of the exchange of women was exploited for power by the Australians in two separate ways: First, 'Since among the Australian aborigines women had a high economic and commercial value, a man who had many sisters or daughters was rich, and a man who had none was poor and might be unable to procure a wife at all' [Frazer, 1919: 198]. Secondly, 'the old men availed themselves of the system of exchange in order to procure a number of wives for themselves from among the young women, while the young men, having no women to give in exchange, were often obliged to remain single or to put up with the cast-off wives of their elders' [Frazer, 1919: 200–201].

In a historical perspective, Frazer may be said to have offered the first theory of social exchange. That theory, moreover, had most of the individualistic characteristics that one finds in Homans' and Blau's exchange theory. Its derivative nature is also to be noted. I summarize Frazer's theory in the following four propositions:

1. *Social exchange processes are developed to serve the economic needs of the population.* In the Australian case, the exchange of sisters or daughters in marriage served the economic needs of the male adult population.

2. *Social institutions are developed to subserve the social exchange processes.* Thus dual organizations arose to facilitate the exchange of sisters and daughters in marriage. *These institutions may be called primary.*

3. *Secondary institutions are shaped to conform to, and to subserve the needs of, the primary institutions.* Thus, the preference for cross-cousin marriage and the prohibition of parallel-cousin marriage conform to and subserve the institutions of dual organizations.

4. *Once established in society, social exchange processes can be exploited by individuals to gain power and status.* Thus old native Australians and those with many sisters or daughters could exploit the social exchange processes for their own individual benefits.

Basic to the theory is the following definition, which should be added to the four propositions stated above.

5. *Exchange items have utilitarian economic values.* Thus women were valued for their commercial and economic worth in native Australian society.

Malinowski and Kula Exchange

Although Malinowski had close ties with Sir James George Frazer, his treatment of Kula exchange in the Trobriand Islands bore no apparent relationship to Frazer's exchange theory of cross-cousin marriage. In his preface to the *Argonauts of the*

Western Pacific, Frazer [1922: x–xi] was careful to note the distinctive contribution Malinowski's treatment of the Kula made to this area of social thought: Malinowski stands out as the first social scientist to draw a sharp distinction between economic exchange and social exchange which he sometimes calls 'ceremonial exchange'. Malinowski's description of Kula exchange is very clear and uncluttered with specialized cultural anthropological terminology:

> The Kula is a form of exchange of extensive, inter-tribal character; it is carried on by communities inhabiting a wide ring of islands, which form a closed circuit . . . Along [the routes of the Kula exchange], articles of two kinds, and these two kinds only, are constantly travelling in opposite directions. In the one direction . . . [Necklaces] of red shell . . . In the opposite direction moves the other kind—[Armlets] [Malinowski, 1922: 81].

Malinowski adds that the exchange of these articles, Necklaces and Armshells, was carefully regulated by rules and rituals. Individuals engage in these exchanges. At any one exchange transaction one partner gives the other an Armshell and the other receives from him a Necklace. These items of social exchange are in constant movement and always in opposite directions.

But the Kula is not an economic transaction. The two items of exchange have symbolic, not economic value; this is not a market-place economic transaction in which one deals with the highest bidder. 'One transaction does not finish the Kula relationship, the rule being "once in the Kula, always in the Kula", and a partnership between two men is a permanent and lifelong affair' [Malinowski, 1922: 82–83]. Economic transactions may be performed under its umbrella, but the non-economic nature of the Kula retains the principal emphasis: 'The ceremonial exchange of the two articles is the main, the fundamental aspect of the Kula. But associated with, and done under its cover, we find a great number of secondary activities and features' [1922: 83]. Moreover, 'The Kula is not done under stress of any need, since its main aim is to exchange articles which are of no practical use' [1922: 86]. 'These objects are not owned in order to be used; the privilege of decorating oneself with them is not the real aim of possession' [1922: 88].

Important for exchange theory is the remarkable distinction which Malinowski stresses between social exchange and economic exchange.[1] As a matter of fact he attributes the distinction to native thought and behavior: 'The natives sharply distinguish it [the Kula] from barter, which they practise extensively, of which they have a clear idea, and for which they have a settled term'[2] [1922: 96]. Malinowski [1922: 95] likens the Kula exchange items to trophies from which the holders get 'a special type of pleasure by the mere fact of owning them, of being entitled to them'. To make a distinction between the utilitarian value of an object of economic exchange and the symbolic value of an object of social exchange is not to imply that symbolic value may not be graded. Gold medals have a greater symbolic value than bronze medals, even though both have only symbolic values to the winners. This gradation of symbolic values of social exchange items is very much recognized in the Kula exchange [Malinowski, 1922: 96].

Two other features of the Kula exchange, at least as interpreted by Malinowski, bear clear emphasis for the sharp contrast they offer to economic conceptions of social exchange. First, Kula exchange items are not to be identified with currency: 'They are neither used nor regarded as money or currency' [1922: 511]. (This is to be contrasted with Homans' [1961: 385] conception of social exchange in which social approval is regarded as a generalized medium of social exchange.) Secondly, in sharp contrast to the rather free-floating conception of economically motivated social exchange, Kula exchange actors are not free to go to the highest bidders since 'Kula transactions can be done only between partners' [1922: 91].

This rejection of economic motives in the Kula exchange is matched by the lack of exploitation of the social exchange relations for power and status differentiations in Malinowski's

---

[1] Firth's [1957] otherwise incisive analysis of Malinowski's interpretation of the Kula not only failed to recognize this distinction between the symbolic value of social exchange and the utilitarian value of economic exchange, but wrongly proceeded to chide Malinowski for not devising a measure of the utilitarian value of the exchange items in the Kula [see Firth, 1957: 220–221].

[2] Cf. Bohannan's [1955: 60] similar distinction among the Tiv of Nigeria: 'Distribution of goods among the Tiv falls into two spheres: a "market" on the one hand, and gifts, on the other. The several words best translated "gifts" apply . . . to exchange over a long period of time between persons or groups in a more or less permanent relationship. The gift may be a factor designed to strengthen the relationship, or even to create it.' On the other hand, 'A "market" is a transaction which in itself calls up no long-term personal relationship, and which is therefore to be exploited to as great a degree as possible.'

interpretation of social exchange. The long-term design of the Kula exchange between permanent partners would itself limit the bid for power [cf. Malinowski, 1922: 91–92; 97–98]. The power and status of chiefs do not emerge from the Kula exchange; rather they validate their power and status by it. Kula exchange items do not uniformly symbolize superiority nor subordination; they serve to cement the existing relations between individuals. Depending on the circumstances, the giving of gifts may be

> the expression of the superiority of the giver over the recipient. In others, it represents subordination to the chief, or a kinship relation or relationship-in-law. And it is important to realize that in all forms of [social] exchange in the Trobriands, there is not even a trace of gain, nor is there any reason for looking at it from the purely utilitarian and economic standpoint, since there is no enhancement of mutual utility through the exchange [Malinowski, 1922: 175].

If economic motives, which Malinowski has so sternly ruled out, do not underlie the Kula exchange what does? Here we come upon a subtlety in Malinowski's sociology: the motives are *social psychological*. The motives for social action, in this case Kula exchange transactions, are at once psychological and social.[1] Critical to Kula exchange is the

> fundamental human impulse to display, to share, to bestow [and] the deep tendency to create social ties through exchange of gifts. Apart from any consideration as to whether the gifts are necessary or even useful, giving for the sake of giving is one of the most important features of Trobriand sociology, and, from its very general and fundamental nature, I submit that it is a universal feature of all primitive societies [Malinowski, 1922: 175].

Homans has repeatedly cited Malinowski's work as providing the charter for what he originally called 'individual self-interest theory' or 'Malinowskian functionalism' [Homans and Schneider, 1955: 15]. If by 'individual self-interest theorist' one means a theorist who assumes that the basic psychological needs of individuals are important for the explanation of social behavior,

---

[1] Malinowski makes clear that the complicated transactions in the Kula are not consciously planned by the actors and that the consequences are not intended: 'Not even the most intelligent native has any clear idea of the Kula as a big, organized social construction, still less of its sociological function and implications' [Malinowski, 1922: 83].

then clearly Malinowski was a leader in that area. But if by that
term we refer to a social theorist who assumes that economic
motives are necessary for the explanation of social behavior,
institutions, and social processes, then obviously Malinowski was
not one. Malinowski's [1922: especially p. 516] indictment against
the assumption of pervasive economic motives in social explanation is second in intensity only to Durkheim's attack on
Spencer's economic assumptions in sociology. What Malinowski's
interpretation of the Kula exchange makes clear is that a social
theorist can be an individualist on only one side of the economic
and psychological approaches to social action and be opposed to
the other side. It further shows that the collapse of the two under
the general rubric of 'individual self-interest theory' can only be
achieved at theoretical peril.

Malinowski's plea and hope that 'the meaning of the Kula will
consist in being instrumental to dispel' the bogey 'conception of
a rational being who wants nothing but to satisfy his simplest
needs and does it according to the economic principle of least
effort' [Malinowski, 1922: 516] has been frustrated in sociology
by modern American social exchange theorists. These Malinowski-
citing social exchange theorists need to pay some attention to
Frazer's own willingness to change his position about the
significance of economic motives in social exchange: 'Dr.
Malinowski's account of the Kula should help to lay the phantom
[of the Economic Man] by the heels; for he proves that the trade
in useful objects, which forms part of the *Kula* system, is in the
minds of the natives entirely subordinate in importance to the
exchange of other objects, which serve no utilitarian purpose
whatsoever' [Frazer, 1922: x–xi].[1]

Malinowski's interpretation of Kula exchange also raises a
matter of central importance for social exchange theory, and
sociology in general. This is the nature of the relationship between
the individual and society. The motives for the Kula are neither
exclusively psychological nor exclusively social, but both of these

---

[1] Frazer's willingness to change his views in the face of convincing evidence,
prominently commended by Freud [1913: 141], is a vanishing virtue in modern
social science. As Frazer [1910: xiii] has put it, 'That my conclusions on these
difficult questions are final, I am not so foolish as to pretend. I have changed my
views repeatedly, and I am resolved to change them again with every change of
evidence, for like a chameleon the inquirer should shift his colours with the shifting
colours of the ground he treads.'

two at once. Useful for analytical purposes, the separation of individual wants and societal needs is empirically unrealistic. Malinowski [cf. 1939: 938] has always sought to steer a middle course between the Scylla of a 'gigantic "Moral Being" which thinks out and improvises all collective events' and the Charybdis of 'the figment of the individual as a detached, self-contained entity'. The hypothesis that is implicit in Malinowski's interpretation of the Kula may be stated as follows: *An institution that both meets the needs of individuals and helps to maintain the society as an on-going concern will be more stable than an institution that insures the one but not the other of these two functions.* Such isomorphism in functionalism has been lent weight in modern sociological theory by Erich Fromm's theory of social character. Thus he argues: 'In order that any society may function well, its members must acquire the kind of character which makes them *want* to act in the way they *have* to act as members of the society or of a special class in it. They have to *desire* what objectively is *necessary* for them to do. *Outer force* is to be replaced by *inner compulsion*' [Fromm, 1944: 380; italics in original].

Uberoi [1962] has discussed what psychological and social needs Kula exchange simultaneously satisfies. He concludes his monograph on the subject as follows:

> This I believe to be the key to the ultimate social importance of the *kula* valuables: that they represent to the normally kin-bound individuals of these small stateless societies the highest point of their legitimate individual self-interest, and also the interest of the widest political association of which they all partake. Armshell and Necklace never function in the *kula* as the simple emblems of the local kin-group which is the basic unit of Massim society. They move, rather, always along the interrelations between groups; and the mechanism of their movement is such that they symbolize, at once, the interests of the narrowest social category operative among the Massim and also the widest: the single individual and the Kula Ring [Uberoi, 1962: 160].

There are special features of the Kula exchange that operate to meet these psychological and social needs simultaneously. Especially outstanding in the Kula is the fact that the exchange items are of two kinds, Armshells and Necklaces, and that each kind constantly moves in one direction while the other con-

stantly moves in the opposite direction. It works as indicated in
Figure 2.1.

FIGURE 2.1

The Armshells and Necklaces in Kula Exchange Flow
in Opposite Directions

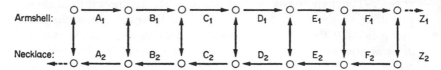

It combines *direct exchange* between any two partners with what
Malinowski [1922: 93] calls *circular exchange* among a large
number of exchange actors. With respect to any two Kula partners,
say A_1 and A_2, in a unit of time and space exchanging Necklace
for Armshell, the exchange is direct and emphasizes the psychological needs of the Kula partners. With respect to any one of the
Kula exchange items, the exchange is spread out in time and
space and moves among a large number of exchange actors
in a form of *circular exchange* to forge, in an incipient form,
an organic solidarity in an otherwise mechanically solidary
society [Malinowski, 1922: 510]. The use of two items in the
Kula exchange is thus not fortuitous. The use of only one item
would rob the Kula of the here-and-now psychological satis-
faction to be derived by individuals from mutual and *direct
exchange*. The two items insure that the needs of social integration
of society and the psychological needs of the individuals in the
Trobriands could be met simultaneously. The use of three items
in the Kula would upset the equality that is assumed to exist
between the exchange partners. Thus the two items represent the
minimum and maximum needed to work out a correspondence
between the needs of individuals and of society.

Marcel Mauss and the Morality of Social Exchange

One of the earliest published reactions to Malinowski's treatment
of Kula exchange is contained in Marcel Mauss' [1925] *Essai sur
le don*, the specific area of concern of which is social exchange. As
Malinowski [1926: 41n] has been careful to note, Mauss came to

some new interpretations of his Kula exchange data, including his incisive remarks about Malinowski's conception of 'pure gifts'. Mauss' 'total sociology' led him to recognize that any one transaction, including the so-called 'pure gifts', could not be isolated from the rest of society [Mauss, 1954: 71].

Mauss' major concern in *Essai sur le don*, however, is not with a general theory of social exchange. It was rather an investigation of the moral and religious foundations and consequences of social exchange processes. His query was: '*In primitive or archaic types of societies what is the principle whereby the gift received has to be repaid? What force is there in the thing given which compels the recipient to make a return?*' [Mauss, 1954: 1; italics in the original]. Mauss was convinced that the discovery of the answer to these questions from comparative data would enable him 'to draw conclusions of moral nature about some of the problems confronting us in our present economic crisis' [1925: 2]. This conviction is predicated on the belief that social institutions in 'primitive or archaic' societies are undifferentiated and are at once 'religious, legal, moral, and economic' and therefore may directly shed light on the interrelationships between economic life and other areas of society. He was interested in discovering the common morality underlying both economic and social life. Social exchange, he assumed, provided that morality.

Essai sur le don is very much in the tradition of Durkheim's [1915] *The Elementary Forms of the Religious Life*. The discovery of basic morality in simple societies will shed considerable light on the moral nature of modern complex societies. The emphasis in Mauss' work conforms to Durkheim's sociology. Psychological factors were largely disregarded. Even when it is apparent in Malinowski's *The Argonauts of the Western Pacific* that the psychological factors of the Kula are emphasized, Mauss could still complain that 'Unfortunately we know very little about the sanction behind these transactions' [Mauss, 1954: 24]. As Firth [1957: 222] has pointed out, Mauss curiously misread Malinowski at some points. The most outstanding misreading is conveyed in his assertion that the '*Kula* trade is aristocratic. It seems to be reserved for the chiefs.' This led him to say that 'The *Kula* is a kind of grand potlach' [Mauss, 1954: 20]. As Firth has also pointed out, the Kula could not be described as aristocratic—not according to Malinowski's data anyway.

But this misreading and misinterpretation of Malinowski's data
falls in line with Mauss' main characterization of social exchange.
In simple societies, which provide examples of fundamental
morality in social and economic life, 'we do not find simple
exchange of goods, wealth and produce through markets established among individuals. For it is groups, and not individuals,
which carry on exchange, make contracts, and are bound by
obligations; the persons represented in the contracts are moral
persons—clans, tribes, and families; the groups, or the chief as
intermediaries for the groups, confront and oppose each other'
[Mauss, 1954: 3].

His definition of social exchange clearly de-emphasizes the role
of individuals in social exchange transactions. In fact, it is *persons*,
not *individuals*,[1] who take part in exchange. The distinction is not
trivial for Mauss, sociologist and philologist at once. *Individuals*
are isolated unit actors unrepresentative of any other units but
themselves. *Persons* are representative of certain social roles and
therefore do not act on their behalf exclusively but on behalf of
social groups in society.

The morality of social exchange, accordingly, is to be sought
in the relationships between groups or subgroups, or between
their representatives. Thus a denial of self-interest is implied in
Mauss' conception of social exchange. The triple obligation of
social exchange—to give, to receive, and to repay—are to be
understood not in the idiom of self-interest but in terms of
interpersonal, hence inter-group, relations. Every social exchange
transaction creates social bonds that not only tie one person to
another and to society but one segment of society to another.
Moreover, the morality that emerges from these social bonds
exists as reality *sui generis* and informs social interactions and
activities in society: 'The pattern of symmetrical and reciprocal
rights [in social exchange] is not difficult to understand if we
realize that it is first and foremost a pattern of spiritual bonds
between things which are to some extent parts of persons, and

---

[1] The distinction between 'person' and 'individual' has been lost in the social
sciences. In its original meaning, the 'individual' denotes that the human being is
isolated from the rest of society, while the 'person' occupies a status position and
is a role incumbent. Thus Park and Burgess [1922: 5] write: 'The person is an
individual who has a status. We come to this world as individuals. We acquire
status, and become persons.' It is in this sense of a role-free and status-free
individual that Marcel Mauss excludes the individual from social exchange processes.

persons and groups that behave in some measure as if they were things' [Mauss, 1954: 11]. That is, the morality of exchange comes to be recognized in its own right and individuals behave in conformity to it in their social and economic activities. Nor is such morality of social action restricted to 'primitive' societies. It informs social action in modern society. In other words, it is fundamental morality that is gained from social exchange processes and it is common to all societies: 'The basis of moral action is general; it is common to societies of the highest degree of evolution, to those of the future and to societies of the least advancement. Here we touch bedrock' [Mauss, 1954: 68].

This survey of Mauss' brief but complicated approach to social exchange yields two conclusions for the comparative study of social exchange perspectives in this book: First, in the hands of Mauss social exchange had come to be invested with a collectivistic robe. Individuals and self-interest have no place in social exchange transactions. It is in terms of groups and of society that one should consider social exchange. Those persons who are engaged in social exchange do so as part of society. Secondly, there is the assumption in Mauss' work that social exchange processes yield for society a special morality that is operative in interpersonal relations as well as in ordinary economic, political, and social activities in society. Although not all such relations and activities are forms of social exchange, the morality, *sui generis*, that flows from social exchange processes inform and guide them. Mauss did not differentiate social exchange processes; but one can infer that the morality that develops out of them is not monolithic. We shall apply this principle later in evaluating Lévi-Strauss' exchange theory.

Part Two

COLLECTIVISTIC ORIENTATIONS
IN
SOCIAL EXCHANGE THEORY

3
Collectivistic Theory of Social Exchange

The French collectivistic tradition in sociology has made a major impact in the area of sociological theory called social exchange. Sociology remains poorer for its failure to exploit this collectivistic orientation in social exchange theory. Beyond adventitious citations of Marcel Mauss' work on social exchange by Homans and Blau, the dominant impression in sociology is that social exchange theory, as a social scientific perspective, is a discovery of professional sociologists and that its discovery dates from Homans' [1958] first statement of his own position on this subject. In fact, however, as I have pointed out more than once in this book, Homans' exchange theory was a reaction to an older theory of social exchange in a different tradition of thought.

A possible reason for the widespread ignorance of collectivistic social exchange theory may be that Lévi-Strauss' work in social exchange has its locus in anthropology. It would not be improper to entitle this chapter 'Lévi-Straussian Social Exchange Theory', since most of what is in it is provoked by his seminal conceptions of social exchange processes. I have, however, given it the broader title of 'collectivistic theory', instead of entirely identifying it with Lévi-Strauss, for some important reasons. First, Lévi-Strauss was not primarily an exchange theorist in the sense of a man who consciously set out to propose a theory of social exchange. His main concern was the explanation of kinship behaviors. Secondly, although I have followed his lead in emphasizing certain points, there are other matters of central concern to Lévi-Strauss that I have ignored—since they are of less relevance for sociology as such. Thirdly, I have moved beyond some of his concepts and propositions to create a few which I judge to be distinctively sociological. Finally, one important reason for choosing the broader title of 'collectivistic social exchange theory' is that I have blended Mauss' emphasis on the morality of social exchange with Lévi-Strauss' theory.

In what follows, I shall identify as clearly as possible Lévi-Strauss' contributions and my own reformulations of some of his points. This chapter deals with a 'collectivistic theory of social exchange' in that the spirit, if not the letter, of Lévi-Strauss' theory is emphasized. It is clearly not in conformity with modern ritualistic expectations of sociological theory as propositional statements, usually numerically and sequentially labelled. This chapter is, as it were, a sociological restatement of an existing theory, with a tradition of concern with substantive issues rather than with matters of sheer logic of science.

Lévi-Strauss' *Les Structures élémentaire de la Parenté* bears a close resemblance to Durkheim's *Le Suicide* in the strategy of theory construction. Durkheim set out to explain variations in suicide rates; in the process he generated a theory of integration that has enjoyed wide applicability beyond the immediate context of suicide rates. His work is sometimes referred to as a theory of suicide but more formally it is a theory of integration. Lévi-Strauss [1949] similarly set out to explain variations in the kinship practices of cross-cousin marriage. In explaining these kinship behaviors he generated a theory of social exchange processes. His theory may more substantively be referred to as a theory of kinship behavior but more formally it is a theory of social exchange processes. Lévi-Strauss' theory has not been widely applied to the study of other phenomena beyond kinship behaviors, but that is perhaps because of its anthropological locus. Anthropologists, at least in the view of this sociologist, seem to be overly concerned with the substantive attributes of the theory and have done little to emphasize its formal structures —beyond its kinship context.

Lévi-Strauss' Structuralism and the Character of Collectivistic Sociology

Lévi-Strauss' writings in social science span many fields and have agitated a large number of intellectuals, including many outside his chosen discipline of anthropology. Although our major interest in his work is limited here to his earliest, more Durk-heimian, emphasis on societies rather than on his later emphasis on the fundamentals of the human mind, it will serve our purpose to indicate in broad strokes the general character of his writings in the context of the French intellectual tradition in sociology. This is all the more important because he heads a movement in French social thought, labelled 'structuralism', which, in its sociological dimension, is an extension and elaboration of French collectivistic sociology and which accordingly stands in sharp contradistinction to Anglo-Saxon individualistic sociology. This latter polemical feature of Lévi-Strauss' work may of course be more apparent to anthropologists who, for example, are exposed to the difficulties the English anthropologists Edmund Leach and Rodney Needham have encountered in winning the agreement of Lévi-Strauss that they correctly represent his thought in their attempts to introduce his structuralism into British anthropology [cf. Lévi-Strauss, 1969: xxx–xxxv]. But thanks largely to George Caspar Homans, a sociologist who is not disinclined to read anthropological works and who is sufficiently capable of reading original French works, Lévi-Strauss' brand of collectivism has surreptitiously seeped into sociology by way of Homans' reaction to his collectivistic social exchange theory. Homans and Lévi-Strauss' disagreements have brought fresh blood to the polemical confrontations between the French collectivistic and the Anglo-Saxon individualistic traditions in sociology. Nor are these sterile polemics: if sociology now enjoys a perspective called social exchange theory, it is because Homans formulated such a theory in reaction to Lévi-Strauss' brand of sociological assumptions in this area of social theory. In reacting thus to Lévi-Strauss' social exchange theory, Homans [e.g., 1962: 31–32] was fully con-vinced that he was fighting a new French Durkheimian sociology which continues to represent the individual as basically non-essential in explaining social processes.

It is true that Lévi-Strauss' *Les Structures élémentaires de la Parenté*, against which Homans has reacted so vigorously and so productively, is largely in a more specialized Durkheimian tradition with greater emphasis on society *sui generis* than are Lévi-Strauss' later writings, especially on myths, in which he sought to transcend spatial and temporal barriers and to discover the fundamentals of the human mind. But as Lévi-Strauss has so often acknowledged, his collectivism—even in his social exchange theory—traces its parentage more from Marcel Mauss than from Durkheim. As Piaget [1968: 97–98] puts it, 'there are at least two differences between [Durkheim-type] structuralism and the deliberate analytic structuralism of, say, Lévi-Strauss':

> First, where the former speaks of 'emergence' the latter speaks of 'laws of composition'; Durkheim's structuralism, for example, is merely global, because he treats totality as a primary concept explanatory as such; the social whole arises of itself from the union of components; it 'emerges'. His collaborator Marcel Mauss, on the other hand, is regarded by Lévi-Strauss as the originator of authentic anthropological structuralism because, especially in his studies of the gift, he sought and found the details of transformational interactions. Second, whereas 'global' structuralism holds to systems of observable relations and interactions, which are regarded as sufficient unto themselves, the peculiarity of authentic (analytic) structuralism is that it seeks to explain such empirical systems by postulating 'deep' structures from which the former are in some manner derivable. Since structures in this sense of the word are ultimately logico-mathematical models of the observed social relations, they do not themselves belong to the realm of 'fact'. *This means, among other things, as Lévi-Strauss points out repeatedly, that the individual members of the group under study are unaware of the structural model in terms of which the anthropologist interprets constellations of social relations* [my italics].

This last inference of Piaget's is worth commenting on. If the individual is considered as underrepresented in the work of Durkheim, his unique existence is considered unimportant for explanatory purposes in Lévi-Strauss'. This is largely because, while Durkheim emphasized the emergence of the *collective conscience* in his attempt to explain social phenomena, Lévi-Strauss thinks that it is the *collective unconscious* of the human mind, buried down deep in common humanity, unknown even to the actor himself, that provides us with an explanation of social phenomena. In its full blown form, which appears more in his study of myths than in his work on social exchange, Lévi-Strauss [1964: 56] typically argues that 'We are not, therefore, claiming to show how men think the myths, but rather how the myths think themselves out in men and without men's knowledge'. Elsewhere, he declares his main concern as an anthropologist to be with the study of the 'unconscious nature of collective phenomena' [1963: 19]. Indeed, in terms of lack of recognition of the role of the individual in the explanation of social phenomena, Durkheim's sociology pales away in the face of Lévi-Strauss' structuralism.

There is one other area in which Lévi-Strauss' collectivistic perspective, or at least the goals of his theoretical concerns, differ markedly from Durkheim's. The latter's collectivism was bounded by space and time considerations. The social phenomena Durkheim sought to delineate were formed by the collective experience of people who lived in the same society, bounded off by the same temporal order. Lévi-Strauss' ultimate ambition is, on the other hand, to achieve the same goal as Durkheim, namely, the understanding of collective social phenomena, without subjecting his inquiries to the restrictions of time and space specifications. To do this, Lévi-Strauss has, in effect, assumed that once humans are differentiated from the world of nature by culture, the phylo-genetic development of the human mind is impossible. The permanency and constancy of the human mind is a crucial assumption in his theory. Like Freud, Lévi-Strauss assumes, as Leach [1970] constantly reminds us, that the human mind is invariant, that the trappings of civilization are mere layers that serve to repress the real configuration of the human mind. In effect, Lévi-Strauss assumes that the key to the understanding of collective social phenomena lies in the collective attributes of the human mind, all human minds. To discover the essence of social phenomena, one must therefore go to 'reduced models' in elementary societies where one does not need to mine deep in order to come upon the core of the human mind.

Perhaps a sociological image of Lévi-Strauss' type of collec-tivism will be gained by resorting to his dissatisfaction with Radcliffe-Brown's interpretation of Durkheim's collectivistic sociology. His chief complaint against the British anthropologist is that his subject-matter, that is, social structure, was too super-ficial and much too limited to observable data. According to Lévi-Strauss [1966b: 117], for Radcliffe-Brown 'structure is of the order of empirical observation' and he charges that Radcliffe-Brown had 'introduced—[structure]—into social anthropology to designate the durable manner in which individuals and groups are connected with the social body'. This factual accent in the meaning of structure, which Lévi-Strauss thinks is unsophisticated, is what Piaget [1968: 102] has negatively commented upon as follows: 'In the Anglo-Saxon countries, the concept of structure tends to be reserved for observable relations and interactions.' On the other hand, for Lévi-Strauss structure has the meaning that is conveyed in Piaget's [1968: 98–99] definition of its use in theory construction: 'The social structure, like causality in physics, is a theoretic construct, not an empirical given. It is related to the observable social relations as, in physics, causality is related to physical laws, or as, in psychology, psychological structures do not belong to consciousness.'

All of these features of Lévi-Strauss' structuralism were least developed in his premier anthropological work *Les Structures élémentaires de la Parenté*. In this book his departure from Durkheim's collectivism is less marked than in his later works, especially in his volumes on myths [Lévi-Strauss, 1964, 1966a, 1968] and in *The Savage Mind*. Piaget's [1968: 108] characterization of Lévi-Strauss' structuralism as being especially 'anti-functionalist' and ahistorical is much truer of these later works than of his study of kinship structures in which he expounds his exchange theory [Lévi-Strauss, 1949]. There seems to be a great deal of justice, therefore, in treating his theory of social exchange in the context of the French collectivistic tradition, without discriminating the various shades of collectivism except to note that in Lévi-Strauss' work the individual is accorded less of a place in social processes than in Durkheim's sociology.

In generalizing social exchange processes beyond the kinship structures from which they were generated, we shall be operating true to Lévi-Strauss' [1963: 276] contention that 'what makes social-structure studies valuable is that structures are models, the formal properties of which can be compared independently of their elements'. The social exchange processes postulated for kinship behavior can operate in other areas of human behavior as well. And it ought to be emphasized that in writing about social exchange, Lévi-Strauss was participating in a stable body of the theory of social exchange to which there are alternative approaches. He was in large part polemically reacting to the British tradition of social exchange—just as his own theory was to be the gadfly that annoyed Professor Homans into proposing a counter-theory of social exchange behavior.

The Polemical Context of Lévi-Strauss' Social Exchange Theory

I know of no other modern work by a social scientist sharing the collectivistic frame of reference in which Durkheim's polemics against utilitarian economic assumptions and psychological reductionism in social explanation are kept as alive as in Claude Lévi-Strauss' *Les Structures élémentaires de la Parenté*. Two assumptions are central to his brand of social exchange theory: first, social exchange behavior is human and therefore sub-human animals are incapable of social exchange and, correlatively, cannot provide a model of human social exchange. Secondly, social exchange is a supraindividual process and individual self-interests may be involved in it but they cannot sustain social exchange processes.

LÉVI-STRAUSS' ANTI-ECONOMIC POSITION IN SOCIAL EXCHANGE

In his social exchange theory, Lévi-Strauss resurrects Durkheim's polemics against the English utilitarians. Spencer is to Durkheim's polemics what Frazer is to Lévi-Strauss':

> Frazer [complains Lévi-Strauss] conceives of exchange of wives as a convenient solution to the economic problem of how to obtain a wife. He repeatedly asserts that the exchange of sisters and daughters 'was everywhere at first a simple case of barter'. He depicts the poor Australian aborigine wondering how he is going to obtain a wife since he has no material goods with which to purchase her, and discovering exchange as the solution to this apparently insoluble problem: 'Men exchange their sisters in marriage because that was the cheapest way of getting a wife.' This economic concept of exchange appears again in Frazer's conclusion: . . . 'For under the surface alike of savagery and of civilization the economic forces are as constant and uniform in their operation as the forces of nature, of which indeed, they are merely a peculiar complex manifestation' [Lévi-Strauss,1969:138].

There are three separate reasons for Lévi-Strauss' disagreement with Frazer. First, as the last sentence in the passage above indicates, Frazer's conception of social exchange theory is deductive. Social exchange laws are to be deduced from economic laws which are in turn to be deduced from more inclusive natural laws of physical and biological sciences. Hence, secondly, Frazer sees no real need to make a distinction between economic exchange and social exchange. Lastly, even if such a distinction were to be conceded in Frazer's work, there is the assumption that social exchange remains a subset of economic exchange: that is, there is no autonomous sphere for social exchange.

On all these grounds, Lévi-Strauss stoutly disagrees with Frazer and, if we are permitted to anticipate a little, with the modern day utilitarian social exchange theorists Homans and Blau. For him, the items of social exchange are culturally defined, and they are remarkable not so much for their economic intrinsic value as for their symbolic extrinsic value [Lévi-Strauss, 1969: 138]. In pointed contrast to the British tradition of social exchange, Lévi-Strauss contends that 'it is precisely from the economic viewpoint that [social] exchange should not be envisaged' [1969: 138] since 'it is the exchange which counts and not the things exchanged' [1969: 139]. At any rate, 'The exchange relationship comes before the things exchanged, and is independent of them. If the goods considered in isolation are identical, they cease to be so when assigned their proper place in the structure of reciprocity' [1969: 139]. In most societies, 'There are certain types of objects which are especially appropriate for presents, precisely because of their non-utilitarian nature' [1969: 55].

LÉVI-STRAUSS' ANTI-PSYCHOLOGICAL POSITION IN SOCIAL EXCHANGE

Lévi-Strauss' rejection of the relevance of psychology for social exchange behavior is on a different level from his attack on Frazer and from Durkheim's previous rejections of psychological explanation of social phenomena. His rejection of psychological reasoning in human behavior is introduced as a heuristic device for advancing his own cultural assumptions of exchange behavior. But they anticipate the opposite assumptions made by Homans [1961] in his exchange theory, with respect to the relationship between human behavior and animal behavior, and are therefore of great relevance in discussing the polemical confrontations between the two types of exchange theory.

For both Lévi-Strauss and Homans the meaning of psychology

in social exchange is in terms of animal behavior and not, as in the case of Durkheim, Spencer, and Comte, the behavior of an isolated individual. As with Leslie White's [1949: 34] contention that 'The behavior of man is of two distinct kinds: symbolic and non-symbolic', Lévi-Strauss [1969: 3] sees 'Man [as] both a biological being and a social individual'. And as in White [1949], Lévi-Strauss argues that it is the social aspect of man that gives him the ability to engage in such distinctively symbolic processes as social exchange. Man may share certain attributes with infran-human animals, but it is what is unique to him as human, not what he shares with animals, that enables him to engage in social exchange processes.

Social exchange can neither be derived from nor ascribed to animal behavior—not even to primates, let alone lower animals as the pigeon [Lévi-Strauss, 1969: 5–6]. On the assumption that what is human is *cultural* and what is non-human is *natural*, Lévi-Strauss [1969: 8] contends that

> No empirical analysis can determine the point of transition between natural and cultural facts, nor how they are connected . . .[1] Wherever there are rules we know for certain that the cultural stage has been reached. Likewise, it is easy to recognize universality as the criterion of nature, for what is constant in man falls necessarily beyond the scope of customs, techniques and institution whereby his groups are differentiated and contrasted.

Social exchange, that is, is normative behavior. Rules govern social exchange. Unlike Homansian social exchange theory in which normative regulations prior to, and brought into, the social exchange interaction are excluded, Lévi-Straussian exchange is defined as a regulated form of behavior in the context of societal rules and norms.

With more pointed reference to social exchange behavior, the difference between culture and nature—between human behavior and non-human behavior—receives an important emphasis in Lévi-Strauss' definitions of the premises of social exchange. Exchange behavior is behaviorally creative and dynamic; animal behavior is static and hence it is incapable of social exchange

---

[1] Cf. White [1949: 35]: 'Because *human* behavior is symbol behavior and since behavior of *infra-human* species is non-symbolic, it follows that we can learn nothing about human behavior from observations upon or experiments with the lower animals'.

behavior: 'The character of nature [represented by animals] is that it can give only what has been received . . . However, in the sphere of culture, the individual always receives more than he gives, and gives more than he receives'[1] [Lévi-Strauss, 1969: 7].

Humans assign meaning to what they give out and what they receive and increase or decrease their interactions with others on the basis of their interpretations. On the other hand, animals cannot initiate a social exchange transaction; nor, of course, do they feel obligated to give back. The principle of reciprocity, so central to Lévi-Strauss' exchange theory, is impossible in animal behavior.

The Institutional Bases of Social Exchange Behavior

Individuals engaged in social exchange activities do not create the norms and values that regulate their behavior. Rather, they carry with them institutional definitions of these norms and values into the social exchange situation. Lévi-Strauss has made many statements about the principles of social exchange that flow from them. I want to consolidate three of these principles that I judge to be of special relevance for sociology.

THE PRINCIPLE OF SOCIAL SCARCITY AND SOCIETAL INTERVENTION

The scarcity of any product that has a symbolic value compels the intervention of society in its distribution. So long as there is an abundance of such product, society leaves its distribution to chance or to natural laws. Its scarcity compels the enunciation of rules of exchange [cf. Lévi-Strauss, 1969: 32–35]. But social scarcity is not economic scarcity. Society regulates the meaning of the former. Thus, exogamy and incest, both of which are

---

[1] Cf. White [1949: 29]: 'The difference between the behavior of man and other animals, then, is that the lower animals may receive values, may acquire new meanings, but they cannot create and bestow them. Only man can do this. To use a crude analogy, lower animals are like a person who has only the receiving apparatus for wireless messages: he can receive messages but cannot send them. Man can do both. And this difference is one of kind, not of degree: a creature can either "arbitrarily impose signification", can either create and bestow values, or he cannot. There are no intermediate stages.'

social inventions that take particular meanings from society to society, make a spouse scarce by excluding certain groups of persons from choice of mate. In social scarcity, desired items may be physically available, but they are barred to some actors by social regulations. One simple way a society creates social scarcity is by denying an individual the consumption of his own product or by making it less valuable. Thus, the present a man buys himself at Christmas is of less symbolic value than the one he receives from a friend or relative.

THE PRINCIPLE OF THE SOCIAL COST OF EXCHANGE

The cost of social exchange is borne by individual givers and attributed to society, *outside of the exchange situation*, rather than to individual receivers *inside the social exchange situation*. The host of a banquet does not attribute its costs to his guests but to the social custom that requires it. The cost of Christmas presents is not attributed to those who receive the gifts bought but to the institution of Christmas. This principle frees particular social exchange transactions from the disruptive consequences of attributing the cost of social exchange activities to those who benefit from them.

THE PRINCIPLE OF RECIPROCITY

This principle defines the patterns of reciprocation practised in social exchange. It is sometimes treated as the norm of reciprocity [cf. Gouldner, 1960] insofar as it states rules of behavior in the social exchange situation and not just generally in social life.[1] Although Lévi-Strauss' principle of reciprocity is widely cited by sociologists, his conception of this principle is not co-extensive with its usage in current sociological theory. As used by Parsons [1951], Gouldner [1959, 1960], or Blau [1964], reciprocity refers to the mutual reinforcement by two parties of each other's actions. The norms governing these two-party reciprocations do indeed represent one meaning of the principle of reciprocity in the social

---

[1] See the section 'Morality of Social Exchange' in this chapter for a distinction between the principle of reciprocity and the morality of exchange.

exchange situation. But it has a wider meaning in Lévi-Strauss' [1949] theory. The principle of reciprocity is also a social usage whereby an individual feels obligated to reciprocate another's action, not by directly rewarding his benefactor, but by benefiting another actor implicated in a social exchange situation with his benefactor and himself. This demands that A gives to C in response to what A receives from B. It consists of what Lévi-Strauss has called univocal or directional reciprocity [Lévi-Strauss, 1969: 178–179]. For consistency of terminology I shall speak of *mutual reciprocity* when the reciprocations involved are limited to two individuals, that is, when, say, A expects to be benefited directly by B whenever A benefits B. On the other hand I shall speak of *univocal reciprocity* if the reciprocations involve at least three actors and if the actors do not benefit each other directly but only indirectly.

There is an important corollary of the principle of reciprocity that I want to stress. The principle of reciprocity operates on the basis of equality between all those interlinked by the cycle of reciprocity. Its malfunctioning leads to inequality, but that is clearly an abnormal situation. Thus in discussing generalized exchange (which operates on the principle of univocal reciprocity), Lévi-Strauss [1969: 266] argues that

> generalized exchange presumes equality . . . For the system to function harmoniously [between, say, three partners] A, B, C shall be of equal status and prestige. By contrast, the speculative character of the system, the widening of the cycle . . . the inevitable preference for certain alliances . . . are factors of inequality, which may at any time force a rupture. Thus one comes to the conclusion that generalized exchange leads almost unavoidably to [status differentiation]; but that at the same time it is at variance with the system of [social exchange], and must therefore lead to its downfall.

Thus, the principle of reciprocity has a built-in change-generating factor. Equality of partnership in social exchange is needed for continuity of social interaction; when this expectation is frustrated the social exchange situation is threatened. This linkage between the principle of reciprocity and the equality of the social exchange partners was discerned by Lévi-Strauss from years of acquaintance with ethnographic data. His conclusions in this matter receive substantial support from Piaget's [1932: 200, 274, 280, 316] varied experiments: according to Piaget's findings cooperation, equality, and reciprocity develop together in the absence of status differentiations. The equalitarian basis of this principle of reciprocity does not necessarily mean that status non-equals do not engage in stable social exchange; they can do so provided status is not a salient issue in the social exchange situation.[1]

At a sociological level, the three institutionalized principles— of social scarcity and societal intervention, social costs, and reciprocity—may be said to provide a minimum definition of a social exchange situation within time and space specifications. Because social exchange transactions are situated in time and space, these parameters become important in social exchange systems. Sometimes the one, sometimes the other, and sometimes both of them together become important in social exchange transactions. Thus some social exchanges call for a time-ordering (e.g., a lapse of one year for the return of Christmas gifts) while in other situations space ordering becomes important.

Types of Social Exchange

Intuitive notions of social exchange have been prevalent since the beginnings of the social sciences. Mutual reciprocities, featuring in social exchange transactions between two parties, were the principal way of conceiving of such social exchange. In anthropology such a conception of mutual reciprocities gained in

---

[1] This formal egalitarian principle in Lévi-Strauss' conception of social exchange is part of a broader view of French 'collectivistic' theory of stratification. Collectivistic sociology regards the social structure as a superordinate order in which individual differences in status are insignificant. At any rate status inequalities are mostly defined according to this view as being disruptive of the harmonious functioning of society. The posture in such French collectivistic sociology is to work down from the interests of the social structure to those of individuals. Even high 'status' individuals are subordinated to the interests of the social structure. It is in this sense that Durkheim [1950: 209-214] condemned large class inequalities as 'unjust' and 'immoral'.

This French collectivistic posture is different from the American 'functionalist' theory of social stratification, as spelt out by Parsons [1940, 1953] and Davis and Moore [1945]. In the American version, the interests of high status individuals are generalized to that of the social structure. Inequality is therefore 'functional', since high-status individuals embody the essential values of society to a greater extent than low-status individuals. In contrast, the internalization of critical values in society is assumed by Durkheim [e.g. 1915] to be uniform to the population and high-status is not judged to be uniquely functional for society.

importance when it was associated with the theory of dual organizations. Thus, Frazer's conception of social exchange was tied into his theory of dual organizations. Lévi-Strauss' place in the development of social exchange theory must be understood in terms of his dissatisfaction with the ability of a model of two-party social exchange transactions to explain his kinship data and his introduction of multi-party social exchange transactions to explain more complex kinship behaviors [cf. Lévi-Strauss, 1969: 144, 220].

I will define these two-party and multi-party social exchange transactions on the basis of the principle of reciprocity. Mutual reciprocities limited to two partners feature in what, following Lévi-Strauss' terminology, I shall call *restricted exchange*. On the other hand, univocal reciprocities involving at least three actors in a social exchange situation, feature in what Lévi-Strauss has called *generalized exchange*. In restricted exchange the two parties to the social exchange transaction benefit each other directly but do not receive or give to any other party as part of the social exchange situation. Thus, for example, given four persons, restricted exchange would operate in two pairs as follows: A↔B and C↔D; or A↔C and B↔D, where '↔' signifies 'gives to and receives from'. In generalized exchange no party gives to the party from whom he receives. Thus, given five persons, generalized exchange operates as a unitary system as follows: A→B→C→D→E→A, where '→' signifies 'gives to'.

Although Lévi-Strauss has not made the point explicitly, the differences in the operation and consequences of the two types of social exchange are qualitative, not quantitative. Two-party or restricted exchange behaviors have certain unique properties that set them apart from any multi-party social exchange transactions. The differences between three- and four-party generalized exchanges are differences of degree, not of kind. Those between two-party restricted exchange and three-party, four-party, etc., generalized exchanges are ones of kind, not of degree. However, the differences here are phenotypic only. Genotypically, there are clear possibilities, to be discussed later, of transmutations from one to the other. These phenotypic differences are analogous to similar distinctions drawn by Simmel [1950: 115–144] in his theory of the group and discovered by Bales and Borgatta [1955] in their small group experiments.

The Structure of Restricted Exchange

As Lévi-Strauss defines it, 'The term "restricted exchange" includes any system which effectively or functionally divides the group into a certain number of pairs of exchange units so that, for any one pair $X - Y$ there is a reciprocal relationship' [1969: 146]. This means 'that the system can operate mechanisms of reciprocity only between *partners* or between *partners in multiples of two*' [1969: 178; italics added]. From a sociological point of view it seems important to make a distinction based on this last definition between a restricted exchange situation in which the actors have no other potential partners, i.e., isolated dyadic social exchange relationships, and that in which the restricted exchange partners are implicated in a larger whole and hence there exists the possibility of change of partners. I shall call the first, i.e., isolated dyadic social exchange relationships, *exclusive restricted exchange* and the second, i.e., multiple restricted exchange relationships, *inclusive restricted exchange*. The former is a purer form of restricted exchange than inclusive restricted exchange.

Perhaps the chief characteristic of restricted exchange is the high degree of accountability in each other's behavior. Even ceremonial gestures that would be ignored in larger groups become emphasized in the restricted dyadic exchange situation [cf. Lévi-Strauss, 1969: 71–74]. The visibility of dyadic relationships makes restricted exchange acquire certain peculiar characteristics. First, there is a great deal of attempt to maintain equality. This is especially the case with repeatable social exchange acts. Attempts to gain advantage at the expense of the other is minimized. Negatively, the breach of the rule of equality quickly leads to emotional reactions. The sensibilities and the emotional loading in restricted exchange can be evidenced in Homans' [1961: 75; 1967: 39] and Thibaut and Kelley's [1959] emphasis on emotional factors in their social exchange theories, both of which deal with forms of restricted exchange. Secondly, there is a *quid pro quo* mentality in restricted exchange activities. Time intervals in mutual reciprocities are cut short and there is an attempt to balance activities and exchange items as part of the mutual reciprocal relations. Some insight into the nature of restricted exchange may be gained by considering the unique features of the dyad. This can be seen in terms of Bales and Borgatta's characterization of the dyad:

> As compared to larger groups, the mean profile for groups of this size [two] has a notably high rate of showing tension, and at the same time low rates of showing disagreement and antagonism. Asking for orientation is uniquely high, and although giving orientation is not uniquely high, it is somewhat higher than would be expected from extrapolating the trend for the remaining group sizes. Similarly, giving opinion, although not uniquely low, is lower than would be expected from extrapolation. Giving suggestion is somewhat on the high side in the sense that it deviates from an otherwise perfectly clear and consistent trend seen in the remaining group sizes [Bales and Borgatta, 1965: 501–502].

On the whole, then, restricted exchange is characterized by attempts to avoid offending the other partner; in spite of that, perhaps because of that fact, it is emotion-laden.

Such great emphasis on emotional factors in restricted exchange leads to characteristic consequences for the larger group and society: its operation is marked by mechanical solidarity. Restricted social exchange relationships are brittle in nature.

The Structure of Generalized Exchange

Generalized exchange operates on the principle of what Lévi-Strauss calls 'univocal reciprocity'. It occupies a unitary system of relationships in that it links all parties to the exchange together in an integrated transaction in which reciprocations are indirect, not mutual. I want to expand on Lévi-Strauss' treatment of generalized exchange because it appears to be far more complex than his seminal conception of the univocal reciprocal process.

There are two basic types of generalized exchange that I want to identify. The first is what we have already encountered and it is the one emphasized by Lévi-Strauss: it is based on what I wish to call *chain univocal reciprocity*. Individuals in the system are so positioned that they operate a chain of univocal reciprocations to each other as individual units in what I shall call (a) *chain generalized exchange*. Thus given five members, A→B→C→D→E→ A, where '→' is short for 'gives to'. There is a second type of generalized exchange not yet covered in the literature. Because of its structure I shall call it *net generalized exchange* and we shall say that it operates on the principle of *net univocal reciprocity*. There are two sub-types of this: individual-focused and group-focused. In both sub-types the individual is placed against the group in contrast to chain generalized exchange. However, the individual units involved are equal, as in chain generalized exchange.

INDIVIDUAL-FOCUSED NET GENERALIZED EXCHANGE

This form of generalized exchange is practised extensively in farming communities in both economic and social exchange terms. The group as a whole benefits each member consecutively until all members have each received the same amount of benefits and attention. In a five-party generalized exchange it operates as follows: ABCD→E; ABCE→D; ABDE→C; ACDE→B; and BDCE→A. Sometimes its operation is limited to special occasions, as when one of the members suffers bereavement. Usually, all members pool their social and economic resources to do benefit to each of the members. A most pronounced example of this process is the Nigerian *esusu*. Part of the operation of the *esusu* involves paying visits of solidarity to each of the members of the group by all other members over a period of time.

GROUP-FOCUSED NET GENERALIZED EXCHANGE

Individuals involved in this type of social exchange successively give to the group as a unit and then gain back as part of the group from each of the unit members. Thus in a five-man friendship group, all the members may each invite all others *together as a unit* to, say, dinner parties over a period of time. If B is invited to dinner (along with C, D, and E) by A, the principle of net univocal reciprocity requires that B reciprocate, not just by inviting A to dinner, but by inviting all of A, C, D, and E *together at the same time and place to dinner*. Hence it operates as follows: A→BCDE; B→ACDE; C→ABDE; D→ABCE; and E→ABCD.[1]

Two points need to be raised about this statement of generalized exchange. First, these types are empirical, not logical. They are the types that exist in various groups and societies. Logically, other cases can be thought up. Secondly, these definitions of generalized exchange strain the conceptions of reciprocity as currently used in sociological theory. As we have said before, that conception of reciprocity is limited to two-party interactions. In such situations, Gouldner [1960: 169] has stated that 'it would seem that there can be stable patterns of reciprocity *qua* exchange only insofar as *each* party has both rights and duties'. The determination of such rights and duties becomes a more complex problem in generalized exchange, largely because it is difficult to exclude the group *sui generis* in its operation. In net generalized exchange the group exists as an entity and opposed to the individuals. The individual has certain duties to the group and his rights are to be defined in terms of the responsibility of the group. The group as such has certain rights and duties. The operation of net generalized exchange leads therefore to the resurrection of the perennial question: is the group real? The answer in terms of this analysis is clearly in the affirmative. For in its operation the individual A who benefits BCDE together cannot press his claims for a return against each of B, C, D, or E, separately but against all of them (BCDE) together.

The matter is far more subtle in the case of chain generalized exchange. What happens if A gives to B and no one else reciprocates univocally to A? Since the group does not operate

---

[1] Sahlins [1965: 141–145] makes a distinction between 'pooling' and 'reciprocity'. What he refers to as pooling seems to be a combination of the two types of net reciprocity that I identify here. He considers pooling as 'centralized movements: collection from members of a group, often under one hand, and redivision within this group [as in diagram]

This is "pooling" or "redistribution" . . . pooling is socially a *within* relation, the collective action of a group. Reciprocity is a *between* relation, the action and reaction of two parties' [Sahlins, 1965: 141]. Although Sahlins' conception of pooling appears insightful, it is doubtful that it is separate from reciprocity as conceived in net generalized exchange.

as a unit the matter may seem precarious. In fact, however, both the chain and net generalized exchange systems operate under what I like to call the law of extended credit: in a generalized exchange situation the receipt of a benefit by any one party is regarded as a credit to that party by all other parties and therefore his reciprocation is regarded as a credit to all of them. Negatively, a breach of exchange rules, for instance the failure to reciprocate to any one individual by another in the generalized exchange system, is regarded not just as the sole business of the cheated individual but of the group. In other words, if A fails to be reciprocated to by B, others in the exchange situation may have to compensate him.

Lévi-Strauss' observations and seminal theoretical formulations have helped a great deal in the conceptualization of generalized exchange. However, a lot remains to be done empirically in the determination of its various forms. It is possible, for instance, that a Bavelas-type [1950] communication patterns analysis may help to clarify the meaning of various forms of generalized exchange. On the basis of several examples in the anthropological literature, it does seem possible at this point to make the following generalization about generalized exchange: as actual examples, e.g., Lévi-Strauss [1969: 245–254], seem to indicate, generalized exchange tends to be more effectively practised in odd-numbered groups than in even-numbered groups.[1] Odd-numbered generalized exchange groups may tend to be more solidary for the important reason that transmutations into inclusive restricted exchange partnerships cannot result without altering the unitary structure of the group by dropping out at least one member, whereas even-numbered groups can be resolved into such inclusive restricted exchange groups without the danger of dropping out a member. At least, odd-numbered generalized exchange systems may manifest a greater degree of social solidarity than even-numbered groups.[2] This position seems to be close to

---

[1] Cf. Lévi-Strauss [1969: 234]: 'Systems of generalized exchange can incorporate any number of sections, but only if a given number is subdivided into an odd number of . . . units . . . can its presence be presumed *a priori*'.

[2] The distinction between odd-numbered and even-numbered generalized exchange may be useful in resolving a problem that hangs loose in Lévi-Strauss' analysis of marriage exchange. Whereas both matrilineal cross-cousin marriages and patrilineal cross-cousin marriages are based on generalized exchange, they insure varying degrees of solidarity, with the former proving to be the superior form.

Bales and Borgatta's [1965: 503] finding that 'groups with even numbers of members [as contrasted with odd-numbered groups] are high in showing disagreement and antagonism, and are low in asking for suggestions'.

As opposed to restricted exchange, the operation of generalized exchange is relatively devoid of emotional loading. Its major attribute is trust of each other in the system [cf. Lévi-Strauss, 1969: 265]. Because the operations of generalized exchange are spread over time and space, trust that it will work seems to be a basic assumption in this type of social exchange. Similarly, as compared to restricted exchange, generalized exchange engenders a high degree of social solidarity.

The Exploitation of Social Exchange

In examining Frazer's and Malinowski's conceptions of social exchange processes, we saw that they had different approaches to the problem of exploitation in social exchange. While exploitation was built into Frazer's theory of social exchange, Malinowski's characterization of social exchange transactions had no room for exploitation of exchange partners. Lévi-Strauss occupies a middle ground between these two positions. He postulates that ideally social exchange processes should be devoid of exploitation if there are to be stable social exchange relations. However, he recognizes that in practice it exists, with the intrusion of exploitation leading to 'pathological' or 'anomic' social exchange relations. Ultimately the exploitation problem leads to the termination of social exchange relations. A common consequence of exploitation in social exchange relations is a new emphasis on economic gains from a transaction marked in the past by symbolic processes. 'The resulting utilitarian, often extravagant, prestations

---

Lévi-Strauss characterizes patrilineal cross-cousin marriage as a 'discontinuous form of exchange for which there is no law' and flatly states that it is 'incapable of attaining a form other than that of a multitude of small closed systems, juxtaposed one to another, without ever being able to realize an overall structure' [1969: 445]. I suggest that the *law* involved is that of even-numbered generalized exchange. Patrilineal cross-cousin marriages seem to be heavily characterized by the conjoining of even-numbers to the exchange system, whereas matrilineal cross-cousin marriage, as actual examples indicate, is usually involved in odd-numbered marriage exchange groups. [Also cf. the diagram in Homans and Schneider, 1955: 11.]

and [economic] exchanges, "debts", claims and obligations [are], in a way, a kind of pathological symptom. But the disorder it reveals and for which it acts as a kind of compensation is inherent in the system; viz., the conflict between the egalitarian conditions of generalized exchange, and its aristocratic consequences' [Lévi-Strauss, 1969: 267].

Thus generalized exchange is seen by Lévi-Strauss in the same terms as those in which Durkheim described the division of labor. Although both generalized exchange and the social division of labor work to insure organic social solidarity in society, they have their pathological and anomic forms, with consequences far removed from their normal or ideal types.

The mention of the 'egalitarian conditions' of generalized exchange by Lévi-Strauss [1969: 266–267] provides the appropriate forum for correcting Blau's misinterpretation of Lévi-Strauss' position as supporting his contention that one of the basic functions of social exchange is to establish superordination over others: 'One of the important functions of social exchange is, in the words of Lévi-Strauss, "to surpass a rival in generosity, to crush him if possible under future obligations which it is hoped he cannot meet, thus taking from him privileges, titles, rank, authority, and prestige" ' [Blau, 1964: 108]. In fact this sentence quoted from Lévi-Strauss is far from Lévi-Strauss' position. He was merely reporting what three ethnographers—D. Davy, H. G. Barnett, and G. P. Murdock—had said of reciprocities in the *potlatch*. The reference to these ethnographers is omitted from the heavily edited 'Principle of Reciprocity' in Coser and Rosenberg's [1957] *Sociological Theory*, from which Blau cited the sentence. Also omitted is the following sentence which immediately follows Lévi-Strauss' statement cited by Blau: 'Doubtless the system of reciprocal gifts only reaches such vast proportions among the Indians of the North-West Pacific, virtuosi who display a genius and an exceptional aptitude for the treatment of the fundamental themes of primitive culture' [Lévi-Strauss, 1969: 53]. This sceptical reception of the 'superordination function' view of social exchange is closer to Lévi-Strauss' position which more or less states that the exploitation of the social exchange situation for power and status differentiation, with its resultant inequalities, is anomic and ultimately leads to the abortion of social exchange relationships.

Structurally, the exploitation of social exchange institutions and relationships result in the transvaluation of the items of social exchange: where before they were weighed entirely in terms of symbolic values, they now come to acquire a utilitarian economic value. The most notorious example of this breakdown in social exchange is in the area of marriages. Where before gifts presented by husbands to their brides' family were symbolic in value, an emblem of the new solidarity between the groups joined by the marriages, they may now come to acquire a utilitarian value. The highest bidder in commercial values may come to dominate the marital scene, thus violating the basic social exchange rule that the partners in exchange are not to be sought for their commercial worth.

The Morality of Social Exchange

We have said that Mauss' chief contribution to social exchange theory lies in his recognition that social exchange processes yield for the larger society a moral code of behavior which acquires an independent existence outside the social exchange situation and which informs all social, economic, and political interpersonal relationships in society. This is what we have called the morality of social exchange. The morality of social exchange is to be distinguished from the principle of reciprocity which operates in the social exchange situation and which defines and regulates social exchange processes. The distinction is by no means trivial. All social interactions are not social exchange—at least according to the perspective I have developed in this chapter. However, much of social life, beyond the immediate social exchange situation, is influenced by social exchange processes through the moral code they yield for the larger society. It plays much the same role as religion in society: even if religion is not practised every day of one's life and even if not everybody is involved in religious matters, the weight of religion is felt by everybody in society through the mode of behavior it sanctions.

Much of what is referred to as the 'norm of reciprocity' [Gouldner, 1960] or 'the principle of give and take' [Malinowski, 1951: 39–49] belongs to what I call here the morality of social exchange. They provide the moral basis for the operation of law, the economy, and politics. All moral values and norms are by their nature interpersonal: they define and control the relationship of the individual to others. The 'norm of reciprocity' and the 'principle of give and take' are moral norms and principles that operate to restrain absolute 'individual self-interest' for the achievement of greater harmonious relationships in social life.

What we can infer from Lévi-Strauss' social exchange theory and my own elaborations of it is that, since social exchange processes are of various types, the moralities that these various types yield will also be different. Especially important is the difference between the morality of restricted exchange and that of generalized exchange. The morality of restricted exchange is bound to be brittle, with little of trust involved. A *quid pro quo* attitude pervades interpersonal relationships and a belief that common investments and goods, from which individuals can gain indirectly and ultimately, are not workable persists in social life. I suggest that the working of 'amoral familism' in Banfield's [1958] *The Moral Basis of a Backward Society* exemplifies such morality of restricted exchange. Those seeking office, for example, are presumed to be exclusively concerned with personal aggrandizement and therefore voters seek to obtain bribes in order to vote them into office.

Wholly different is the operation of the morality of generalized exchange. Trust of others; trust that others will discharge their obligations to the enrichment of society rather than for their exclusive narrow self-interests; the willingness to give to others the benefit of the doubt: these are the true attributes of the morality of generalized exchange. Societies with a morality of generalized exchange enjoy a *credit mentality*: the belief that individuals are credit worthy and can be trusted to pay back what they owe. Similarly, contributions to causes that do not yield immediate and direct benefits to the contributor, with only the hope that they will ultimately and indirectly come to benefit him or his family after a lapse of time, are characteristic of social relationships in which the morality of generalized exchange operates.

We have said that generalized exchange is differentiated. On the one hand there is chain generalized exchange; on the other hand net generalized exchange. These are areas in which empirical research needs to be carried out, but I wish to enter some permissible speculations with respect to the moralities of these generalized exchange systems. I shall limit myself to the moralities of net generalized exchange. We have already made a distinction between individual-focused net generalized exchange and group-focused net generalized exchange. I speculate that the morality of the former will be more receptive to a social welfare ideology than the morality of group-focused net generalized exchange. Similarly I speculate that group-focused net generalized exchange may yield a morality that emphasizes duties more than it emphasizes rights, at least much more than would be the case with individual-focused net generalized exchanges.[1]

---

[1] This conception of the morality of social exchange has some bearing on the burgeoning study of the modernization of traditional societies. Much of the motive force for industrialization, and modernization generally, is usually attributed to individual personality attributes and to innovating changes in the character structure of individuals [cf. especially McClelland and Winter, 1969: 1–37; Hagen, 1962]. Underemphasized is the role of the interpersonal bases of modernization and industrialization. Modernization and industrialization would be impossible without the trust of others or without a basic willingness to cooperate—even if the requisite individual character structure was available in any society. I contend that the elaborate social exchange processes in various traditional societies help to build a foundation of trust and cooperation necessary for the modernization of these societies.

Belshaw [1965: 12] remarked rather casually of the Trobrianders who practiced Kula exchange: 'It should be noted in passing that in 1964 the ceremonially oriented Trobrianders participated with the rest of the peoples of New Guinea in the first election by universal suffrage of representatives to the Legislative Council'. It would be of great sociological interest to find out how their political attitudes and orientations have been affected by the history of their traditional Kula exchange.

4
Social Exchange and
Social Solidarity

One of the most vexed issues in Lévi-Strauss' exchange theory concerns the relationship between the two forms of social exchange he has applied with such insight in the study of kinship behaviors and Durkheim's conceptions of mechanical solidarity and organic solidarity. The problem is that Lévi-Strauss likens restricted exchange to mechanical solidarity and generalized exchange to organic solidarity in analogical terms. There was no analysis carried out to demonstrate these relationships. Subsequently, twenty years after suggesting these relationships, Lévi-Strauss [1969: xxxiii–xxxiv) has grown suspicious of them and has indeed cast doubt on them. There is need for some fresh attempt at analysis. Durkheim's *The Division of Labor in Society* focused attention on differentiation in industrializing societies and only treated traditional societies as a baseline from which to proceed to an analysis of the emergent attributes of a changing society. On the other hand Lévi-Strauss' [1949] exchange theory focused attention on the integrative forces of social exchange processes in traditional societies. A full view of social solidarity would seem to require a synthesis of the two approaches. In other words, there is need to move beyond the separate searches for the sources of social solidarity in traditional and industrialized societies to a more comprehensive theory of social solidarity. This chapter attempts such a theory. The cultural *integrative* basis of social exchange in Lévi-Strauss' theory is meshed with the concern with *differentiation* arising from the division of labor in Durkheim's theory.

Lévi-Strauss' Position

From our analysis of what I have called collectivisitic social exchange theory, it should be apparent that there are suggestive similarities between the social conditions underlying restricted exchange and those of mechanical solidarity on the one hand and conditions underlying generalized exchange and those of organic solidarity on the other. For instance, the emotional loading of the former seems significantly higher than that of generalized exchange and organic solidarity. But this is not the type of parallel between the two sets of constructs that impressed Lévi-Strauss. Rather, he emphasized the fragility of mechanical solidarity and of the social relationships predicated on restricted exchange as contrasted with the elasticity and flexibility of organic solidarity and of the social conditions of generalized exchange. In this regard at least, Lévi-Strauss is a functionalist in the classical Durkheimian sense of the word, and his arguments about the social dynamics of the two types of social exchange are cast in functionalist reasoning. But his functionalism is untouched by the familiar latter-day 'four-functions' assumption introduced into functional analysis by Parsons [e.g., 1961a; 1971: 4–28]. Lévi-Strauss' [cf. 1969: 441–448] overall position is that social exchange performs an integrative function for society. The differences between generalized exchange and restricted exchange are thus to be seen in terms of the degree of integration each type achieves for society:

> There is thus a basic difference between direct and indirect exchange in that the former is extremely productive as regards the number of systems which can be based upon it, but functionally is relatively sterile . . . The development of restricted exchange goes hand in hand with the admission of [a great] number of local [i.e. structurally separate] groups participating in the exchange . . . Organic solidarity (i.e. development in the degree of integration) goes hand in hand with a mechanical development (i.e., the numerical increase in the number of participants). Conversely, generalized exchange, while relatively unproductive in the matter of the system (since it can engender only one single pure system), is very fruitful as a regulating principle: the group remaining

unchanged in extent and composition, generalized exchange allows the realization of a more supple and effective solidarity within this mechanically stable group [Lévi-Strauss, 1969: 441].[1]

This passage deserves careful interpretation. It is based on a distinction that has not been emphasized in modern functional analysis of social dynamics. It is a distinction between structural integration and functional integration. Several units of a social system can be brought together mechanically without affecting the functions ordinarily performed by each of them and without enhancing their total functional output and the overall harmonious functioning of the group. I shall call this *structural integration*. In structural integration new or different fuctions are not involved in the rearrangement of the parts. On the other hand, several units or parts of the social system can be brought together in such a way that not only is unity of structure achieved but also unity of functions is enhanced. The functions of the different parts may be coordinated in such a way that the total functioning of the social system is enhanced over and above the level achieved in functions by the disparate parts. Moreover, new emergent functions may follow the social arrangement that brought the parts together. I shall call this *functional integration*. The hypothesis implicit in the passage quoted above is that functional integration leads to the realization of a greater level of social solidarity than structural integration. As a matter of definition, the point may be made that the working of restricted exchange involves structural integration while the working of generalized exchange involves functional integration.

The point deserves to be repeated that the significance of social exchange for social dynamics lies in its integration of society, not its differentiation of society. In this regard at least, Homans and Schneider [1955: 10] misinterpreted Lévi-Strauss' work when

---

[1] Similarly the differences between patrilateral cross-cousin marriage (predicated on what Lévi-Strauss characterizes as 'discontinuous exchange') and matrilateral cross-cousin marriage (based on generalized exchange) are seen in terms of the level of integration they attain: 'If, then, in the final analysis, marriage with the father's sister's daughter is less frequent than that with the mother's brother's daughter, it is because the latter not only permits but favors a better integration of the group, whereas the former never succeeds in creating anything but a precarious edifice made of juxtaposed materials, subject to no general plan, and its discrete texture is exposed to the same fragility of the little local structures of which ultimately it is composed' [Lévi-Strauss, 1969: 448–449].

they ascribed to his social exchange theory Durkheim's emphasis on differentiation:

> Lévi-Strauss is a French social scientist, and the parentage of his theory is clear. In the language of the turf, it is by Émile Durkheim out of Marcell Mauss's *Essai sur le don*. According to Durkheim in *De la Division du travail* a society is organically solidary to the extent that its individual members or subgroups are specialists and so dependent on one another, a further implication being that a solidary society is one showing a capacity to maintain itself in the face of disruptive tendencies. While Durkheim is talking for the most part about occupational specialization (the division of labor), Lévi-Strauss is talking about the specialization of one group with respect to others in giving women in marriage, but we believe the two men mean the same thing by *organic solidarity*. For Lévi-Strauss the greater the marriage specialization of each of the kin-groups in a society, the greater the dependence of each upon all, and hence the greater the organic solidarity.

In actual fact the items for exchange in Lévi-Strauss' social exchange theory have symbolic value and are of the same type, thus leaving no room for specialization. Lévi-Strauss has rightly rejected Homans and Schneider's interpretation of his position. But in doing so he leaves unresolved the nature of the relationship between social exchange and social solidarity:

> [a fundamental misunderstanding is bound to arise from] the likening of restricted exchange to mechanical solidarity and of generalized exchange to organic solidarity, adopted without discussion by Homans and Schneider. If a society with restricted exchange or generalized exchange is envisaged as a whole, each segment fulfils an identical function to each of the other segments. Consequently what we are dealing with is two different forms of mechanical solidarity. I dare say I myself have repeatedly used the terms 'mechanical' and 'organic' more loosely than Durkheim intended and than is generally accepted [Lévi-Strauss, 1969: xxxiii–xxxiv].

What Lévi-Strauss rejects in this passage is the attribution of social differentiation to his exchange theory. But his further comments pertaining to Durkheim's theory seems to imply that he accepts Homans and Schneider's interpretation of Durkheim's theory of social solidarity. I think that theory does more than link specialization or differentiation with organic solidarity. I shall argue that the integrative processes of social exchange have a part to play in the emergence of organic solidarity.

The Bases of Social Solidarity

In *The Division of Labor in Society*, Durkheim sought to establish the conditions that contributed to the emergence of different types of social solidarity in society. The dependent variable in his analysis is social solidarity for which the 'visible symbol is law' [1933: 64]. There are two types of social solidarity: organic solidarity characteristic of industrialized societies and symbolized by restitutive law and mechanical solidarity characteristic of traditional societies and symbolized by repressive law. But what are the independent variables that determine these types of social solidarity? At this point we run into unsatisfactory answers. Durkheim says that mechanical solidarity derives from the predominance of a common conscience in society and 'is at its maximum when the collective conscience completely envelops our whole conscience and coincides in all points with it' [Durkheim, 1933: 130]. On the other hand organic solidarity flows from the division of labor in society. This would mean that the two types of solidarity derive from different sources: mechanical solidarity from the *integrative* forces of *conscience collective* and organic solidarity from the social *differentiation* of society occasioned by the division of labor. But do integrative processes have anything to do with organic solidarity and does differentiation have anything to do with mechanical solidarity? The answer is by no means obvious.

The possibility of two separate sets of independent variables for the emergence of mechanical solidarity and organic solidarity would appear partially plausible in view of the evolutionary model posited by Durkheim: the latter replaces mechanical solidarity as society experiences industrialization. But there is a strong case for arguing that Durkheim's evolutionary 'replacement theory' of social solidarity is limited. This is the way Ralph H. Turner [1967: 62, 63] sees it:

> Instead of Durkheim's replacement theory, mechanical solidarity is viewed as a continuing requirement for the development and maintenance of organic solidarity. Organic solidarity cannot

replace mechanical solidarity. Instead, organic solidarity requires, in addition to the division of labor, an effective substratum of mechanical solidarity. And the division of labor fails to operate without a working mechanical solidarity [p. 62].

Among many reasons why the division of labor requires a substratum of mechanical solidarity we single out three. First, each participant in a division of labor must neglect *some* essential tasks in order to perform his own tasks. He can only do so when he has confidence that the neglected tasks will be performed by others. The most basic source of such confidence is the assurance that people share common sentiments, including duty and responsibility. Second, the usefulness of most specialized tasks is not obvious, especially as they become more highly fractionated. Hence the individual must depend upon group consensus to validate his claim to be doing something useful, and to supply the self-respect which motivates him at his work. Third, the individual is unable to control the over-all direction of group effort under divided labor. If the division of labor is to produce organic solidarity, there must first be confidence that the general direction in which the group product is moving is a desirable one [p. 63].

Seen in such contextual terms, mechanical solidarity and organic solidarity may well have a common basis for their existence. At least one student of Durkheim's thought has implied that the legal structure is in fact an independent variable and not just an index of social solidarity:

One of Emile Durkheim's remarkable insights concerned the role of integrative mechanisms during periods of growing social heterogeneity. Attacking the utilitarian view that the division of labor would flourish best without regulation, Durkheim demonstrates that one concomitant of a growing division of labor is an *increase* in mechanisms for coordinating and solidifying the interaction among individuals whose interests are becoming progressively more diversified. Durkheim locates this integration largely in the legal structure; however, similar kinds of integrative forces can be discerned elsewhere in society [Smelser, 1966: 41].

According to Smelser's interpretation the legal structure represents an independent variable, which was perhaps not as clearly specified by Durkheim as he did specify the division of labor. This would indicate that organic solidarity is determined not just by differentiation in society but by the interaction of *processes of differentiation* (in this case the division of labor) and some form of *integrative processes.*[1]

The same argument may be put forward concerning the determination of mechanical solidarity. The integrative mechanisms of *conscience collective* do not operate in the absence of the processes of differentiation. In a little known passage in *The Division of Labor*, Durkheim makes an important distinction between the simple division of labor and the compound division of labor in society:

> reciprocity is possible only where there is cooperation, and that, in its turn, does not come about without the division of labor. To cooperate, in short, is to participate in a common task. If this is divided into tasks qualitatively similar, but mutually indispensable, there is a simple division of labor of the first degree. If they are of a different character, there is a compound division of labor, specialization properly called [Durkheim, 1933: 124].

Durkheim of course focused his attention on 'the compound division of labor' in which the tasks (or, more formally, functions) performed by the subunits of the social system are specialized, as in an industrialized society. He was less interested for his purposes in the 'simple division of labor', the type one finds in traditional societies, in which the subunits of the social system do not have specialized functions to perform. At least, then, a type of division of labor exists for societies in which mechanical solidarity exists and, presumably, it works in interaction with the integrative forces of the *conscience collective* to determine the mechanical solidarity of traditional societies.

Beyond what Durkheim [1933: 124] says in the passage cited above, what are the formal properties of the simple division of labor and of the compound division of labor? As Durkheim [1933: 131, 353–354] intimates, the simple division of labor comprises *structural differentiation* or 'differentiation pure and simple' [p. 353] but not *functional differentiation.*[2] In the simple division of

---

[1] When one moves beyond *The Division of Labor in Society* and considers Durkheim's work as a totality, the impression remains strong that ultimately the principal source of social solidarity is the moral principles of the *conscience collective* type. As Parsons [1937: 321] has remarked, 'In a sense reversion to mechanical solidarity represents the authentic line of Durkheim's own development.'

[2] The distinction drawn here between structural differentiation and functional differentiation is not identical with Parsons' distinction between segmentation and differentiation: 'Differentiation is distinct from *segmentation*. Both processes involve

labor new structures emerge which do not contribute new or different functions to the working of the social system but rather are nourished at the expense of the parent functions [Durkheim, 1933: 354]. In the compound division of labor, old as well as new differentiated substructures contribute specialized functions, which are new or different, to the social system in concert with other specialized functions performed by other parts of the social system.

In sum: to rephrase Smelser [1966: 41], social solidarity is the result of an interplay 'between differentiation and integration' of social *structures* and social *functions*. I believe this to be a logical development of Durkheim's theory of social solidarity. It is at variance with the modern analysis of social dynamics [cf., e.g., Smelser, 1966] which is limited to the differentiation and integration of structures to the exclusion of those of functions, under the assumption that functions in society are functions are functions are functions and therefore do not change. To justify my departure from the Parsonian strategy and my return to what I believe to be classical Durkheimian functional analysis, I shall devote the next section to an examination of the limitations of the 'four-functions' Parsonian assumption that now dominates the modern functionalist analysis of social dynamics.

Differentiation and Integration in Functional Analysis

Modern functionalism in sociology developed out of Durkheim's work. But certain changes in assumptions have been introduced into it and what we know as functional analysis today, particularly

---

an increase in the number of distinct units or subsystems. But segmentation is the process by which one unit divides into two or more structurally and functionally equivalent smaller units . . . In the process of differentiation, on the other hand, the new units are neither structurally nor functionally equivalent, but each contributes different specialized ingredients to a more general function' [Parsons and Smelser, 1956: 256]. In Parsons, differentiation does *not* involve *new* or *different* functions, since all functions already exist in every social system. It is this assumption that I reject in the present discussion. Parsons seems to have been aware of the fact that Durkheim himself made the distinction emphasized here between 'functional differentiation' and 'structural differentiation'. [See Parsons, 1937: 321-322 where he talks of 'differentiation of function' and of 'social differentiation' in Durkheim's *The Division of Labor in Society*.]

the Parsonian brand of functionalism, is different from Durkheim's original position in important ways. Originally Durkheim [1938: 95] talked of function in terms of a correspondence between the activity of a phenomenon and 'the general needs of the social organism'. This trite definition attains more meaning if we examine the other contexts in which the term 'function' was used in *The Rules of Sociological Method*. In all cases there is the strong implication that these needs of the 'social organism' (or, in modern terminology, the social system) vary according to the complexity and size of the society involved. Thus he says, 'For example, we have explained the constant development of the division of labor by showing that it is necessary in order that man may maintain himself in the new conditions of existence as he advances in history' [Durkheim, 1938: 92]. In other words the division of labor performs a function that was not in existence in traditional societies. Elsewhere in *The Rules*, Durkheim [1938: 96] writes:

> in proportion as the social milieu becomes more complex and more unstable, traditions and conventional beliefs are shaken, become more indeterminate and more unsteady, and reflexive powers are developed. Such rationality is indispensable to societies and individuals in adapting themselves to a more mobile and more complex environment.

That is, as in the case of the division of labor, the emergence of rationality fulfills a function that was absent in the more primitive level of social life. In general then, specific functions may be present or absent from a society, depending on the simplicity or complexity of that society. This is the most important hypothesis in Durkheim's functionalism.

The first major change in Durkheim's conception of functional analysis was introduced by Radcliffe-Brown. His 'elaboration' of Durkheim's conception of 'function' needs to be cited because it is the beginning of some radical changes that have been introduced into functional analysis:

> Durkheim's definition is that the 'function' of a social institution is the correspondence between it and the needs of the social system. This definition requires some elaboration. In the first place, to avoid ambiguity and in particular the possibility of a teleological interpretation, I would like to substitute for the term

'needs' the term 'necessary conditions of existence' or if the term 'need' is used, it is to be understood in this sense. It may be noted, as a point to be returned to, that any attempt to apply this concept of function in social science involves the assumption that there *are* necessary conditions of existence for human societies just as there are for animal organisms, and that they can be discovered [Radcliffe-Brown, 1935: 178].

This is really more than an elaboration of Durkheim's position. The unwitting but critical change in this 'elaboration' is that Radcliffe-Brown seems to be generalizing to 'human societies' as a generic type and 'the necessary conditions' therefore appear to refer to *the least common functions of all human societies.* Lost in it is Durkheim's central emphasis on the differentiated needs of societies at different levels of development. Certainly, Durkheim treated industrial societies as a type and 'primitive' societies as another type, with needs and, therefore, functions specific to the types. Radcliffe-Brown's position was to lead in the direction of the search for what are the most elementary functions in the abstraction of all societies, namely, the social system, and the assumption that the same functions exist in all societies of whatever complexity.

Aberle *et al.* (1950) made one of the earliest detailed attempts to advance the conceptualization of these 'functional pre-requisites of a society'. Altogether, they named nine such 'functional prerequisites'.[1] But they were careful enough to caution that 'Any formulation of functional prerequisites depends for its categories on the theory of action employed' [Aberle *et al.*, 1950: 100]. In other words, their nine functional prerequisites are not an empirical statement of all functions in every society, but only a heuristic statement intended to help the sociologist to understand his problem area of investigation. Depending on the 'theory of action employed' the functional prerequisites could be more or less. The other point to be noted about their attempt is that they were talking about a 'society' defined as 'a group of human beings sharing a self-sufficient system of action which is capable

---

[1] These are (1) provision for adequate relationship to the environment and for sexual recruitment; (2) role differentiation and role assignment; (3) communication; (4) shared cognitive orientations; (5) a shared, articulated set of goals; (6) the normative regulation of means; (7) the regulation of affective expression; (8) socialization; and (9) the effective control of disruptive forms of behavior.

of existing longer than the life-span of an individual, the group being recruited at least in part by the sexual reproduction of the members' [Aberle *et al.*, 1950: 101]. Needless to say, their time and space specifications are broader than those of most ordinary groups studied by the sociologist.

Parsons' attempt at the formulation of the 'functional prerequisites' is designed to meet the needs of all sociologists. His unit of enquiry, the social system, is more analytical and more abstract. Both Bales' small groups, limited in time and space, and American society as a whole constitute such a social system. The result is that Parsons looked for functional prerequisites that are more elementary, the *least common functions of the social system*. This search led him initially to three social system functional prerequisites of goal-attainment, integration, and pattern-maintenance corresponding with three subsystems: 'the individual actor, the interactive system, and a system of cultural patterning' [Parsons, 1951: 27]. Subsequently, Parsons [1961a] increased them to four, by adding a new category of 'adaptation' corresponding to the behavioral organism as a subsystem. Since this [1961a] position has been adopted ten years later [Parsons, 1971: 4–28], we may be satisfied that for Parsons' action theory all the functional prerequisites needed are those of integration, pattern-maintenance, goal attainment, and adaptation. It is this four-functions assumption that now dominates the functional analysis of social dynamics in sociology.

This *de facto* restriction of functions in society to four in number has serious consequences for the analysis of social dynamics or social processes generally. The burden of change comes to rest exclusively on social structures, with new and different structures emerging and being reintegrated. But no new or different functions can emerge, since all the functions are presumed to exist *a priori* even in the most elementary social system. The differences between an Eskimo fishing village and General Motors must be discovered not in terms of the numbers or types of functions performed by each of them, but rather in terms of the variations in the substructures and how these latter perform the four basic functions in each social system. As Smelser [1959: 12] so bluntly put it, 'The functions are constant over time, no matter what the composition of a given social system'. Social change must therefore be seen in terms of structural differentiation and integration involving *new* and *different* substructures, but never in terms of functional differentiation and integration involving *new* and *different* subfunctions or functions [cf. Parsons, 1961c, 1966; Parsons and Smelser, 1956: Chap. V; Smelser, 1959, 1966; Bales and Slater, 1953].

Dissatisfactions with the four-functions assumption remain one of the principal reasons for the common complaints against the structural-functionalist analysis of social change [cf. Lauer, 1971; Blain, 1971]. Such dissatisfactions also lead to the suggestion of alternative approaches, notably among them Etzioni's [1966: 3] conception of epigenesis 'according to which "adult" units emerge through a process in which parts that carry out *new* functions are added to existing ones, until the entire unit is assembled'. While there is much to be said for such alternatives, they fail to face up to the fact that the weaknesses they seek to correct are an artifact of the 'four-functions' assumption and that this assumption is only a heuristic device intended to help the analyst in his attempt to understand social reality. It is clearly not an empirical statement of a scientific truth. As a heuristic device its continued existence in analysis is strictly subject to its utility in social research. I dare suggest that the Parsonian 'four-functions' assumption is now standing in the way of explaining relevant data in sociology [cf. Etzioni, 1964: 483–484] and should be abandoned in preference for Durkheim's conception of functions as specific to the level of civilization and industrialization attained by a society.

Sociology is not unique in facing the problems that arise from limiting assumptions in functional analysis. As Clara Thompson [1950] has so brilliantly shown, Freud's original conception of personality dynamics was heavily based on the assumption that the sex instincts were exclusively responsible for neurosis. When faced with war-time data which his theory could not explain, Freud expanded his assumptions and took the significant step of including aggression instincts in his functional analysis of personality. Nearer our field, Hullian functionalism in psychology had discouraged the intensive investigation of specialized themes and it was only after the rejection of its assumptions that such new areas as McClelland's rich research in achievement motivation were possible. McClelland's thought here is worth quoting for the light it sheds on this matter in sociology:

> Influenced by Hull and other functionalists, many of us for a long time tended to think of motives or drives as if they were functionally interchangeable. . . . All motives are functionally equivalent and vary only in intensity. A motive is a motive is a motive is a motive . . . Today as we have begun to study motivation in its own right, and not just a convenient construct to explain learning, such a point of view seems painfully inadequate [McClelland, 1955: 43–44].

The similarity of this situation in psychology to the Parsonian 'four-functions' assumption should be obvious. Specific functions do not count beyond their significance as representatives of the four functions.

Two changes in assumptions are called for. First, not only *new* and *different* structures but also *new* and *different* functions emerge in the process of societal change. Secondly, as a strategy in analysis, we should pay more attention to *specific* functions (e.g. communications, socialization) than to conglomerate functions (e.g. the Parsonian social system four functions). Both changes mark a retreat to Durkheim's original position: The functions of subunits of the social system are determined by the needs of the total system. As societies change new and different needs arise and old subunits as well as emergent subunits perform new and different functions (in addition to the old ones) in order to meet these needs.

Social Exchange and the Division of Labor

The rationale for this argument is not to establish a new methodology for the analysis of social dynamics but to state my reasons for rejecting the dominant mode of functional analysis of social dynamics and for staying with Durkheim's original position. My interpretation of Durkheim's and Lévi-Strauss' theories is that social solidarity is the result of two separate, but closely related processes of differentiation and integration. While the division of labor supplies the processes of differentiation, Lévi-Strauss' work stresses that social exchange transactions supply integrative mechanisms in society. I have drawn a distinction between functional integration and structural integration in Lévi-Strauss' exchange theory. Restricted exchange involves structural integration while generalized exchange involves functional integration. Similarly, I have made a distinction between structural differentiation and functional differentiation in Durkheim's work. The simple division of labor involves structural differentiation while the compound division of labor involves functional differentiation.

Together, Durkheim's conception of the division of labor in industrialized societies and Lévi-Strauss' conception of social exchange behavior in non-industrialized societies yield a more complete picture of social solidarity. Durkheim wrote his *The Division of Labor in Society* at a time when the poverty of data on non-Western societies made it fashionable to make sweeping and rather simplistic generalizations about 'primitive societies'. Evidence since accumulated by anthropologists cast doubt on Durkheim's [1933: 148] judgement 'that in the lower societies, where solidarity rests solely, or nearly so, upon resemblances, breaks are more frequent and easier to bring about'. Not only centralized traditional states as the Ashanti and the Yoruba [see Busia, 1951; and Lloyd, 1962] but also stateless traditional societies as the Tiv and the Tallensi [see Fortes, 1945, 1949, 1960] have been shown to have a degree of social solidarity and stability unimaginable in Durkheim's life time. Similarly, even as Durkheim's own treatment of anomic division of labor suggests, not all industrialized societies, with a high degree of differentiation, have experienced organic social solidarity. There is therefore need to move beyond Durkheim's blanket distinction between mechanical solidarity and organic solidarity.

Durkheim considered organic solidarity as primarily resulting from functional differentiation in society. I suggest that ideally the growth of this differentiation is within a cultural matrix infused with a morality of generalized exchange. This suggests that ideally the growth of differentiation goes hand in hand with the growth of integrative mechanisms in society. The whole process may be diagrammed as follows:

FIGURE 4.1

The Generation of Social Solidarity in Industrialization

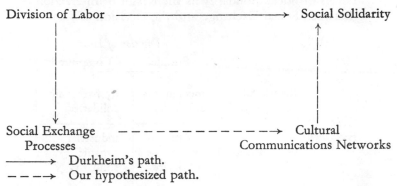

Division of Labor ⟶ Social Solidarity

Social Exchange Processes — — — — — — — — — — —→ Cultural Communications Networks

⟶ Durkheim's path.

— — —→ Our hypothesized path.

Social exchange processes, together with the morality *sui generis* that flow from them, and the cultural communications networks which they promote and sanction, act as intervening variables between economic specialization and the degree of social solidarity that grows out of the industrialization process.

We have said that Durkheim was principally concerned with industrializing societies, where occupational specialization was gaining ground. However, social exchange processes do operate independently in non-industrialized, i.e., traditional societies, to create cultural bonds of social solidarity. Social solidarity in such traditional societies owes a great deal of its existence to the lines of communications opened up by social exchange processes. The level of specialization may be elementary, limited to 'a simple division of labor', but such 'simple divisions of labor' may work in interaction with the integrative forces of social exchange in promoting the cohesion of traditional society, thus leading to an incipient form of organic solidarity in society.

In general, then, we may conceive of social solidarity as the product of interaction between the processes of differentiation and integration in society. As represented at our empirical level of concern, the interaction of the social processes of the division of labor with those of social exchange, together with the *sui generis* morality that flow from social exchange processes, determine the level of social solidarity in society. I present the more concrete form of this interaction in Figure 4.2 and its more formal aspects in Figure 4.3.

FIGURE 4.2

Levels of Social Solidarity as the Result of Interaction
Between Social Exchange and the Division of Labor

		Division of Labor	
		Simple	Compound
	Restricted	mechanical solidarity	dysharmonic solidarity
Social Exchange	Generalized	traditional organic solidarity	industrial organic solidarity

FIGURE 4.3

Levels of Social Solidarity as the Result of Interaction
Between Integration and Differentiation Processes

		Differentiation	
		Structural	Functional
	Structural	mechanical solidarity	dysharmonic solidarity
Integration	Functional	traditional organic solidarity	industrial organic solidarity

MECHANICAL SOLIDARITY

This is the type of social solidarity in non-industrialized societies
that approximates Durkheim's description of the same type in
The Division of Labor in Society. Integration and differentiation are
structural, not functional. Fragility of the social system is not
only possible but probable. Since individuals do not have any
specialized functions, their loss is not damaging to the group.

When individuals do come together, the functions they perform remain unaffected because they do not complement each other.

DYSHARMONIC SOLIDARITY

This is the industrial counterpart of mechanical solidarity, a result of some form of the 'anomic division of labor'. The division of labor attains functional differentiation, but integrative mechanisms are weak and are arrested at the structural level. In the language of political science, the criss-cutting networks in memberships of groups that make a pluralist society are absent. A *quid pro quo*, here-and-now, attitude pervades interpersonal transactions. It is dysharmonic because integration has not matched the growth of differentiation in the rise of new functions.

TRADITIONAL ORGANIC SOLIDARITY

This is what Durkheim overlooked in his classification of social solidarity—a type representing the stable traditional, non-industrialized societies, of antiquity and of the recent past in Asia and Africa. The division of labor is simple, i.e., differentiation is structural. However, integrative forces are strong and, in part at least, flow from social exchange processes and the ensuing morality of generalized exchange. In other words, integration is functional. This type of social solidarity is, as it were, a step removed from organic solidarity in industrialized societies.

INDUSTRIAL ORGANIC SOLIDARITY

This represents Durkheim's classical type of organic solidarity. Differentiation and integration are functional. Specialization of tasks is matched by pluralistic criss-crossing integration of society. Social relationships are infused with a high degree of the morality of generalized exchange, accompanied with a high degree of trust of other actors in society.

To sum up: both Durkheim [1933] and Lévi-Strauss [1949] had theories that emphasized social solidarity as the result of interactive processes in society. While Durkheim emphasized differentiated economic activities of various groups and individuals in society, Lévi-Strauss' social exchange theory deals with the integrative cultural bonds provided by the networks of communications, which social exchange promotes and sanctions. The former represent the *intensive*, the social exchange processes the *extensive*, aspects of social solidarity. Together the two perspectives yield a more complete picture of social solidarity, in both traditional and industrialized societies, than we can obtain from any one of them by itself.

Part Three

INDIVIDUALISTIC ORIENTATIONS IN SOCIAL EXCHANGE THEORY

Introduction

Modern individualistic social exchange theory, initiated by Homans [1958, 1961], has readily found its way into the mainstream of sociology. Its popularity and acceptance cannot be entirely explained in terms of its content. It is finicky in its claim to propositional theory construction and even boring to those used to other types of theory more grounded in sociological data. But its perspective gains some broader significance when it is viewed in the light of the utilitarian tradition, of which it is a brand, and against the polemical context from which it arose in the hands of the man who initiated it, George Caspar Homans.

A series of broad-minded observers of the American scene, beginning with Lowenthal [1944] and including Riesman [1950], Wolfenstein [1950], Whyte [1956], and Miller and Swanson [1958] have been pointing to the decline of the Protestant ethic and the rise of a substitute ethic in industrial U.S.A. Much of traditional sociology, stretching into the present, has been written as if the Protestant ethic reigns supreme. But little by little, sociological research of organizations, at the level of observation at any rate, have been pointing to a major breach of one of the tenets of the Protestant ethic: consistently it is found that work and play, seriousness and pleasure, can no longer be separated but that success dictates that they must be fused. The emergence of this 'fun morality', to use Martha Wolfenstein's felicitous phrase, has hardly found its way into sociological theorizing. I submit that modern individualistic social exchange theory (as distinguished from the older conceptions of individualistic social exchange by Spencer, Frazer, or Malinowski) represents the first theoretical system in sociology to capture the spirit of this 'fun morality' in American society. In a sense it is a theory of 'post-industrial society', likely to appeal more to Americans and Swedes than to sociologists in societies not so industrialized.

Traditional utilitarian thought gave prominent recognition to the quantitative value of goods and services, in the material sense, in its theoretical system. But as in the case of Spencer's [1896: 390–391] conception of social exchange processes, it could not include 'immaterial' fun items in its inventory of these 'goods and services'. The strain of the Protestant ethic in it compelled a distinction between play and work, and between past-time and work-time. Its motif was, 'work while you work and play while you play'. That famous admonition to schoolboys, 'all work and no play makes Jack a dull boy' at least recognized a distinction between 'work' and 'play'. And as Martha Wolfenstein has pointed out, the Protestant ethic compelled a distinction between 'needs' and 'wants'.

All such distinctions have been lost in modern, post-industrial, American 'fun morality'. Americans now like their work if 'it's lots of fun'. Mothers no longer tell their children: 'that is what you *need*'; rather it is now: 'if that is what you *want*'—indicating, as Martha Wolfenstein has observed, that in 'fun morality' no distinction is made between 'needs' and 'wants'. Above all, feelings and sentiments now occupy a prominent place in serious work. This is clearly more than traditional 'self-interest'. The new 'fun morality' tends to fuse together what might be separately called 'psychological self-interest'—with an emphasis on the here and now—and 'economic self-interest'—involving a postponement of immediate gratifications for the sake of greater benefits in the future. As a theoretical system, modern individualistic social exchange theory is the first to give expression to this 'fun morality'. Its acclaimed subject-matter is social behavior seen as the exchange of goods, 'material and non-material' or 'tangible or intangible'. In fact, however, it is specializing on the intangibles; or, rather, what traditional utilitarian thought regarded as intangibles—smiles, hand-shakes, nods, and such other sentiments—have been converted, in individualistic social exchange theory, into tangibles and brought into the mainstream of theoretical sociology. All of them have been invested with utilitarian value. The point of emphasis here is not the technological problem of measuring such sentiments—there is measure for everything in this age. What I emphasize is the fact that theoretically the new post-industrial 'fun morality' in the U.S.A. has been incorporated into a sociological theoretical system. Individualistic social exchange theory is a sign of the times.

Every major theoretical perspective in sociology has usually arisen as a reaction to an older dominant perspective. Most commentators on social exchange theory [see especially Mulkay, 1971] give the impression that Homans developed his social exchange theory in reaction to Parsons' functionalism. In the narrow canvas of American sociology, this may appear to be the case. Certainly, within the politics of American sociology, Homans [e.g., 1964a] gives that impression. But Homans is as much a European scholar as an American sociologist. His direct attacks on Durkheim have been far more persistent than his criticism of Parsons' strategy in theory construction. With more pointed reference to social exchange theory, Homans' individualistic social exchange theory arose from a polemical confrontation with Lévi-Strauss' collectivistic social exchange theory of cross-cousin marriage. Parsons' work, it seems to me, had very little to do with the particular direction that Homans' exchange theory has taken.

Of course once a perspective becomes established, there is a broad tendency for its adherents to be unaware of, or at least to be unconcerned with, its polemical origins. This tendency is heightened in the case of individualistic social exchange theory by the fact that the work of the man who, negatively, spurred the direction of Homans' exchange theory was written in French and in a different academic discipline, let alone the fact that Lévi-Strauss' [1949, 1969] book on social exchange is written in a difficult style—more in the devious style of Durkheim's *The Elementary Forms of Religious Life* than in the lucid style of *Suicide*. But it seems to me that the larger significance of individualistic social exchange theory in social thought will be lost if this polemical context of Homans' work is not kept in mind.

5
Homans' Social Exchange Theory

Homans' Encounter with Lévi-Strauss' Exchange Theory

The impression is strong among sociologists, largely because Homans [1961: 8–16] says so, that *Social Behavior: Its Elementary Forms* is a natural development from *The Human Group*. It is true that in terms of levels of explanation reached, *The Human Group* is limited to what Abraham Kaplan [1964: 327–335] has called 'pattern explanation',[1] while in *Social Behavior* Homans attempted a deductive model of explanation. To the extent that the history of attempted levels of explanation by the same author represents progression *The Human Group* may justifiably be called a forerunner of *Social Behavior*. When, however, Homans' writings and his reactions to other social scientists' writings on social exchange, are considered as a substantive area, then it is clearly his *Marriage, Authority and Final Causes* [Homans and Schneider, 1955][2] that is the precursor to *Social Behavior*. Indeed any worthwhile evaluation of Homans' exchange theory should take into account the polemical significance of *Marriage, Authority, and Final Causes* for

---

[1] Cf. Kaplan [1964: 333]: 'According to the pattern model [of explanation] something is explained when it is so related to a set of other elements that together they constitute a unified system.'

[2] I shall refer to *Marriage, Authority, and Final Causes* as if it is Homans' work rather than a book jointly written by him and Schneider. The main reason for my style of reference to this book is that many of the theoretical statements with which I am concerned have been integrated into Homans' later work. At any rate it has also been reprinted in *Sentiments and Activities* [Homans, 1962] where it appears as Homans' work.

Homans' exchange theory. It was in it, for the first time, that Homans publicly reacted to an explicit social exchange theory.[1] Furthermore, virtually all the major aspects of sociology with which Homans has become identified crystallized first in *Marriage, Authority, and Final Causes*: the organized attack on functionalism; psychological explanation; and, above all, to repeat, social exchange theory.

This sixty-four page book is indeed one of the first criticisms of Lévi-Strauss' [1949] exchange theory of cross-cousin marriage. However, Homans' attack was mainly directed at the implications of the theory. The central assumption that Homans attacked is Lévi-Strauss' argument that institutions based on generalized exchange are superior to those based on restricted exchange, because generalized exchange works more effectively for the integration of society: 'All we are concerned with is the *nature* of Lévi-Strauss' theory. We argue that, to account for the adoption by a society of a particular institution, it is, in principle, never sufficient to show that the institution is in some sense good for the society, however that good may be defined' [Homans and Schneider, 1955: 17]. Homans' preference is for an 'efficient cause', or, as he has more frequently expressed it, 'individual self-interest theory' [1955: 15] that would derive the patterns and the adoption of a social institution from individual motivations [1955: 20, 28].

Homans' reaction to Lévi-Strauss' exchange theory as such is mostly muted, but it is significant on three counts. First, he was irritated by what Lévi-Strauss regarded as his chief contribution to social exchange theory, namely, the introduction of the concept of generalized exchange into social exchange theory: 'It might be argued,' Homans says of Lévi-Strauss' effort in this connection, 'that in extending the idea of exchange this way [to generalized exchange], Lévi-Strauss has thinned the meaning out of it' [Homans and Schneider, 1955: 7]. Homans' own theory [1958, 1961], first spelt out three years after this harsh assessment of generalized exchange, was careful to exclude this concept and to

---

[1] This sentence is written on the face of full awareness by this writer of Homans' own claim that 'So far as I know, the only theoretical work that makes explicit use of [exchange] is Marcel Mauss's *Essai sur le don*' [Homans, 1958: 598]. Homans' claim is puzzling in the light of his excellent review of key aspects of Lévi-Strauss' exchange theory in *Marriage, Authority, and Final Causes*.

limit the social exchange process to a two-party interaction.

Secondly, Homans also showed some dissatisfaction with the restriction of the items of social exchange to one kind, namely women, in Lévi-Strauss' theory. The strategy of limiting the items of exchange to one or a few kinds (e.g., Necklaces and Armshells in Malinowski [1922] and women in Lévi-Strauss [1949, 1969]) is in effect challenged by Homans: 'Of course some of the tribes following this rule [of generalized exchange] say they exchange women for *goods*, but when Lévi-Strauss talks about marriage exchange he always means the exchange of women for *women*, whether recognized as an exchange or not' [Homans and Schneider, 1955: 7]. This terse reaction has two important connections with Homans' own exchange theory. The first is that in his theory Homans expanded the range of social exchange items to all activities—almost without limit. Although he was later to state that these involved 'tangible or intangible activities', his theory seems to be specializing on intangible activities—in sharp contrast to Lévi-Strauss'. Similarly, his reaction is an implied rejection of Lévi-Strauss' non-utilitarian interpretation of social exchange. In Lévi-Strauss' exchange theory women were exchanged not for economic gain but rather for the symbolic value derived from the social exchange relationships for the benefit of the wider society. In reacting thus, Homans, like Frazer [1919] before him, is indicating that the purpose of social exchange is utilitarian—in sharp contrast to Lévi-Strauss and Malinowski [1922]. Homans' own exchange theory has come to emphasize this utilitarian attribute of social exchange.

Thirdly, in reacting to Lévi-Strauss' exchange theory Homans indicated that the meaning of 'individual self-interest' is a combination of economic and psychological needs. This point is worth emphasis, because the relationship between economics and psychology has fluctuated a great deal in Homans' thought. His first characterization ever of what he was later [1962: 23–35] to call 'psychological functional statements' was in reaction to Lévi-Strauss' exchange theory and Homans put it this way: 'An institution is what it is because it results from the drives, or meets the immediate needs, of individuals or subgroups within a society. Its function is to meet these needs. We may call this an individual self-interest theory, if we remember that interests may be other than economic' [Homans and Schneider, 1955: 15]. The combination of psychological needs and economic needs was to be central to Homans' own exchange theory.

It is not unimportant to note that in the period between *Marriage, Authority, and Final Causes* [1955] and *Social Behavior* [1961], Homans was absorbed with his own formulation of social exchange theory. It should be clear from his own theory that Lévi-Strauss' theory had no positive influence on him. But it is more than likely that Lévi-Strauss influenced the formulation of Homans' individualistic social exchange theory by way of reaction. I list the following attributes as the possible products of this reaction formation in Homans' exchange theory: (1) face-to-face relations; (2) restricted exchange, limited to two individuals; (3) the double emphasis on psychological and economic needs, and (4) the utilitarian value of exchange items. At the very least, it may be said that if Homans had not read Lévi-Strauss' *Les Structures élémentaires de la Parenté*, these themes might have received degrees of emphases different from Homans' present theory of social exchange. In all these respects Homans' exchange theory stands in sharp contrast to Lévi-Strauss'.

It is important to take note of the following point: in no other social exchange theorist is there such an explicit combination of psychology and economics. Homans stands out as an 'individualist-oriented', or, in his own words, 'an individual self-interest theorist' *par excellence*. While Frazer [1919] before him emphasized economic issues in social exchange and was silent on psychological needs, and while Malinowski [1922] emphasized psychological needs but was antagonistic to economic interpretations of exchange behavior, Homans, as we shall see, boldly combines both. In this respect especially, he stands on a different plane from Lévi-Strauss. Or if you will, Lévi-Strauss' position retains the French collectivistic orientation, while Homans advocates the individualistic orientation in social exchange processes. As in the days of old—in the days of Comte, Spencer, and Durkheim—they do not disregard each other, but actively seek out each other in an ongoing polemic that has fertilized the fields of theoretical sociology.

Homans' Philosophy of the Social Sciences

Homans' encounter and dissatisfaction with Lévi-Strauss' collectivistic social exchange theory was not an accident in his development as a sociologist. As he himself has told it in his 'Autobiographical Introduction' to *Sentiments and Activities* [1962: 31–34], his reading of Lévi-Strauss' *Les structures élémentaires de la Parenté* was the last straw that broke his patience with functionalism of the Durkheimian type. His dissatisfaction with collectivistic thought began early in his life as a student of sociology at Harvard. Homans had become convinced that Durkheim's collectivistic assumptions were a direct attack on what he believed to be an unstated assumption in Western intellectual life—'the notion that the nature of individuals determined finally the nature of society'. Homans' generalization of this specialized view of Western civilization to intellectual pursuits in sociology consistently put him in opposition to what had become the dominant mode of sociological imagination, thanks to Durkheim's burgeoning influence in sociology. I cite below Homans' feelings on this matter, because I suspect that they are very important in understanding his social exchange theory as a joint product of a commitment to an individualistic tradition and an opposition to a collectivistic orientation in sociology. Writing about his graduate work under Mayo he recalls that

> In the course of an essentially literary education [before being involved in sociology], I had absorbed one of the unstated assumptions of the Western intellectual tradition, the notion that the nature of individuals determined finally the nature of society . . . Both [Durkheim's] *Suicide* and the *Rules* implied that the unstated assumption should be turned around and—to put the matter as naïvely as I then saw it—that the nature of society might determine the nature of individuals. As for the *Elementary Forms* . . . it suggested, as the latter did, that the purpose or function of human institutions was not—to put the matter naïvely again— the satisfaction of human needs but the maintenance of society . . . Durkheim upset me. His was a revelation, but a revelation I never was quite comfortable with. Though at the time I did not see what was wrong, he started an itch [in me] [Homans, 1962: 8].

Ultimately, Homans' exchange theory was a reaction to the itch that Durkheim started. What is at stake here, however, is not the narrow province of social exchange theory but broader confrontations in traditions of thought. Homans' philosophy of social science, as it has evolved over the years, is after all a reflection of his view of what the tenets of Western civilization are and it has been determined in large measure by his reaction to the views opposed to his own. Along with his broad dis-satisfaction with Durkheim's line of sociological imagination, he was more particularly upset by the type of functionalism encour-aged and sanctioned by Durkheim's work, the functionalism that argued that 'an institution was functional for society in the sense of helping to maintain the society as an ongoing society' [Homans, 1962: 24]. Again I cite Homans' own words, since the intensity of his feelings can hardly be captured by a mere paraphrase: 'I was never happy with [this type of] functionalism. I was suspicious of it from the beginning without knowing why. It has been a splinter under my skin that it has taken me a long time to get out' [Homans, 1962: 23].

After years of private debate with himself, it was no longer any surprise when Homans [1962: 29] publicly 'rejected as having no final truth . . . Durkheim's assertion that society was an entity *sui generis* and that sociology was not a corollary of psychology'. Groping for a position that he believed to be the correct one, Homans came to the opposite conclusion that 'Sociology was, Durkheim to the contrary, a corollary of psychology' [1962: 48]. After years of harsh rejection of Durkheim, mostly in footnotes, Homans [e.g., 1969: 17–20] has more recently tried to be fair to him by stating what he believes Durkheim meant by psychology and the limitations he believed his times imposed on the pioneer French sociologist. According to Homans, the meaning of psychology has changed since Durkheim's days: 'What he [Durkheim] conceived to be psychology was a sort of instinctual psychology, and it certainly assumed that human nature was the same the world over . . . Sociology is surely not a corollary of the kind of psychology Durkheim had in mind. But this does not mean that it is not a corollary of, cannot be derived from, another psychology'[1] [Homans, 1969: 18–19]. The substitute psychology

---

[1] This writer is unable to reconcile the characterization of a psychology as 'instinctual' with its definition as assuming 'that human nature [is] the same the world over'. Instinctual psychology would be interested in studying instinctual behavior in animals, for example, hoarding habits of squirrels. The uniformities in human behavior as an area of study for *a* psychology would belong to what Redfield [1957] has referred to as 'developed human nature'—and it is certainly not instinctual psychology.

In actual fact Durkheim's rejection of psychology in sociological explanation is

S.E.T.–4*

that Homans has in mind is, of course, behavioral psychology, the model of which is supplied by animal behavior. It would even be more revolting to Durkheim!

Homans' conception of what psychology means is even more difficult to come to terms with for the important reason that Homans has made use of *three different conceptions of psychology* in the years he has been arguing with the shades of Durkheim. (a) Before being influenced by Skinner's behavioral psychology [see Homans, 1962: 47], Homans' conception of psychology was entirely in distinctively human terms as *the behavior of the individual in the group*. His earliest statement of this was that of a psychology focussing on 'individuals and three elements . . . of the behavior of individuals in groups [which] will be called operation, sentiment, and interaction' [Homans, 1947: 14]. It was subsequently amplified in *The Human Group* and this conception of psychology in Homans' work was still active by 1954 (Riecken and Homans) and 1955 (Homans and Schneider).¹ Thereafter

---

based on a confusion of Comte's and Spencer's two, though undifferentiated, conceptions of psychology. Durkheim [1938: 97–100] initially presented Comte's and Spencer's arguments on the explanatory power of (developed) human nature. Then he adds, 'This principle is not only at the basis of these great doctrines of general sociology, but it likewise fathers an equally large number of specific theories. Thus domestic organization is commonly explained by the sentiments parents have for their children' etc. [Durkheim, 1938: 100]. In doing so, Durkheim switched to the psychology of the individual in the group and it was on this basis that he proceeds to 'refute' Comte's and Spencer's claim on the explanatory power of psychology for sociology [1938: 101–124]. Given Durkheim's argument, it is doubtful that any type of psychology—whether behavioral psychology, or the psychology of human nature ['original or acquired', as he himself refers to it, 1938: 100]—would be acceptable to Durkheim. Indeed behavioral psychology and the psychology of human nature, as the common attributes of men, would even be more alien to Durkheim's sociology.

¹ At this early stage of his evolution as a sociologist, Homans sounded very much like Parsons in his pronouncements concerning the relationships between the individual and society. Thus he writes in *The Human Group*: 'If we examine the motives we usually call individual self-interest, we shall find that they are, for the most part, neither individual nor selfish but that they are the product of group life and serve the ends of a whole group not just an individual . . . That both self-interest *and* something else are satisfied by group life is the truth that is hardest for the hard-boiled—and half-baked—person to see. As Mayo says, "If a number of individuals work together to achieve a common purpose, a harmony of interests will develop among them to which individual self-interest will be subordinated. This is a very different doctrine from the claim that individual self-interest is the solitary human motive"' [Homans, 1950: 95–96].

It is embarrassing to any claims to purity in individualistic sociology on Homans' behalf that Sheldon Wolin [1960: 357, 493] cited part of this passage in *The Human Group* as indicative of the disregard of individual motives in the 'age of organization'.

Homans changed the meaning of psychology to (b) *an area of study of behaviors common to animals and humans, or behavioral psychology* [Homans, 1958, 1961, 1967b, 1969]. (c) Lastly, scattered in many discussions of what Homans meant by psychology are references to the behavior of 'men as men', belonging to the 'human species'. Unlike the psychology that studies the behavior of individuals in the group, this psychology studies the behavior of men *qua* humans as opposed to nonhumans. Its definition of men excludes nonsocialized men (e.g., children, psychopaths) and focuses on the behavior of adult humans who have been socialized. This psychology studies what Redfield [1957] has called *developed human nature*. Cooley has made some of his greatest contributions to it. While Cooley [1909] emphasized universal sentiments (e.g., incest) and Redfield [1957] universal 'intellections' (e.g., the self concept) as prominent parts of developed human nature, Homans [e.g., 1967b: 38–39, 1971: 23] seems to be emphasizing universal motivations in men as the springboard of action.

I do not say that Homans has made these distinctions or that he is aware of them. His predilection for deductive reasoning has apparently led him to believe that there is only one valid psychology, namely, behavioral psychology, and that it encompasses any other type of psychology.[1] But the distinction is important for my evaluation of Homans' social exchange theory and for assessing its limitations. Especially problematic in Homans' conception of the scope of psychology is his contention that there are no exclusively human processes, such as social exchange behaviors, and that human behavior can ultimately be reduced to the laws of behavioral psychology derived from animal behavior. Homans has brought this strong Skinnerian reductionism into sociology via his social exchange theory. I shall later on show how this posture has influenced Homans' social exchange theory and I shall argue that Homans has not limited himself to its strictures.

At this point, however, I am more concerned with Homans' formal advocacy of *behavioral* psychological reductionism in

---

[1] Cf. Homans [1969: 12]: 'To support the propositions of behavioral psychology there is a vast body of evidence, both clinical and experimental, for man and other animals. Indeed there is some question whether there is any other general psychology . . . Even Freudian psychology, so far as it is subject to test, is behavioristic.'

sociology. Most sociologists would of course be more receptive to Homans' arguments if his meaning of psychology were that of the behavior of individual men in the group or that of developed human nature. But by psychological reductionism[1] Homans ultimately means that human behavior and social institutions and organizations can only be exhaustively explained, without residue, by invoking the principles of psychology yielded by animal behavior, as in Skinner's experiments with pigeons. At least this is what he means by applying his argument of psychological reductionism in his social exchange theory. As further developed under his sponsorship with the grand name of 'behavioral sociology' [see Burgess and Bushell, 1969], this position denies that there is a *qualitative* difference between animal behavior and human behavior—insisting on the contrary that the differences are *quantitative*. As Blain [1971b] has pointed out, this form of reductionism is far more 'radical' than most sociologists imagine.

But Homans' crusade for behavioral psychological reductionism has simply ignored an old controversy. It has revived Watson's position without mentioning the established opposition to his intellectual pursuits, notably by the so-called scientists of culture led by Leslie A. White [e.g., 1949], who argue that the symbolic

---

[1] Homans [1964a: 817; 1967b: 80–87; 1969: 15–17; and 1971: 24] has increasingly become more reluctant to use the term 'reduction'—thus backing away at the level of terminology, anyway. This reluctance appears to have grown out of his changing conception of psychology. When he was interested in the psychology of the individual in the group, Homans [e.g., 1958] judged sociology capable of yielding general reducible propositions; but when his interests shifted to a general psychology, encompassing all human behavior, his doubts about the capacity of sociology to yield general propositions developed.

There is an unfortunate tendency for different writers to invest the term 'reductionism' with different meanings and connotations. Some theorists [e.g. Scott, 1971: 13] equate reduction with routine explanation in which the integrity of the *explanans* and the *explanandum* is left untouched by the process of reduction. But this is not the meaning of reduction that provokes disagreement from, say, vitalists in biology or collectivists in sociology. What they reject is the corollary of any program of reduction, which is that the body of propositions that one seeks to reduce to another level does not have an autonomous existence of its own apart from the more general principles of which they are a part. Contrary to Scott [1971: 13], all explanations are *not* reductions. 'Explanation' has the *positive* connotation of seeking to understand one phenomenon in terms of another phenomenon. 'Reductionism' has the *negative* connotation of attacking the autonomous existence of one phenomenon as unnecessary and scientifically unjustifiable. It is in this sense that Scott's [1971: 13–14] contention, that 'psychology' and 'sociology' are mutually reducible to each other, is misleading.

nature of man sets him apart from all other animals and that the reduction of the behaviors of men *qua* human acts to animal behavior cannot be achieved without the loss of all that is essentially human in men.[1] Moreover, Homans' arguments for the reduction of social phenomena to behavioral psychological principles seems unresponsive to two counter-currents in the philosophy of science. First, there is the growing dissatisfaction among established philosophers of science with the inadequacy and irrelevance of the traditional physicalistic view of science. This dissatisfaction is best exemplified by the varied contributions of eminent scientists in Europe and America to the Alpbach Symposium *Beyond Reductionism* [see Koestler and Smythies, 1969]. Thorpe's [1969: 428] summary of their views with respect to reductionism should be of some interest to sociologists. In effect he says that the reductionist appeal has an ideological side to it, persisting long after its value has been diminished by new emphases in science:

> many of us hold that because in the last three hundred years the scientific technique of reductionism has been so successful in gaining control over the forces of nature, our present society is far more receptive to rationalistic-mechanistic philosophies than to others simply because it considers such views as more 'scientific' than other alternatives. Much of society's acceptance of this is, in fact, based on a misunderstanding of the nature of science itself. Reductionism is only one aspect and not the most fundamental aspect of the activity of scientists and the progress of science.

Of special relevance for sociology are the reasons given by Bertalanffy [1969: 58–60] for dissatisfactions with reductionism in psychology and the social sciences. The classic mechanistic view of science is now inadequate in both fields because the problems that the social sciences face nowadays are no longer ones of '*process laws* such as Newton's laws or the laws of electro-dynamics' but rather they are faced with '*problems of organized*

---

[1] The attempt to ignore opposed points of view is far more prominent in the 'behavioral sociology' adherents of Skinner and Homans than in Homans' work. In *Behavioral Sociology*, to which twenty-three behaviorists made contributions, there was no noticeable mention of opposed views except in Homans' paper; one cannot find any reference to Leslie A. White or any other 'scientists of culture', or to the chief advocate of the methodology of symbolic interactionism, Herbert Blumer. [See Burgess and Bushell, 1969.] Apparently, 'behavioral sociologists' hope to establish their point by overwhelming readers with 'quantitative' results.

complexity', which require a new strategy and a new emphasis in scientific pursuits [Bertalanffy, 1969: 59]. This is saying that modern social science is a different type of science because the type of problems it faces require laws of organized wholes, not the nihilist reduction of organized wholes to their simplest units. The model of physics—Homans' model of science—would be inadequate for the social sciences. Bertalanffy's point would hardly be invalidated by advancing the view that the social sciences may have to follow the footpaths of the physical sciences by hacking through the elementary routes which the physical sciences followed before facing the problems of organized wholes. His point, to repeat, is that the nature of the social sciences— perhaps indeed much more than that of the physical sciences— requires laws of organized wholes and would benefit least from an evolutionary appeal to Newtonian physicalism.

The second counter-current against Homans' position is within the social sciences. According to the phenomenologist view of science, humans form a unique type of subject-matter for science. In order for social scientific interpretations to be adequate social scientists must include in their *action-meanings*—their scientific interpretations of their data—the individual's *act-meanings*—the subject's own interpretation of what his activity means.[1] This is a problem that the physicist, the geologist, or the animal psychologist does not have to face. This phenomenologist view of the social sciences militates against the reduction of human behavior to animal behavior, since *act-meanings* will be lost in the process.[2]

---

[1] Cf. Kaplan [1964: 32]: 'The data for behavioral science are not sheer movements but actions—that is, acts performed in a perspective which gives them meaning or purpose. Plainly, it is of crucial importance that we distinguish between the meaning of the act to the actor (or to other people, including ourselves, reacting with him) and its meaning to us as scientists, taking the action as subject-matter. I call these, respectively, *act meaning* and *action meaning* . . . behavioral science is involved in a double process of interpretation, and it is this which is responsible for such of its techniques as are distinctive. The behavioral scientist must first arrive at an act meaning, that is, construe what conduct a particular piece of behavior represents; and then he must search for the meaning of the interpreted action, its interconnections with other actions or circumstances.'

[2] Cf. Frankl's [1969: 402–403] prosaic illustration of this point: 'Those people, those behaviourist psychologists or whatever they call themselves, who insist that what is observable in a man must also be observable in animals, and who wish to derive from this attitude a justification for reductionism or subhumanism, these people remind me very much of the rabbi in a Viennese joke. There were two neighbours; one of them contended that the other's cat had stolen and eaten five

More than in anything else, Homans is pre-eminently Skinnerian in his belief that human behavior can, perhaps should, be reduced to principles of animal psychology in order to be fully understood.[1] Skinner and Skinnerians, like the behaviorists before them, have attempted to discredit the phenomenologist characterization of unique human behavior by rejecting the validity of 'act-meanings' as matters of objectionable 'conceptual inner causes' [Skinner, 1953, e.g. p. 31], or 'introspection' [Scott, 1971: 21–28]. Their insistence on limiting the scope of scientific pursuits to observable phenomena in effect denies the validity and the usefulness of theoretical constructs in science and theory construction, and is directly responsible for Homans' crusading resistance to the conceptualization of society as an entity *sui generis*, apart from and beyond the individuals in society. This behaviorist view is, as Piaget [1968: 102] has remarked, more pronounced (in the social sciences, at least) in 'the Anglo-Saxon countries [where] the concept of structure tends to be reserved for observable relations and interactions' than in the French intellectual tradition in which non-observable theoretical constructs are not only accepted as legitimate but even expected as a useful aid in theory construction. In short, the issue concerns not so much the logic of science as it is a doctrine of science to which intellectuals have been persuaded and which they may have been socialized to accept. Insofar as the Skinnerian position is based on the logic of science it consists of the following view: animals have no mentality; we should assume that humans have

---

pounds of his butter; there was a bitter argument and finally they agreed to seek the advice of the rabbi. They went to the rabbi and the owner of the cat said: "It cannot be, my cat doesn't care for butter at all", but the other insisted that it was his cat and so the rabbi decided: "Bring me the cat." They brought him the cat and the rabbi said: "Bring me the scales." And they brought the scales and he asked: "How many pounds of butter?" "Five pounds." And believe it or not, the weight of the cat was exactly five pounds. So the rabbi said: "Now I have the butter, but where is the cat?"

'This is what these people remind me who say in fact: we have some type of conscience in the animal as well; so whatever we find in humans may be found in animals as well. And then they ask: we have this behaviour in man, we have these "innate releasing mechanisms" and so forth, but where is man? The humanness of the human phenomena has necessarily disappeared.'

[1] Skinnerians have in this matter been far less cautious than Skinner himself. His try-and-see doctrine that was repeatedly asserted in *Science and Behavior* has been converted into a creed adopted by many Skinnerians in their attempt to reduce human behavior to the principles of animal psychology.

no mentality: after all it is as impossible to observe the mentality of men as it is impossible to see the non-mentality of animals. Accordingly there is no barrier between human behavior and animal behavior and the former can be fully understood by invoking the principles of animal behavior. Those who accept the legitimacy of theoretical constructs in science would point out that their validity is established by their results—that the mentality of humans can be validated through the consequences of that construct,[1] which is absent in animals. In the long run the Skinnerian position is predicated on the conception of humans as 'empty organisms', lacking in 'mental states'—in contradistinction to, for example, the Piagetian assumption of innate sensori-motor abilities unique to humans and the Freudian assumption of human mentality. To point out these differences is to invite the reader to make his choice, for in matters of doctrine, be it of religion or of science, the weight of an argument is never totally impressive to those opposed to it.

But the limitations of Homans' philosophy of social science are beyond the logic and doctrine of science. If the issues raised previously cannot be resolved on the basis of the logic or doctrine of science, perhaps one can apply a more pragmatic test of how best to benefit the social sciences by involving psychological principles. But because of his doctrinaire commitments to behavioral psychological reductionism, Homans has ignored the persuasive pleas of Alex Inkeles that a viable alternative exists for engaging psychological variables in sociological theory and research without the implausibility of psychological reductionism and without posing any threat to the social essence of sociological explanation. (It is true that by 'psychology' Homans and Inkeles refer to different subject-matters: for Homans, at least after his conversion to Skinnerian behaviorism, psychology refers to the area of behavior common to animals and humans; whereas Inkeles' conception of psychology is in terms of human personality variables. But there is little doubt that Inkeles' logic for inter-relating sociology with psychology would be productive even to those whose conceptions of psychology are different from

---

[1] Cf. Professor Penfield's remark cited by Professor Joseph Wood Krutch in his foreword to Barnett [1967: viii]: 'It is much easier to explain all the data we have regarding the brain if we assume an additional phenomenon "mind" than it is to explain all the data if we assume only the existence of the brain.'

his.) According to the Skinnerian program of reductionism which Homans adopts, the explanation of social processes and institutions requires that we seek the *explanans* in the principles of behavioral psychology and that in their analysis we seek the independent variables also in behavioral psychology. Inkeles suggests that a more productive line of reasoning for sociology would consist of maintaining both the dependent and independent variables in social analysis at the sociological level, while the sociologist introduces psychological variables by treating them as intervening variables between the sociological independent and dependent variables. As Inkeles [1959a, 1959b, 1963] has persistently pointed out, such an approach to theory and research has the great advantage of pointing up avenues to new knowledge. Perhaps the worth of his approach can be best highlighted by giving two examples of its use. The first and the most famous is David C. McClelland's interpretation of Weber's theory of the rise of the Protestant ethic in terms of the psychological construct of achievement motivation. McClelland [1955; 1961: 45–52] retains Weber's original independent variable of Protestantism and his dependent variable of 'spirit of modern capitalism', but between these two McClelland attributes two inter-related psychological processes of 'socialization to independence and mastery training' by Protestant parents *and* the resulting high achievement motivation in their sons. In this psychological interpretation of the Weber thesis, we come to acquire a richer understanding of the sociological processes which the German sociologist sought to establish—for instance, we gain a clearer understanding of the inter-generation time dimension of the emergence of the Protestant ethic. Similarly, and this is Inkeles' own example, Henry and Short [1954] have enriched our sociological understanding of Durkheim's theory of suicide, by retaining his original independent variable of integration experienced by actors as responsible for the dependent variable of the rates of suicide in groups, and by interposing between them the intervening variables of childhood socialization types of punishment (i.e., whether physical or psychological) and the resulting tendency to assume responsibility. As a result of this approach Durkheim's original theory has been broadened to the explanation of the rates of homicide without thereby destroying the sociological essence of the phenomenon.

I have sought to highlight the significance of Alex Inkeles' method here in order to point up the fact that to doubt the validity of Homans' psychological reductionism is not to deny the value of psychological variables in sociological theory and research. Ironically, the most effective piece of work ever done by Homans, and combining theory and research at once, is in this tradition of psychological interpretation of sociological theories. The explanation of cross-cousin marriage offered by Homans and Schneider in *Marriage, Authority, and Final Causes* had a sociological dependent variable (cross-cousin marriage) and a sociological independent variable (jural authority), with interpersonal contacts and the sentiments they generate between individuals acting as the intervening variables in the explanation of cross-cousin marriage. This is at least what Homans [1962: 33] says he has done:

> Ours was a tested structural proposition: it stated a relationship between two kinds of institution: the locus of jural authority and the form of unilateral cross-cousin marriage. What is more, our explanation why the relationship existed, though far from being thoroughly spelled out, appeared to be made of psychological statements about the behavior of men as men, as members of a species, specifically statements about the reactions of men to the behavior of others placed in authority over them.

Is Homans' reductionism, then, really a formal statement of ideals to which his work has not corresponded? This is what I hope to establish: to the extent that Homans—as a theorist and researcher concerned with *what is* rather than as a philosopher of science concerned with *what ought to be*—has been successful in explaining anything (and his attempts are impressive) he has done so only by being false to his ideals of psychological reductionism.

Animal Behavior and Human Behavior

On the very first page of *Social Behavior: Its Elementary Forms*, Homans makes a statement that most sociologists would be uncomfortable with. He says the physicist, apparently the model scientist *par excellence*, studies the 'social behavior of particles in the atom'. It is only natural then that he should later say with so much ease that 'the pigeon is thoroughly social' [1961: 31]. Sociologists who believe that the subject-matter of their investigation is exclusively 'social behavior'—that the physicist and the animal psychologist who, respectively, study atoms and pigeons have a different area of concern—will not find a great deal of support in Homans' social exchange theory. In that theory, anyway, Homans' meaning of 'social behavior' is elaborated in terms of animal 'social behavior', not in terms of 'social behavior in atoms'.

But Homans does little to say why he considers what occurs in the atom 'social behavior' or why he considers as 'social behavior, or true exchange' situations in which 'the activity of each of at least two animals reinforces (or punishes) the activity of the other, and where accordingly each influences the other' [Homans, 1961: 30]. Rather he assumes that there is a 'family likeness' between animal behavior and human behavior [1961: 31]. At least if the action of two men interacting in a given situation can be considered 'social' by a sociologist, so must he consider the action of two animals acting together in a situation.

What then is *social* behavior? There is no full answer to that question in Homans' social exchange theory, largely because he does not attempt to delineate the scope of social behavior as such but rather of *elementary* social behavior. His meaning of social behavior may be inferred from his definition of this elementary social behavior. The subject-matter of his social exchange theory, elementary social behavior, is delimited as follows: 'First, the behavior must be social, which means that when a person acts in a certain way he is at least rewarded or punished by the behavior of another *person*, though he may also be rewarded or punished by the non-human environment.' 'Second, when a person acts in a certain way toward another person, he must at least be rewarded or punished by *that* person and not just by some third party.' 'Third, the behavior must be actual behavior and not a norm of behavior' [Homans, 1961: 2,3]. It is these attributes of social behavior that animals are assumed by Homans to share with humans.

Homans does not mean to imply that animal behavior is identical with human behavior. Rather, fundamental or elementary human behavior can ultimately be traced to animal behavior. In other words, when complex human behavior has been derobed of its secondary acquisitions, it primarily remains animal behavior. Moreover, complex human behavior, as compared to elementary human behavior, is derivable from, or else reducible to, animal behavior. The characteristics of elementary social behavior, thus possessed in common by animals and humans, 'are shared by all mankind' [1961: 6]. It seems proper to remind the reader that the animals Homans is writing about are not primates, but all animals, even the lowest forms of animals. It is pigeons, not any primates, that furnishes Homans with the model of human exchange.

Once these similarities between animal and human behaviors are understood, Homans imagines that two successes can be scored by seeking to understand human behavior from the patterns of animal behavior. First, 'some of the propositions [of social exchange] that we shall use in describing and explaining the behavior of men are more firmly established for other animals, because investigators can more often experiment with animals under controlled conditions than with men. Second, anyone concerned with the unity of science ought to show, when he can, that the propositions holding good within his special field of interest illustrate those holding good within a wider one' [Homans, 1961: 17]; hence, that is, the propositions of behavioral psychology should be used to illustrate those of sociology.

Naturally, Homans has stated his case in terms of the similarities between animal behavior and human behavior. What then are the differences between them and what effect do these differences have in any attempt to generalize from animal behavior to human behavior? He sees quite a few differences—differences in organs and the accompanying differences in verbal skills and activities [1961: 29]. But the nature of these differences does not receive a clear-cut characterization. In what must be regarded as a fit of theoretical absent-mindedness, Homans [1961: 29] declares, 'so great are these differences that they make, if we please to say so, a qualitative difference in behavior'. I understand this sentence to mean that differences between animal and human behaviors are *qualitative* because they are *quantitative*. That is, of course, not what Homans had meant to say. Rather, his position is that the differences between animals and humans, however great, are *quantitative,* not *qualitative*; differences of *degree*, not of *kind*. This is a hallowed position associated with eminent scientists—and Homans is in good company. In *The Descent of Man*, Charles Darwin concluded that 'there is no fundamental difference between man and the higher mammals in their mental faculties; [the differences between them consists] *solely* in [man's] almost infinitely larger power of associating together the most diversified sound and ideas . . . the mental powers of higher animals do not differ in *kind*, though greatly in *degree*, from the corresponding powers of men' [Cited in White, 1949: 23]. Nearer our times Ralph Linton [1936: 79] has argued that 'The differences between men and animals in all these respects [of behaviors] are enormous, but they seem to be differences in *quantity* rather than in *quality*' (my italics).

I have cited these sources to clarify Homans' position. The implication is obvious. If the differences between animal behavior and human behavior are only quantitative, not qualitative, then fundamental human behavior can best be studied by resorting to animal behavior—to a point where animal behavior and human behavior meet in fundamentals. This strategy is of course more appealing to a scientist like Homans whose meaning of theory is expressed in terms of deductive processes. Thus Homans declares the behavior of the pigeon as capable of providing the sociologist with a model of human social exchange behavior. So ultimately Homans makes two crucial assumptions: first, 'social behavior', involving two actors (animals or humans), is totally reducible to the behavior of individual actors; and second, animal behavioral principles are generalizable to human behavior. The validity of these assumptions seems critical to Homans' exchange theory and I prefer that the reader hear from him:

> In this book [*Social Behavior: Its Elementary Forms*] we are less interested in individual behavior than in social behavior, or true exchange, where the activity of each of at least two animals reinforces (or punishes) the activity of the other, and where accordingly each influences the other. Yet we hold that we need no new propositions to describe and explain the social. With social behavior nothing unique emerges to be analyzed in its own terms. Rather, from the laws of individual behavior [as in the behavior of the individual animal] follow the laws of social behavior . . .
>
> Not only shall we adapt the propositions of individual behavior to the social situation, but propositions about pigeons to the human situation . . . Taking our departure, then, from what we know about animal behavior, we shall state a set of propositions that seem to us fundamental in describing and explaining human social behavior, or true exchange [Homans, 1961: 30–31].

These, then, are the premises of Homans' exchange theory. It is as social as animal behavior is 'social' and it sees no generic differences between the behavior of an individual (animal or human) and 'social behavior' (of two or more animals or humans rewarding or punishing each other).

With respect to these premises regarding the similarities and differences between human behavior and animal behavior, Homans has apparently rejected the arguments of the science of culture. As, for example, White [1949: 34–35] and Hartung [1960] see it, man shares certain types of behavior with animals but a great deal of his activities derive from distinctively human behavior, exclusive to man. I will illustrate these differences and similarities, as seen through the point of view of science of culture, with the help of a Venn diagram:

FIGURE 5.1

A Venn Diagrammatic Illustration of Similarities and
Differences between Animal Behavior and Human Behavior

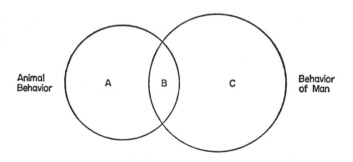

A = Instinctual Behavior: Distinctive to animals
B = Conditioned Behavior: Common to animals and humans
C = Symbolic Behavior: Distinctive to men

Three types of behavior represent the range of behaviors under consideration. First, distinctively animal behavior, outside the reach of man's behavior,[1] is *instinctually* determined. A squirrel,

---

[1] Cf. Barnett [1967: 122]: 'One reason why species characteristic [instinctual] behavior patterns make such an impression on us, is that we almost entirely lack them ourselves.'

whether reared in the laboratory or in its natural habitat in the forest, will hoard in the summer in preparation for the winter, out of sheer instinct. Secondly, there is behavior that is common to animals and humans which is learned through rewarding or punishing past experiences. This is *conditioned* behavior. Thirdly, there is *symbolic* or human behavior, completely outside the reach of animal behavior. As White [1949: 22] has said, 'All human behavior consists of, or is dependent upon, the use of symbols. Human behavior is symbolic behavior; symbolic behavior is human behavior. The symbol is the universe of humanity'. Conditioned behavior represents only a small part of the total behavior of man; symbolic behavior is by far the most outstanding attribute of men.

Let us recast the matter as follows: the lowest form of animal behavior is instinctual behavior; the highest form of animal behavior is conditioned behavior. On the other hand, the lowest form of man's behavior is conditioned behavior; the highest form of man's behavior is symbolic behavior. The theorem of science of culture with regard to the relationship between animal behavior and human behavior may be stated as follows: *It is possible to generalize from conditioned animal behavior to conditioned behavior in men; but it is impossible to generalize from conditioned animal behavior to symbolic or human behavior.*

It is perhaps important to re-emphasize at this point that the type of distinction drawn here between animal behavior and human behavior is partial to a school of thought and has been rejected by behavioral sociologists. The distinction faces opposition from two inter-related views: First, there are theorists who would freely accept that the differences between conditioned animal behavior and symbolic human behavior are, or could be, qualitative, but they deny that such differences debar generalizations from animal behavior to human symbolic behavior. This position is implicit, for example, in John Finley Scott's [1971] theory of moral learning. Although his theory is about humans and although many constructs of the theory—conscience, guilt, moral commitment—are distinctively human, he has no hesitation in inferring the principles of these distinctively human constructs from those of behavioral psychology derived from animal behavior. Such a position is fraught with methodological difficulties. One may ask, why do animals not develop moral commitment since they are presumed to possess the fundamentals necessary for its development? Humans are moral, to stick to Scott's concerns, not because they are like animals but rather because of their distinctive human attributes. A more forthright opposition faced by the distinction between conditioned animal behavior and symbolic human behavior and its stated theorem of non-generalizability from the former to human behavior is that which rejects it as completely mistaken by stating flatly, as Homans was shown to have done above, that these differences are not only quantitative but that indeed animal behavior provides an adequate basis for understanding human behavior. Although this latter position is identified with eminent scientists —ranging from Charles Darwin to B. F. Skinner—it needs to be said that it is based more on philosophical suasion than on the weight of scientific demonstration.

Sociologists are apt to react to all this by saying that this matter has an old-fashioned ring around it, that the issues involved have been well argued in previous controversies. Unfortunately most sociologists tend to see this matter from a limited vantage point by opposing symbolic interactionism to Skinnerian or Watsonian behaviorism. In doing so they assume, if they happen to be aware of its separate existence, that the science of culture, as developed by anthropologists, is nothing more than symbolic interactionism. I see an important difference between the two—at least as far as the issues outlined here are concerned. The science of culture regards as problematic—as critical to its survival—the demonstration of the fact that animal behavior is qualitatively different from human behavior and that, therefore, the generalization of animal behavior to men is limited to the sub-human facets of the behavior of men. On the other hand, symbolic interactionism sometimes assumes that the differences between animal behavior and human behavior are qualitative—but this is not critical to its survival as a distinctive perspective. Indeed Mead saw enough similarities between his position and that of the behaviorists to label his theory 'social behaviorism'.[1] When, for instance, John

---

[1] As Mead [1934] contended, he sought to be a better 'behaviorist' than Watson: 'The common psychological standpoint which is represented by behaviorism is found in John B. Watson. The behaviorism which we shall make use of is more adequate than that of which Watson makes use. Behaviorism in this wider sense is simply an approach to the study of the experience of the individual from the point

Finley Scott [1971] argued that there is no fundamental difference between learning theory, derived from animal studies, and symbolic processes in humans, he may win some points only when the position of Meadians are considered, but clearly not when the position of the science of culture, all too often neglected by sociologists, is considered.

A possible source of confusion in this matter is the meaning of some of the terms used with reference to Figure 5.1. For instance, Skinner's definition of a symbol misses what is most essential in its meaning. According to Skinner [1953: 293]: 'A symbol, as the term was used by Freud in the analysis of dreams and art, is any temporal or spatial pattern which is reinforcing because of similarity to another pattern but escapes punishment because of differences.' What is missing in this definition is the important distinction between *symbols* and *signs* that is always implied in any adequate definition of the symbol. 'Symbols' are a human invention and have an arbitrary quality in that men may

---

of view of his conduct, particularly, but not exclusively, the conduct as it is observable by others. Historically, behaviorism entered psychology through the door of animal psychology. There it was found to be impossible to use what is termed introspection. One cannot appeal to the animal's introspection, but must study the animal in terms of external conduct. Earlier animal psychology added an inferential reference to consciousness, and even undertook to find the point in conduct at which consciousness appears. This inference had, perhaps, varying degrees of probability, but it was one which could not be tested experimentally. It could be then simply dropped as far as science was concerned. It was not necessary for the study of the conduct of the individual animal. Having taken that behavioristic standpoint for the lower animals, it was possible to carry it over to the human animal' [Mead, 1934: 2]. There seems to be little doubt that 'symbolic inter- actionism', as it has developed under Herbert Blumer's tutelage, has a different polemical focus than Mead's original writings [Cf. Scott, 1971: 4n, 64n]. Perhaps this point can be best established by considering the three types of 'false' approaches to social psychology which Blumer [1937] urged should be rejected and replaced with the symbolic interactionist view. In this pedagogically influential article, in which the term 'symbolic interactionism' was used for the first time [cf. Blumer, 1969: 1n], Blumer berated three false approaches to social psychology: these were 'biological determinism' in the form of the 'instinct doctrine'; 'cultural determinism' as in Levy-Bruhl's collectivistic theory of pre-logical knowledge; and the 'stimulus- response' approach of behavioral psychology. As Blumer [e.g. 1937: 160] makes clear, however, the force of his polemical attacks was directed at the 'stimulus- response' approach of the behaviorists, whereas Mead's sought accommodation with the behaviorists by seeking to elaborate their theory. It would appear that Mead's polemical attacks were more totally directed against the 'cultural deter- ministic' view [cf. 1934: 379–389]. The sharpness of Blumer's and other symbolic interactionists' more recent polemics against 'the cultural determinist' approach would appear to be in reaction to the ascendance of Parsonian sociology.

decide to change their meanings. A grade of 'A' is a symbol, arbitrary as it is, for excellence in American schools. There is no physical, immanent, relationship between 'A' and 'excellence' and if educators wish they can change the symbol to 'Z' for the referent 'excellence'. 'Signs' physically represent their referents, as clouds indicate rain, and are not amenable to arbitrary manipulation as is the case with symbols. Thus, the 'similarity' and 'differences' in Skinner's definition would refer more strictly to 'signs'. In 'symbols', differences can be converted to similarities and vice versa, without incurring punishment. It is said that during World War II Americans changed the term 'frankfurter' to 'hot-dog' because of anti-German feelings. 'Frankfurter' was, just as 'hot-dog' has become, a verbal symbol for some food. The point is that animals lack such arbitrary and inventive codes called symbols.

The confusion, sometimes the bold-faced distortion, in the behaviorist definition of the 'symbol' can be effectively exemplified in John Finley Scott's treatment of the matter. Here is his discussion of a 'symbol':

> Here is a good place to define two popular concepts: 'symbol' and 'meaning'. These in particular need attention, because many sociologists believe that they cannot be interpreted in reductive or learning-theoretical terms. A 'symbol' may be defined as a stimulus whose reinforcing value is based on conditioning rather than on unconditioned effects. Symbols generally are considered to possess meaning. Symbols may be defined as 'meaningful' to the extent that they elicit a consistent response independent of other reinforcers or stimuli with which they may be variably associated. *Thus the sound of the bell was a symbol to the dog who had been conditioned by it, and it meant that food was on its way* [my emphasis]. The dog showed the meaning of the bell by responding, as it were, to food. Some epistemological conservatives speak as if signs operate by a *natural* association between the sign and the thing signified, and symbols by an *artificial* and somehow non-natural relation; but this distinction makes sense only if we assume that human society is non-natural [Scott, 1971: 50].

The problem with Scott's refusal to acknowledge any difference between a 'sign' and a 'symbol' is that it blurs the significant fact that man *creates* symbols whereas, in the case of the dog, the association between the sound of the bell and the food is created for it. The truth of the matter is that 'human society is non-natural' in that it is a network of symbols created by men who then make use of them in their behaviors. It does not follow, however, that 'symbols' are *artificial*, as Scott has put it; they are *arbitrary* in the sense that they are created by men in an extra-natural fashion. To denote that fact by the term 'symbol' and to differentiate it from the *natural* communications involved in 'sign' associations in animal behavior seems legitimate. It is because behavioral sociologists refuse to differentiate 'symbols' from 'signs' that they consider the associated distinction between symbolic behavior in humans and conditioned behavior in animals as untenable.

At any rate, the theorem derived from this distinction, namely, that the principles of conditioned animal behavior can only be generalized to sub-human conditioned behavior in men but not to symbolic behavior in men, seems crucial to an evaluation of Homans' social exchange theory. I shall therefore expand on the implications of the theorem by pointing to a few differences between conditioned behavior and symbolic behavior. It serves good purpose to note that these are not new issues but old ones which need to be reviewed precisely because they are being overwhelmed by the resurgence of 'behavioral sociology'.

The first difference that may be noted is this: *in conditioned behavior, past experiences are necessary conditions of present activities.* Conditioned behavior relates present activities to past experiences and is only meaningful in terms of these past experiences. It is however incapable of relating present activities to future possibilities. On the other hand, *in symbolic behavior, past experiences are neither necessary nor sufficient conditions of present activities.* Although symbolic behavior may include past experiences in its repertoire of responses, its chief characteristic is the capacity to relate present activities to future possibilities. If exchange behavior were in fact to be conditioned behavior, then we must assume that social exchange processes do not include future anticipations. This attribute of symbolic behavior in relating present activities not only to past experiences but also to future possibilities means that it can make use of 'selective choice' from a wide range of past experiences and future possibilities and that it can take into consideration 'probable future consequences'. Unlike conditioned behavior, symbolic behavior can make 'use of reflective choice in selecting the alternative that will finally be the response. The utilization of reflective choice means that the completion of an act (response) is delayed until the alternatives are more or less thoroughly tested symbolically' [Hartuung, 1960: 233].

There is a crucial difference between this attribute of symbolic behavior to reach into the future, sometimes in spite of or even in the absence of similar past experiences, and what Skinner [1953: 126–128; 180] considers 'anticipation' in which delayed present responses are firmly tied to past learned experiences. The power of symbolic behavior, over conditioned behavior, is that it is capable of transcending past experiences in guessing what the *unknown future* may bring.

Secondly, *symbolic behavior is behaviorally creative; conditioned behavior is static.* Symbolic behavior can and does result in new behavior; conditioned behavior is repetitive of old behaviors. This attribute of symbolic behavior is the one most emphasized in sociology, because the symbolic interactionist perspective specializes in it. In symbolic behavior, definitions and interpretations of the intentions of other actors serve as intervening variables between stimulus and response. It is on this score that symbolic interactionist sociologists frown on Homans' behavioral psychological interpretation of human behavior [cf. Blumer, 1969: 64n], since in conditioned behavior an individual does things not because he interprets the intent of other individuals but rather because he is responding to past experiences. In fact, behavioral sociologists dismiss 'intentions' as 'internal states' and thereby as 'fictions' not amenable to scientific investigation. Thus Scott [1971: 50] avers: 'Behavior rather than intent gives the symbol its meaning'; of course the symbol means nothing more than a 'signal' to the behavioral sociologist. In this type of construction, however, no *new* behavior can result, since all activities must be tied to the past.

A corollary of the behaviorist view on this matter ought to be noted: In contending that there is no qualitative difference between animal conditioned behavior and human symbolic behavior, behavioral sociologists frequently point to the fact that animals can be taught 'sign language'.[1] But human behavior would hardly be claimed to constitute a unique type if all humans

---

[1] In actual fact, the so-called 'sign-language' in animals is limited to the understanding of the immediate environment and does not transcend time and space.

were capable of was learning what they were being taught. In symbolic behavior, individuals not only can *be taught*, but they can *teach* as well—often adding *new* dimensions to behavior in the process.

Thirdly, *symbolic behavior is normative behavior shared by persons within a value system; conditioned behavior is nonnormative behavior and is an attribute of the individual.* Since conditioned behavior is an individual experience, learned through sheer experience, it is non-transmissible. To give an example, one may train an intelligent animal to do something ingenious by rewarding it; but the off-spring of that animal cannot be socialized by its animal mother into that pattern of behavior. It has to be trained all over again. Symbolic behavior is transmissible. For instance, the norm of reciprocity, whether conceived as a supra-individual universal norm [Gouldner, 1960] or as an emergent group norm [Blau, 1964a: 92], relates to symbolic behavior and is transmissible from one person to another. To treat exchange behavior as conditioned behavior, one would have to exclude normative behavior, as indeed Homans [1961: 5] has sought to do.

Other behavioral sociologists, less sensitive than Homans to the moral nature of society, have indeed tended to emasculate the meaning of normative behavior by seeking to show that it is not necessarily symbolic. Thus, Scott, who has attempted to formulate a behavioral sociological theory of normative behavior, believes that it is possible to advance a conceptualization of the *norm* 'in which symbolic form, though included in the concept, is not its criterion'. Scott only recognizes a pattern of behavior as normative if it is accompanied by sanctions consisting of apparently individually learned experiences: 'As a pure symbol', Scott [1971: 73] writes, 'the statement of the norm is always impotent; any potency it has derives from a sequence of learning that began with a non-symbolic conditioner.' Two conclusions would seem to follow from this grosser form of behavioral sociological conception of normative behavior (to which, be it emphasized, Homans' work does not entirely succumb).[1] First, although Scott does not

---

[1] Homans' [1961: 46] definition of the norm is: 'A *norm* is a statement made by members of a group, not necessarily by all of them, that its members ought to behave in a certain way in certain circumstances.' The difference is that Homans appears to treat the *norm* as an attribute of the group, while Scott treats the *norm* as an attribute of the individual. Homans' posture here borrows from his former more Parsonian emphasis on the group as, for instance, in *The Human Group*.

explicitly make the point, the *norm* is not unique to humans and could also be found in animal behavior. Secondly, since the norm is individually learned, borne out of sheer experience—with no relation to society or the group as such—it is an attribute of the individual rather than of society. As a result, it is not transmissible from one generation to another or from one person to another; rather, the *norm* must be individually acquired by each individual from brute confrontation with 'nonsymbolic conditioners'. This behavioral sociological conception of 'nonsymbolic' normative behavior is clearly in opposition to our view as stated above. As Davis and Blake [1964: 457] have so cogently put it, such behaviorist 'biologizing' of human behavior and human society is a 'fallacy [that] is no less bizarre than the opposite—namely, an explanation of some aspect of insect or animal society in terms of presumed norms governing behavior'.

Fourthly, *symbolic behavior makes use of time and space conceptions; on the other hand conditioned behavior cannot make use of time and space conceptions.* In symbolic behavior it is possible to generalize across time and space—especially to include a conception of the future. This is impossible in conditioned behavior. Its emphasis is on the here-and-now. Correlatively, the conception of alternatives, absent from the view of the individual, is symbolic behavior, not conditioned behavior.

Let us now relate these views of the science of culture—emphasizing in effect that the differences between conditioned behavior and symbolic behavior are qualitative, not quantitative—to Homans' exchange theory. Is the distinction drawn here between animal behavior and symbolic behavior irrelevant for Homans' theory? I do not think so. Many of the attributes of the subject-matter of Homans' exchange theory, namely, elementary social behavior are, as he defines them, more like conditioned behavior than symbolic behavior: the nonnormative nature of social exchange [1962: 3, 5]; the emphasis on the here-and-now, face-to-face interaction [1962: 3, 4]; and the emphasis on past experiences, on what has actually been learned. But Homans did not limit himself in his social exchange theory to the principles of behavioral psychology. His behavioral psychological statements of these principles of conditioned behavior seemed to have played a part only in the formal statement of his social exchange propositions. Homans was apparently not satisfied that behavioral psychology could yield all the propositions to which to reduce human behavior. Instead, he sought to combine behavioral psychology with elementary economics. We now turn to that attempt and the difficulties it creates for Homans' social exchange theory and his crusade for the behavioral psychological reduction of human behavior and institutions.

Behavioral Psychology and Elementary Economics

Neither 'utilitarian' nor 'hedonistic' is an adequate epithet for describing Homans' social exchange theory. If by 'utilitarian' one means, as in economics, that a man makes his calculations in the market in terms of both *gains* and *loss*, with the aim of maximizing profits, then clearly Homans' social exchange theory is less than that. If by 'hedonistic' one means, as in psychology, the *seeking of pleasure* and the *avoidance of pain* with the pleasure principle emphasis on the here-and-now, then equally clearly Homans' social exchange theory was intended to be more than that. From its inception, Homans' intent was to make the theory both of these at once. While proclaiming himself as an 'ultimate psychological reductionist' [1958: 597], he also thought that 'an incidental advantage of exchange theory is that it might bring sociology closer to economics—that science of man most advanced, most capable of application and intellectually most isolated' [Homans, 1958: 280]. That initial attempt at a theoretical conception of social exchange left the relationship between economics and psychology ambiguous: how are they related to each other and to social exchange behavior? The position of economics was at that time [1958] only marginal to the theory, with the principal burden of the explanation of the 'view that interaction between persons is an exchange of goods, material and immaterial' principally assumed by psychology. In pointing out these facts, it is not my intention to imply that one expects Homans to spell out every relationship in a premier article. Rather, it is to indicate my conviction that Homans changed from being 'an ultimate psychological reductionist' in 1958 to a psychological-with-economic reductionist in 1961 when the full statement of his exchange theory was presented in *Social Behavior*. It would be most interesting if one could find out from Homans why the change occurred; my suspicion is that he recognized in the interval that the 'ultimate behavioral psychological reduction' of human behavior is impossible and that he had to augment his arguments by including elementary economic principles in his theory.

Simply stated, Homans set out in *Social Behavior* to combine behavioral psychology and elementary economics for the purpose of explaining 'social behavior, or true exchange'. The change from the 1958 position is significant. Far from suspecting [as in 1958: 597] that the 'more general set [of propositions for explaining sociological propositions] will turn out to contain the propositions of behavioral psychology', Homans [1961: 12] had come to believe that these 'empirical [sociological] propositions may most easily be explained by two bodies of general propositions already in existence: behavioral psychology and elementary economics'. What is the warrant for this belief in the ability of a combination of two sciences so far removed intellectually to offer such ease in the explanation of human behavior? Homans' thought here bears close scrutiny, and since it is relevant for my own arguments I shall quote a whole paragraph from him, a paragraph by the way that has not been given the critical attention it deserves in the various reactions to Homans' work:

> It is true that both sets of propositions will take a little extrapolating before they are ready to explain what is observed of elementary social behavior. Behavioral psychology is a set of propositions that come mostly from experimental studies of animals, usually in nonsocial situations. It must be extrapolated— and this is quite a distance—to men and to a social situation: one in which the behavior of one person affects, and is affected by, the behavior of another. As for elementary economics, it is a set of propositions describing the behavior of men exchanging material goods for money in a so-called perfect market: one in which the behavior of any one buyer or seller has little effect in determining the market prices. Elementary economics does deal with men and with a social situation, for exchange is obviously social; and to serve as an explanation of elementary social behavior it needs a different kind of extrapolation from that which behavioral psychology needs. From apples and dollars, physical goods and money, it needs to be extrapolated so as to apply, for instance, to the exchange of intangible services for social esteem in a market that is far from perfect. As the two sets of propositions, behavioral psychology and elementary economics, are stretched in these

respective directions, they seem to me to mesh with one another and form a single set; but rather than trying to prove that this is so, I shall later suggest what the set might be [Homans, 1961: 12–13].

It is important to understand what Homans says he wants to achieve here. He wants to extrapolate *independently* from behavioral psychology and elementary economics to 'elementary social behavior'. Apparently the extrapolation of behavioral psychology consists of *upgrading* animal behavior 'usually in non-social situations' 'to men and to a social situation'. The extrapolation of elementary economics, on the other hand, consists of *downgrading*, if you please, from the tangible to the intangible; from a perfect market in which individual characteristics do not influence the final outcome to an imperfect market in which individual sentiments and activities are of the utmost importance. However, Homans apparently feels that there is no extrapolation needed to mesh behavioral psychology and elementary economics together. We are told to take it on faith that 'behavioral psychology and elementary economics . . . mesh together and form a single set'. Far from agreeing with Homans that this is the case, I shall take as problematic for Homans' exchange theory this attempt to mesh these disparate sciences. For the truth is that, although Homans has not tried to prove that behavioral psychology and elementary economics do mesh together, he has tried to reconcile them. The strength or weakness of his theory depends very much on this exercise at combinations.

Before probing the strength of the theory on this basis, I will seek to highlight another problem. As he has defined it—when translated into our terminology—behavioral psychology studies conditioned (nonsymbolic) behavior in animals, whereas 'elementary social behavior' is symbolic, studying men 'in social situations'. If, as has been argued, it is understood that such symbolic behavior is generically unique to men and that, there-fore, it is qualitatively different from animal behavior, then Homans' position in seeking to achieve such extrapolation amounts to an argument that *it is possible to upgrade the nonsymbolic to the symbolic, to generalize from conditioned behavior in animals to symbolic behavior in humans*. This is a large assumption.

Still more problematic is the assumption that elementary economics and behavioral psychology mesh together. Stated in our terms, it is an argument that symbolic and nonsymbolic behaviors can be combined together for the sake of better explaining another form of symbolic behavior. One might indeed ask, why is it necessary to combine elementary economics and behavioral psychology—two sciences at opposite ends of the complexity of human behavior? Or to put the question more directly, could either of elementary economics or behavioral psychology by itself explain human exchange? There would of course be no need for the combination if it could. At any rate the position I wish to develop here is that there is a *qualitative* difference between them—with one specializing in the study of time-laden symbolic behavior while the other, behavioral psychology, specializes in the study of nonsymbolic behavior with no conception of time—and that a combination of the two to form explanatory propositions for human or symbolic behavior is not possible. Whether one accepts this position or not may well depend on one's attitude to the distinction drawn here between symbolic and nonsymbolic behavior. Irrespective of one's position in such matters, however, Homans' strategy in combining elementary economics with behavioral psychology calls for an examination.

Homans combined the two sciences to form explanatory propositions for his social exchange theory by a method that might be called *conceptual articulation*.[1] Some selected key concepts in the two sciences are either reconciled by defining one in terms of the other or else are assumed equivalent with no attempt to reconcile them. The criteria for selecting these concepts are not clear. One must assume that those selected for the theory are concepts nearest elementary human behavior and that those left out are concepts which are unimportant for elementary social behavior. In Figure 5.2 I present the range of concepts mentioned in Homans' [1961] social exchange theory according to whether Homans (a) tries to reconcile them, (b) assumes them to be equivalent, without discussion, or (c) mentions one set of concepts but makes no attempt to relate them to their counterparts in the other science.

---

[1] Smelser [1967; Wallerstein and Smelser, 1969] has been active in recommending a method of 'complementary articulation' as a way of combining the resources of different social sciences in theory building. One aspect of that method, as between sociology and psychoanalysis anyway, is the articulation of 'conceptual resources' of both disciplines [Wallerstein and Smelser, 1969: 698].

FIGURE 5.2

The Range of Concepts from Behavioral Psychology and
Elementary Economics in Homans' Social Exchange Theory

Behavioral Psychology	Elementary Economics
a. Reconciled Concepts	
Punishment	Cost
b. Concepts Assumed Equivalent	
Reward (Reinforcement)	Reward
c. Equivalence Not Specified	
Stimulus	Demand
Response	Supply
(no equivalent)	Investment
(no equivalent)	Profits

The only concepts that Homans [1961: 24–27; 57–61] seriously
attempted to reconcile are *psychological punishment* and *economic
costs*. He apparently assumes that 'costs' are more inclusive than
'punishments' [1961: 58]. What he did do was to define 'punishment' in terms of 'costs'; in effect psychological punishment,
usually considered as a sensuous physical negative feeling of
deprivation, is endowed with the symbolic meaning of a 'value
forgone' [p. 58] or 'forgone rewards' [p. 26]. Homans, the honest
scientist that he is, however, gives us good reason for doubting
the validity of this transformation of non-symbolic here-and-now
psychological punishment into non-physical, nonsensuous, symbolic economic costs. I quote him:

> Since the emission of any reinforced activity prevents by that fact the simultaneous emission of an activity leading to an *alternative* reward, and thus amounts to the withdrawal of the alternative reward—that is, to a punishment—we might argue that costs, or unavoidable punishment, of any one activity include the withdrawn or foregon rewards of an *alternative* activity. *But we doubt that pigeons act as if they were aware of this* [Homans, 1961: 26; italics added].

Indeed not! Pigeon behavior would be symbolic behavior if it was aware of alternatives, i.e., if it was capable of 'selective choice' from a range of possibilities not *physically* available before it. To assume that a pigeon, or any other animal, operates on the principle of opportunity costs is to say that the pigeon has a conception of time and space—that it can generalize across time and across space. There is no basis in Homans' or Skinner's work for such an assumption. There seems little doubt that this attempt at the articulation of the two concepts from behavioral psychology and elementary economics has not been very successful.

But 'costs' and 'punishments' are not the most important concepts in Homans' social exchange theory. The most important concepts, rather, are *psychological rewards* and *economic rewards*—or what Homans has massed together as 'rewards' [cf. Abrahamson, 1970]. Curiously Homans makes no attempt to reconcile them, most probably because he does not see any differences between them—thanks to workaday English language that confuses the two concepts while semantically separating psychological 'punishments' from economic 'costs'. But a scientific enterprise must cut through the impurities of the English language. Psychological *rewards* are nonsymbolic, usually sensuous, activities. Thibaut and Kelley [1959: 12] offer a definition of psychological rewards as follows: 'By rewards, we refer to pleasures, satisfactions, and gratifications the person enjoys. The provision of a means whereby a drive is reduced or need fulfilled constitutes a reward.' Even Skinner [1953: 185] ties 'rewards' to the presentation of a 'stimulus'; i.e., it has a physical basis. On the other hand, economic rewards are symbolic experiences of benefits, usually of non-sensuous kind, involving an outlay of resources and time. Economic rewards need not involve 'pleasures, satisfactions, and gratifications', nor the reduction of a drive. Consequently, it is not usual to discuss economic rewards in terms of 'satiation', whereas the amount of psychological rewards depends on the physical needs of the subject and hence 'satiation' is very relevant in understanding psychological rewards [Homans, 1961: 19]. Homans, as we have said, never differentiated between these two types of rewards. Accordingly, he has usually switched from the one to the other and he is able to claim at the same time that he is dealing with the psychological reduction of human behavior to behavioral psychological principles based on 'psychological rewards'.

Thirdly, Homans has made use of concepts from one of the two sciences that he believes mesh together without reference to their counterparts in the other science. 'Stimulus' and 'response' from behavioral psychology are used without their counterparts in economics, 'demand' and 'supply'. More revealing of the difficulties involved in Homans' exercise at conceptual combinations is the fact that he has used two concepts in elementary economics that do not have equivalents in behavioral psychology. These are 'investments' and 'profits'. Both are symbol-encrusted conceptions that psychologists have not attempted to approximate in their study of animals. Homans' extrapolation from economics to behavioral psychology in the realm of 'profits' sounds unconvincing: 'psychic profit [is] reward less cost' [Homans, 1961: 61].

This survey leaves us with only one conclusion: *behavioral psychology and elementary economics do not mesh together*. But they did guide Homans separately to formulate the five explanatory propositions that make up his social exchange theory in a curious way. The first four propositions are patterned on behavioral psychology; the fifth on economic symbolic arguments. Thus the first four propositions relate present activities to past experiences but not to future possibilities or future probable consequences. The fifth proposition, based on the distributive justice principle, clearly relates present activities not only to past experiences but also to future possibilities and it is based on the symbolic concept of 'expectations'. This distinction seems to be the essence of Morton Deutsch's [1964: 158] perceptive remark:

> The first four propositions of Homans are attempts to restate in everyday language a Skinnerian [behavioral psychological] viewpoint about the interrelated effects of deprivation or satiation and

of frequency and quality of a given behavior. The fifth is un-adulterated Homans.

Nor is there an ecological fallacy involved in pointing out that the first four propositions were presented together within three pages [1961: 53–55] while the fifth proposition is separated from the others by full twenty pages within which are introduced such key variables in Homans' exchange theory as 'costs', 'profit', 'total reward', and 'distributive justice'.

I now present Homans' five explanatory propositions of social exchange behavior:

(1) If in the past the occurrence of a particular stimulus-situation has been the occasion on which a man's activity has been rewarded, then the more similar the present stimulus-situation is to the past one, the more likely he is to emit the activity, or some similar activity, now [1961: 53].

(2) The more often within a given period of time a man's activity rewards the activity of another, the more often the other will emit the activity [1961: 54].

(3) The more valuable to a man a unit of the activity another gives him, the more often he will emit activity rewarded by the activity of the other. ['Value' refers to the degree of reinforcement or punishment that is received from a unit of another's activity, p. 40] [1961: 55].

(4) The more often a man has in the recent past received a rewarding activity from another, the less valuable any further unit of that activity becomes to him [1961: 55].

(5) The more often to a man's disadvantage the rule of distributive justice fails of realization, the more likely he is to display the emotional behavior we call anger. [The rule of distributive justice is stated as follows: 'A man in an exchange relation with another will expect that the rewards of each man be proportional to his costs—the greater the rewards, the greater the costs—and that the net rewards, or profits, of each man be proportional to his investments—the greater the investments, the greater the profit'] [1961: 75].

To sum up, let us ask: is Homans a psychological reductionist? Unfortunately, there is no ready-made answer to this question. As he has more recently conveyed the matter, the social sciences—including 'psychology, anthropology, sociology, economics, political science, and probably linguistics'—can all be explained by invoking the principles of behavioral psychology [Homans,

1967b: 3, 43]. Note that rather than mesh elementary economics with psychology, Homans seeks more recently to reduce economics to behavioral psychology. But there is a clear change—and something of growing confusion—in Homans' conception of what behavioral psychology is all about. More recently, he says now that the propositions of behavioral psychology 'hold good of all human beings and indeed of all the higher animals, modified in the case of the animals by mechanisms called instinctual that are rather more specific in their operation than such mechanisms in men' [1967b: 42]. Note that sentence well. It represents a change: it seems as though humans are being studied in their own right and the generalizations are not derived from animal behavior and ascribed to human behavior. Homans, I dare say, is still a psychological reductionist but the inevitable line of development is away from the psychology of animal behavior to the study of human behavior as an autonomous area, independent of, qualitatively different from, animal behavior. At least behavioral psychology now seems to refer to the *higher* animals—no more to pigeons. Homans continues to confuse 'psychological rewards'—with an emphasis on what has actually been experienced—with 'economic rewards'—involving a calculation of possibilities and uncertainties in the future. At the very least his social exchange theory as presented in *Social Behavior* was not intended to be solely behavioral psychological reductionism, but rather psychological-with-economic reductionism. But because the two could not mesh together as easily as he had hoped, they show their separate and uneven influences on the theory.

Homans' Social Exchange Theory Minus Behavioral Psychology

My search into Homans' writings convinces me that he had intuitively formulated a conception of human social exchange behavior before he became a Skinnerian intellectual convert [cf. Homans, 1962: 47–48]. I want to develop the view that if Homans had not read Skinner he would still have formulated a theory of social exchange but that its formal statements would have been different. My assumption is that Homans sought a scientific legitimation of his intuitive conception of social exchange by employing the principles of Skinner's behavioral psychology. The essential difference would have been that if he had not sought a scientific legitimation of his theory in terms of an esthetically appealing behavioral psychology, Homans' social exchange theory would have stressed what he has come to emphasize of late, namely, the psychology of what Robert Redfield [1957] has characterized as 'developed human nature', specializing in what is common to all socialized adult men.

The painful contradiction in Homans' social exchange theory is that he believes he is dealing with a psychology, behavioral psychology, that studies men as men, as members of the human species, and yet it is a psychology that takes its principles from animal behavior. Even more glaring is the fact that Homans misses what is perhaps most essential in man: unlike animals men's actions are not *necessarily* tied to their past but men can act now in spite of their past provided their calculations of future possibilities are in their favor. If, in fact, Homans' various attempts to explain behavior were derived from his behavioral psychological explanatory propositions of exchange theory, then one must conclude that his exchange theory is incapable of explaining human behaviors based on calculations of future possibilities, independent of past experiences.

But at this point one is likely to be involved in an endless terminological argument with Homans and his 'behavioral sociology' adherents. For behavioral psychology, the principles of which were first stated with modesty, has now come to embrace every form of behavior in men. We are now told that 'Behavioral psychology seems to include within itself the so-called theory of rational behavior' in that behavioral psychology embraces the rational choice of alternatives [Homans, 1969: 13]. And yet Homans is insistent on his emphasis on the necessity of past experiences for present activities[1] [1967b: 39; 1969: 13] while leaving the weight of calculations of future possibilities undefined.

The critical questions for Homans' exchange theory to answer

---

[1] Thus Homans points up what he considers to be the limitations of 'rational theory' of behavior: 'the rational theory is obviously more limited than behavioral psychology. Though it recognizes the importance of perception, and assumes that a man is rational in acting in accordance with his perceptions even though in the eyes of persons better informed his perceptions may be incorrect, it simply takes the perceptions as given and *does not tie them back, as behavioral psychology does, to past experience* [Homans, 1967b: 39; my italics].

are these two: First, is the theory one of men as men, as members of a distinct species [1961: 6; 1967b: 35; 1971: 23]? Second, do the principles of animal behavior explain such universal human behavior? Homans' answers to both questions are in the affirmative. Here lies his weakness. Homans [e.g., 1967b: 35–36] believes that the answers to the problem of the psychology of human nature have been well developed in behavioral psychology. As Redfield [1957: 156] has more cautiously noted, although 'developed human nature' is a reality in the sense that 'in whatever established group [men] develop, certain outcomes of the development are always the same', 'it is not a reality that is easily amenable to investigation by precise method and subject to dependable proof. The intuitions as to its reality are stronger than the demonstration of its content. It is something we know but do not reduce easily to formal propositions' [Redfield, 1957: 156]. That is, while Redfield and Homans, writing about the same time, define the same area of study of universal human behavior, Redfield believed it was an area that was still to be developed, Homans that it has been developed.

Let me illustrate the difficulty in Homans' position by pointing up the limitations of his *success* proposition. He states it so: 'When a response is followed by a reward (or 'reinforcement'), the frequency or probability of its recurrence increases' [1967b: 36–37; 1969: 11]. What if a person meets a new situation, dissimilar to the ones whose reward patterns he knows so well? *Homans' theory does not tell us what the individual will do in new situations.* Or what will happen if the individual believes that future possibilities will be different from the reward patterns that he has been used to? *Homans' theory does not tell us about the behavioral consequences of the individual's changed evaluations of future possibilities.* And yet the behavior of men *qua* human is determined more by the *hope* of success than by the *past experiences* of success. The emphasis here is on the prospects of, the hopes of, success as the motivating force in human behavior. Behavioral psychology, if by that we mean the psychology that wholly or partially derives its principles from animal behavior, is incapable of handling such future calculations as the motive force in human behavior.

But Homans claims to have explained a variety of human behaviors in terms of the principles of behavioral psychology. I submit that he has not done so. Homans has usually explained

S.E.T.–5*

human behavior in terms of future possibilities and consequences, not in the behavioral psychological terms of past experiences. Part of the problem is that he has freely changed the meaning of rewards from 'psychological rewards' to 'economic rewards'. Let me illustrate with Homans' [1964c: 968; 1967b: 43–46] example of the retreat of William the Conqueror from Scotland. As Homans presents it:

1. The more rewarding men find the results of an action, the more likely they are to take this action.
2. William the Conqueror was a man.
3. Therefore, the more rewarding William found the results of an action, the more likely he was to take this action.
4. In the circumstances, he did not find the conquest of Scotland rewarding.
5. Therefore, he was unlikely to take action that will win him Scotland [Homans, 1964: 968].

The problem here is that 'rewards' could have one of two meanings. The first proposition, which Homans [1964c: 968] says is the major psychological premise, could either read as (a) 'The more rewarding men find the results of a certain action *taken in the past*, the more likely they are to take this action now' or as (b) 'The more rewarding men *judge* or *expect* the results of some future action (yet to be carried out) will be, the more likely they are to take this action now'. In (a) present activities are predicated on past experiences and 'reward' is that in behavioral psychology. In (b) present activities are predicated on the symbolic process of calculations against uncertainties and possibilities in the future and the meaning of 'rewards' here is fully in accord with the meaning of economic rewards. As it turns out the meaning of 'rewards' in Homans' explanation of William the Conqueror's retreat from Scotland is (b) economic, not (a) psychological—certainly not behavioral psychological.

What could have have happened if Homans had not tied his social exchange theory to behavioral psychology with so much weight attached to the necessity of past experiences in the explanation of present activities and so light weight attached to calculations of future possibilities? I detect some shifts in Homans' work and in the absence of behavioral psychology they could have been much better developed. I believe the following formulation approximates what Homans' exchange theory would have been when freed from behavioral psychology.

Assumption 1. All socialized men (i.e., humans) are motivated by the hope of success [cf. Homans, 1971: 23].

This assumption is becoming ever more prevalent in Homans' writings. Like the other two assumptions to follow, it belongs to what Redfield [1957] refers to as 'developed human nature'— true of all socialized human adults and untrue of animal adults.

Proposition 1. When a person is confronted with a range of choices for a course of present action, he is more likely to choose the one he believes will bring him success.

Social Exchange Derivation 1. A person will enter into a social exchange transaction with others if and only if he believes the exchange transaction will bring him success.

Assumption 2. Men's past experiences reduce their uncertainty in making a choice for present action from a range of future possible sources of success.

Proposition 2. When a person is confronted with a range of possibilities for present activity, all of which could bring him success in the future, he is more likely to choose that possibility that has proven successful in the past.

Social Exchange Derivation 2. When a person chooses from a range of persons with whom to enter into social exchange transaction he is more likely to choose a man who has rewarded his activities in the past.

Assumption 3. Men like to maintain a relationship that is rewarding to them.

Proposition 3. When confronted with a choice between a new relationship with uncertain results and continuing present relationship with certain benefits, a person will choose to maintain the present one.

Social Exchange Derivation 3a. When social exchange interactions prove rewarding to a person, he emits behavior that he believes will sustain the social exchange process.

Social Exchange Derivation 3b. When social exchange interactions are rewarding to a person, he will seek to increase his reciprocal rewarding activity to the other person with whom he is in the social exchange relationship in order to sustain the social exchange transaction.

I offer these statements as a correction to Homans' extravagant emphasis on the necessity of past experiences for human exchange.

I do not deny that the past influences the present: that is what men share with animals. But any theory that seeks, as Homans says his does, to study men, as men, should emphasize the attributes that are unique to men. The assumptions above belong to such unique characteristics of men. The propositions and the derivations assume that social exchange is symbolic or human behavior that is out of reach of animal behavior.

I want to emphasize that I am not proposing a new theory. This is an exercise in what could have been. It is not *my* theory. But I believe these statements convey my impression of the shortcomings of Homans' behavioral psychological formulation of human exchange behavior.

Restricted Exchange and Generalized Exchange

I have already quoted Homans' response to Lévi-Strauss' extension of the concept of social exchange to generalized exchange involving at least three parties: 'It might be argued,' Homans had written, 'that in extending the idea of exchange in this way, Lévi-Strauss has thinned the meaning out of it' [Homans and Schneider, 1955: 7]. Clearly, restricted exchange limited to two persons had great appeal to Homans. That this is so is made clear in *Social Behavior*. Homans' [1961: 378] avowed concern is with 'an exchange of rewards (or punishments) between at least two persons; the exchange is direct rather than indirect; and it is actual behavior and not just a norm specifying what behavior ought to be.' His exchange theory is limited to restricted exchange between two individuals both in time and space: 'Here social behavior is elementary in the sense that the two men are in face-to-face contact, and each is rewarding the other directly and immediately: each is enabled to do his work better here and now' [1961: 4]. The legacy of animal psychology can be felt here.

Homans did not mean that that is all there is to social exchange. He, as Blau [1964a] after him, has a concept of *indirect exchange*. But this is totally different from what Malinowski called circular exchange and Lévi-Strauss generalized exchange. These sociologists refer to circular or generalized exchange in terms of the number of people involved in unit time and space in the same social exchange transaction. On the other hand, in Homans indirect exchange is equivalent to the 'complexity of exchanges' in the sense of the degree of sophistication of the things exchanged: these are 'processes by which institutions develop out of elementary social behavior—the increasing roundaboutness of the exchange of rewards, which is sometimes called the increasing division of labor' [1961: 385]. According to this view indirect exchange is a complex form of human behavior involving the division of labor. That is not what Malinowski means by circular exchange; and that is not what Lévi-Strauss has called generalized exchange. As used by these writers, generalized exchange is as elementary social behavior as restricted exchange. If A gives to B, B gives to C, and C gives to A, we have generalized exchange. Malinowski regards it as circular exchange if the same item is thus being exchanged. If, on the other hand, A gives to B and B gives to A—thus exhausting the exchange process—we have restricted exchange. What makes the difference is the number of people involved, not what Homans calls 'the complexity of rewards'.

Does Homans deal with generalized exchange? He says he does not. Indeed all five explanatory propositions of his theory are limited to two-person interactions. We have said that the differences between restricted exchange and generalized exchange, in a phenotypic sense, are qualitative, not quantitative. Accordingly, we should assume that Homans' exchange propositions are only capable of explaining exchange transactions between two persons. Here, immediately, we arrive at another contradiction in Homans' theory. Although it is stated in dyadic terms, the evidence offered to validate the theory is in connection with multi-person interactions. Unless it can be shown, against the evidence presented by Simmel [1950: 122–142] and Bales and Borgatta [1955], that the differences between dyads and multi-person groups are quantitative and, therefore, one can generalize from two-person interactions to multi-person interactions, Homans' explanations of small group behavior in terms of his social exchange theory would appear questionable. But Homans sees very little difficulty in invoking multi-person interaction in support of his dyadic theory. It is significant nevertheless, indeed a tribute to the man, that he was sensitive to this issue. In spite of the large number of small group experimental results available to him for his study [cf. 1961: 12], Homans could find no direct evidence in support of his dyadic theory of social exchange behavior and he had to resort to larger groups: 'We do not, I think, possess the kind of studies of two-person interaction that would either bear out these propositions [of exchange behavior] or fail to do so. But we do have studies of larger numbers of persons that suggest they may apply' [Homans, 1958: 599].

Ironically these lines were written in a number of *The American Journal of Sociology* dedicated to Georg Simmel. Surely Simmel's position, essentially supported by Bales and Borgatta, that there is a qualitative difference between two-person and multi-person interactions would seem to militate against Homans' attempt to generalize across the dyadic–multi-person distinction.

True, Homans became more cautious in *Social Behavior* in this attempt to generalize from two-person interactions to larger-group interactions. He did so *by reducing all multi-person interactions to multiple dyadic relationships or what we have called inclusive restricted exchange.* This reduction is a major characteristic of Homans' interpretation of small group experimental results:

> We have stated our propositions as if they applied to the behavior of a single pair of men, Person and Other, with the Third Man brought in from time to time. But the laboratory research is seldom designed to study the influence upon one another of individuals forming a single pair . . . And the question then comes up whether propositions about a single pair could possibly apply to the research. The only answer is to see if in fact they do. We have the more reason to expect they will, in that the circumstances of many of the experiments turn them, in effect, into studies of a number of separate pairs, each made up of the experimenter plus one of the subjects, and minimize the influence of the subjects on one another [Homans, 1961: 84–85].

As we shall see, Homans reduced these multi-person relations to dyadic relationships, not just between the experimenter and the subjects, but between the subjects themselves. This is clearly a case where one's theory guides one's perception of social phenomena.

6

The Pitfalls of Homans' Social Exchange Theory: Comparison and Justice

I want to continue with an examination of Homans' social exchange theory by focusing on two themes in the theory. First, I want to offer evidence that there is a disjunction between Homans' dyadic propositions of social exchange and the empirical data he offered to validate these propositions. I argue that *Homans forced these data to fit his theory by reducing multi-person interactions to multiple dyadic interactions.* My point here is that Homans' multi-person small group experimental data are based on generalized exchange and, therefore, that they are inappropriate for illustrating his dyadic propositions of restricted exchange. In arguing this case I point out that generalized exchange and restricted exchange respectively emphasize two distinct types of comparison: intrapersonal and interpersonal. These types of comparison are also involved in, indeed critical to, Homans' social exchange theory. Secondly, I argue that the distributive justice principle, based on the concept of fair exchange, is divorced from the first four propositions of Homans' theory, based on the concept of profitable exchange. Furthermore, I argue that the distributive justice principle represents in Homans' theory an intellectual justification of the exploitation of social exchange relationships and that on the whole it is more conservative than the conceptions of distributive justice in social welfare economics and philosophy, which partially see distributive justice as an egalitarian principle or at the very least as a principle for reducing social inequalities.

Intrapersonal and Interpersonal Comparisons in Social Exchange

After presenting the first four propositions of his theory in *Social Behavior*, Homans spends some seventeen pages of tough argument to prepare his readers for the important principle of distributive justice and the less important fifth 'anger' proposition [1961: 75–76]. In these seventeen pages something important, which is liable to be missed because it is not stressed, happened. All the first four propositions [1961: 53–55] had referred an individual's (Person's) responses on the basis of his past experiences to another person's (Other's) stimuli. These responses were determined entirely by considerations of what rewards Person got from the transaction. The rewards that Other got from the interaction were unimportant for Person's responses. The activities of Other in propositions 1 through 4 were neutral stimuli—those of any other individual could have been substituted for them. With the introduction of the distributive justice principle we see a change. The rewards the Other gets becomes important in what Person does.

To prepare the way for this transition from exclusive *intrapersonal* considerations to relative *interpersonal* considerations, two unemphasized propositions are introduced. First, the concept of profit is extended into an interpersonal mechanism. 'We define profit,' Homans [1961: 61] writes, 'as reward less cost, and we argue that no exchange continues unless both parties are making a profit.' In other words, the individual's response in social exchange transactions is not entirely determined (as in the case of the first four propositions) by considerations of his own rewards but also in part by the rewards his partner in exchange gets. We are now told an open secret hidden from the first four propositions: 'The open secret of human exchange is to give the other man behavior that is more valuable to him than it is costly to you and get from him behavior that is more valuable to you than it is costly to him' [1961: 62]. Social exchange is not so selfish after all and it is not really so 'behavioral psychologically conditioned', as we had been led to believe by the first four propositions.

Secondly, Homans performs a brilliant magic. Hitherto [e.g.,

1961: 38–39] Third Man was a phantom absorbed by Other and Person for social analysis. But now [1961: 66] we need him urgently as an individual and lo! he is alive. 'We shall remember that we made him just the same as Person' [1961: 66]. But now he is separate from, if not equal to, Person and Other. Person now has to take into consideration not just his own interests, not just how much Other is getting in relation to him, but also his relationship at the same time to this new potent Third Man [1961: 67–68]. Here for the first time Homans stretches his restricted social exchange theory and we begin to see the hidden contours of generalized exchange in his theory. We now learn, for instance, that 'when each man [in a three-man interaction] is being rewarded by some third party, he will expect the third party to maintain [proportionate rewards] between the two of them in the distribution of rewards' [1961: 75].

This transition from exclusive intrapersonal concern in social exchange to relative interpersonal concern was marked by Homans himself in not so hidden terms:

> At this point, a new effect makes the question of maximization . . . somewhat irrelevant. It should be clear by now that Person and Other have two other kinds of bargain to strike . . . over the monetary rate of exchange . . . and over the total amount of activity each gives the other over a long period of time such as a day. Into both bargains intrudes a problem we have not so far considered. It is the problem whether or not each party considers he is getting not just a profitable exchange but 'fair exchange', and to this problem we now turn [Homans, 1961: 72].

Immediately after the above statement follows the treatment of distributive justice. The two types of exchange mentioned here— profitable exchange and fair exchange—need to be emphasized. They refer to two types of comparison involved in social exchange transactions. In the first case, *profitable exchange*, the individual is comparing his own rewards with his own costs. This is an intra-personal comparison. In the second case, *fair exchange*, he is comparing his rewards, costs, or profits—either jointly or severally— with those of his exchange partner in arriving at his own assessment of his position. It is this fair exchange, involving interpersonal comparisons, that the Distributive Justice Principle was intended to bring out. The intriguing thing in *Social Behavior* is that Homans dropped the concept of 'profitable exchange' as soon as 'fair exchange' was introduced. Never again was any attempt made to redeem it. If we like we can say that *Social Behavior: Its Elementary Forms* is two books. The first book ends at page 61 and deals with *profitable exchange*. The second book begins at page 72, with an introduction on pages 61 to 72, and deals with *fair exchange*. No attempt was ever made to find a common ground between these two parts of Homans' *Social Behavior*.

This is not a trivial distinction. Whether comparisons are intrapersonal or interpersonal may depend on the size of the group in which social exchange transactions take place and, therefore, on the type of exchange involved. In two-person groups, in which restricted exchange is practised, comparisons tend to be interpersonal. The reason is that comparisons can be direct and one can immediately assess the elements of 'fair exchange' of the partners: costs, rewards, and profits. In multi-person groups, on the other hand, comparisons tend to be intra-personal: an individual engaged in multi-person or generalized exchange tends to compare his rewards with his costs for the important reason that comparisons with others of their rewards, costs, or profits become unmanageable in large groups. If individualism has any meaning in social exchange it is in the fact that the individual arrives at conclusions on the basis of such intrapersonal comparisons. This argument is in line with our contention that restricted exchange is more characterized by emotions than generalized exchange.

Now, Homans' exchange propositions refer to dyadic relation-ships and hence comparisons tend to be interpersonal. In the distributive justice principle Homans enunciates such rules of interpersonal comparison: the exchange partners evaluate their rewards and profits in relation to the relative efforts they command in the social exchange situation:

> A man in an exchange relation with another will expect that the rewards of each man be proportional to his costs—the greater the rewards, the greater the costs—and that the net rewards, or profits, of each man be proportional to his investments—the greater the investments, the greater the profit (Homans, 1961: 75].

Two statements seem to summarize this principle of distributive justice: 'the greater the rewards, the greater the costs'; and 'the greater the investments, the greater the profit'. The first of these is clearly an interpersonal rule, since in individual intrapersonal calculations of gain, one expects that rewards will be increased while costs are decreased, that is, the greater the rewards, the less the costs. That intrapersonal concern was conveyed in Homans' definition of 'profit as reward less costs'. Homans [1961: 72] says in effect that the operation of 'fair exchange' or distributive justice 'makes the question of maximization [i.e. reward less cost] . . . somewhat irrelevant' in a social situation in which intrapersonal comparisons of costs with rewards are suspended in the interest of 'fair exchange' and distributive justice. In this latter situation comparisons are interpersonal.

What Homans failed to do is to reconcile these two situations in which 'profitable exchange' and 'fair exchange' operate. A man may be engaged in 'profitable exchange'—in which his rewards are in excess of his costs—but he considers it 'unfair exchange' because compared to his exchange partner he is not faring very well and he may accordingly withdraw. He may also withdraw because he judges his interactions as resulting in 'unprofitable exchange' even though it is a 'fair exchange'. The optimum point of interaction, Homans' theory implies, is that point where 'profitable exchange' and 'fair exchange' meet.[1] Rather than suspend considerations of profitable exchange for considerations of fair exchange, the line of development of Homans' exchange theory required that the two should be considered together. This is of course what Homans has not done.

I wish to suggest an alternative way of looking at the matter. Profitable exchange, involving intrapersonal comparisons of rewards and costs, and fair exchange, in which one compares one's rewards, costs, or profits with those of one's exchange partner, are emphasized in separate contexts. *In two-person groups, whose members are engaged in restricted exchanges, interpersonal comparisons and fair exchange prevail. In multi-person groups, with an emphasis on generalized exchange, intrapersonal comparisons and profitable exchange prevail.* This is where I believe there has been a mix-up in Homans' theory. Because his exchange propositions, especially the dis-

---

[1] The interaction of 'fair exchange' with 'profitable exchange' may well be relevant in the determination of what Thibaut and Kelley call 'the *comparison level for alternatives* (or CL$_{alt}$), the standard the member uses in deciding whether to remain in or leave the relationship' [1959: 21].

tributive justice principle, are dyadic and because he apparently sees no qualitative differences between the operation of dyads and larger groups, he assumes that interpersonal comparisons and fair exchange are emphasized in multi-person groups in the way that his theory would predict. Hence he argues that in such groups, the rules of fair exchange dictate that the greater the rewards the greater the costs. While I believe that that rule is valid for dyads, in multi-person groups the individual is more concerned with his profit and hence he strives to attain a position in which the greater his rewards the less his costs.

Evidence from Small Group Experimental Results

Homans [cf. 1961: 83] relied heavily on small group experimental results from various researchers, particularly from the 'Festinger Group' (p. 85), to support his social exchange propositions. I believe that the first four 'conditioned behavioral psychological' propositions have nothing to do with Homans' interpretations of these results. Invariably they involve comparison and such other symbolic processes as conformity, influence, competition, and cooperation—all out of the reach of behavioral psychology. Within the domain of human behavior, the dominant assumption made by Homans is that interpersonal comparisons and the rules of fair exchange will always prevail.

The best way of gaining an insight into Homans' thought in this regard, however, is by searching into the reasoning underlying the two model interaction matrices [1961: 191–193] which he constructed to illustrate the principles of group behavior. This is so because, unlike the actual small group experiments, the two models were deliberately designed by Homans to illustrate not only how elementary social behavior works but also how it does *not* work. The first of these, presented here as Table 6.1, was a strawman six-person matrix intended to show the *wrong* way of conceiving of group interaction [1961: 191]. It was constructed on the principle of generalized exchange multi-person interaction in which some individuals were receiving rewarding activities from those they do not directly reward.

TABLE 6.1

(Reproduced from Homans' *Social Behavior*, p. 191)

A Model Interaction Matrix

| | | \multicolumn{6}{c}{Interactions received} | *Total given* |
		O	P	Q	R	S	T	
Interactions given	O		5	4	3	2	1	15
	P	5		4	3	2	1	15
	Q	5	4		3	2	1	15
	R	5	4	3		2	1	15
	S	5	4	3	2		1	15
	T	5	4	3	2	1		15
Total received		25	21	17	13	9	5	

Homans condemns this strawman matrix because, he argues in effect, it is unfair exchange to have one member emit certain activities to another without *directly* receiving an equivalent amount from that member:

> Plausible as it may appear at first glance, our matrix [Table 6.1] does not correspond to any real state of affairs, and that for a very obvious reason. It shows, for instance, member T addressing interaction to member O five times, but O addressing interaction to T only once. But is this a realistic result? . . . In real life we should expect, as the group moved toward practical equilibrium, either that O would increase the returns he made to T . . . or that T would decrease the number of attempts he made on O . . . In either case the two members would become nearly equal in the interactions each addressed to each other . . . the interactions each gives to the other will tend toward something like equality . . .
>
> If what must happen in any one pair happens also in other pairs in the group, we should expect that members who receive much will also give much [Homans, 1961: 191–192].

The flaw in this argument is that Homans is considering interactions in the group as if they were in isolated dyadic relationships. Remember that Homans' [e.g., 1961: 2] definition of social exchange insists that it is only between two persons—and so he has, in his model interaction matrices, ruled out the possibility of generalized exchange multi-person interactions. In fact, however, in a six-man group if T rewards O, O does not have to get his reward directly from T but possibly from other actors. At any rate Homans' dyadic social exchange theory bars such a possibility. So let us follow his reasoning further. He insists that his matrix [in Table 6.1] must be corrected. His 'Corrected Interaction Matrix' [p. 193] follows:

TABLE 6.2
(Reproduced from Homans' *Social Behaviour*, p. 193)
Corrected Interaction Matrix

		O	P	Q	R	S	T	Total given
				Interactions received				
Interactions given	O		30	24	18	12	6	90
	P	25		20	15	10	5	75
	Q	20	16		12	8	4	60
	R	15	12	9		6	3	45
	S	10	8	6	4		2	30
	T	5	4	3	2	1		15
Total received		75	70	62	51	37	20	

Homans reasons that this corrected matrix is more realistic because it represents 'fair exchange' and the members deal with each other directly:

> Let us, therefore, make an assumption that will bring the matrix closer to real life. Let us assume that the more interactions a member receives, the more he also gives, and correct the matrix accordingly . . .
> In the new and corrected matrix [Table 6.2] . . . the two members of many pairs are much more nearly equal in the number of interactions each gives to the other than they were in the original matrix [Table 6.1]. For instance, T gives five interactions to O, but he gets 6 back instead of only one . . . On these counts . . . the new matrix is more realistic than the old one [Homans, 1961: 192–193].

I believe Homans is wrong in offering these corrections. And he is wrong because, true to his social exchange theory, he is reducing multi-person interactions to multiple dyadic relationships under the assumption that all social exchange processes must be direct, not indirect. I think I can show that Homans' condemned matrix, based on the principle of generalized exchange, is correct while his favorite toy 'corrected' matrix, based on restricted exchange, is wrong. I shall do so by comparing these two matrices with all other multi-person interaction matrices in *Social Behavior*. Homans [1961: 193–200] did compare these two toy matrices with other multi-person matrices. But we shall use a more objective criterion provided, but not used, by Homans himself: the rate of exchange. Homans [1961: 55] defines it so: 'The number of units of activity Person emits within any limited period of time in return for a specific number of units emitted by Other we shall call the *rate of exchange.*'

This is a ratio of 'costs' to 'rewards'. Although it is stated in dyadic terms—as all Homans' social exchange terms—we shall treat it here as the ratio of 'total costs' to 'total rewards' for each actor. Since the important point is that of which matrix is more realistic we should expect this ratio to be similar for the correct matrix and the other actual small group matrices. If Homans' position—the greater the rewards, the greater the costs—proves to be the correct one then we expect that his 'corrected matrix' and the actual small group results to show that this ratio is equal for all members of the group—or at least that the rates of exchange will run the same course in all of them. On the other hand, our position is that Homans' condemned matrix is the right one and we accordingly expect—based on the multi-person interaction assumption of the greater the reward, the less the costs—that the ratio, that is, the rates of exchange, in the condemned matrix will run the same course as the actual small group results. For the purposes of this matrix only total 'activities' received and given by each individual actor are important. I have accordingly reproduced these for the two Homans' toy matrices and for the only other comparable multi-person interaction matrices in *Social Behavior*. They are all six-person groups. One of them is not quite a real life small group. It is a matrix that Homans [1961: 228] modelled on the study of choices and rejections in women dormitories in a women's college by Lemann and Solomon [1952]. The only other multi-person toy interaction matrix in *Social Behavior* [p. 330] is a pure product of Homans' assumptions

and is very much like his 'corrected matrix'. Since it does not have
anything different to offer more than the other 'toy' matrices
constructed by Homans, I have left it out.

Here then are the matrices of interaction with 'totals given'
and 'totals received' and the rates of exchange expressed in per-
centages for each actor by rank.

TABLE 6.3[1]

(From *Social Behavior* Table 12, p. 191—Condemned by Homans)

	Units of Activities		
Actors by Rank	Total Given 'Costs'	Total Received 'Rewards'	Rate of Exchange (%)
1	15	25	60
2	15	21	71
3	15	17	88
4	15	13	115
5	15	9	164
6	15	5	300

[1] This table and the following four were first presented in Ekeh [1968].

TABLE 6.4

(From *Social Behavior* Table 13, p. 193—Preferred by Homans)

	Units of Activities		
Actors by Rank	Total Given 'Costs'	Total Received 'Rewards'	Rate of Exchange (%)
1	90	75	120
2	75	70	107
3	60	62	97
4	45	51	89
5	30	37	81
6	15	20	75

TABLE 6.5

(Actual Small Group Results: From *Social Behavior*
Table 14, p. 194)

Units of Activities
Total Given

Actors by Rank	(a) *Total Individuals* 'Costs'	(b) *Grand Total*	*Total Received* 'Rewards'	*Rate of Exchange* (%) (a)	(b)
1	3506	9167	5203	68	176
2	2778	3989	2313	120	173
3	2285	3027	1944	118	156
4	1676	2352	1306	128	180
5	1141	1584	872	135	182
6	819	1192	565	145	326

TABLE 6.6

(Actual Small Group Results: From *Social Behavior*
Table 15, p. 198)

Units of Activities

Actors by Rank	*Total Given* 'Costs'	*Total Received* 'Rewards'	*Rate of Exchange* (%)
1	.47	.81	58
2	.46	.61	76
3	.47	.43	110
4	.38	.30	127
5	.34	.21	162
6	.29	.07	415

TABLE 6.7

(Actual Small Group Results: From *Social Behavior*
Table 18, p. 228)

Units of Activities

Actors by Rank	Total Given 'Costs'	Total Received 'Rewards'	Rate of Exchange (%)
1	15	18	83
2	15	17	88
3	15	16	94
4	15	16	94
5	15	13	115
6	15	10	150

The evidence may not be strong enough to be totally impressive, but the trend is clear. Homans' favorite 'corrected' interaction matrix [Table 4] is unlike the actual small group experimental results while his condemned toy matrix [Table 3] is like them. Two factors are responsible for this outcome. First, he has treated interactions in six-man groups as if they were a cluster of dyadic relationships, thus limiting interactions to restricted exchange interpretations. In actual fact these are generalized exchange multi-person interactions in which one does not have to give to the person one receives from. Secondly, Homans has based his reasoning on 'fair exchange' and he has disregarded the operation of 'profitable exchange': hence he assumes comparisons in groups to be interpersonal, but not intrapersonal. The truth for multi-person interactions is that intrapersonal comparisons tend to be more salient. To repeat a significant point here: the following 'fair exchange' statement which dominates *Social Behavior* may be true of dyadic interactions but not of multi-person groups: *the greater the rewards the greater the costs*. For multi-person groups the correct statement is: *the greater the rewards the less the costs*. The former is derived from an emphasis on interpersonal comparisons, the latter from an emphasis on intrapersonal comparisons.

Homans' Conception of Distributive Justice

By far the most popular part of Homans' exchange theory,

perhaps also the area of the theory most appealing to sociologists interested in status differentiations, is the principle of distributive justice. In general, sociologists have not questioned what Homans says about distributive justice on the assumption, it seems, that it is right. As I have previously emphasized, the first four propositions of Homans' exchange theory hang together, refer to nonsymbolic behavior and have little to offer in the understanding of interpersonal relations, especially in the matter of status differentiations. It is the distributive justice principle that offers such understanding. It does so largely because it is built on such economic concepts as 'profit', 'investments', 'rewards', and 'costs', whereas the first four propositions are all predicated on the single psychological concept of 'rewards'. The general characteristic of Homans' statement of distributive justice is that it translates the principles of behavior in the general society into interpersonal relationships. For instance, social welfare economics sees 'economics of distributive justice as embracing the whole economic dimension of social justice, the entire question of the proper distribution of goods and services within society' [Rescher, 1966: 5; cf. Ryan, 1916). What Homans has done in effect is to substitute rewarding and profitable *activities* for 'goods and services' and *interaction* for 'society'.

Homans' items for distribution are 'rewards' and 'profits', that is, activities that are rewarding and profitable. To repeat the best known statement of his distributive justice:

> A man in an exchange relation with another will expect that the rewards of each man be proportional to his costs—the greater the rewards, the greater the costs—and that the net rewards, or profits, of each man be proportional to his investments—the greater the investments, the greater the profit [Homans, 1961: 75].

So stated, the principle is incomplete and Homans elaborates it further in a whole chapter of *Social Behavior*. According to him, rewards in a social interaction are proportioned according to the following three rules of justice: 'The first rule of distributive justice . . . might be put as follows: the value of what a member receives by way of reward from the members of the group in one field of activity should be proportional to the value [i.e., reward] to them of the activities he contributes in another field' [Homans,

1961: 234]. In other words, rewards should be apportioned according to the amount of contribution to the group by each of the members. 'The second rule of justice is this: the value [i.e., reward] of what a member of a group receives from other members should be proportional to his investments' [Homans, 1961: 237]. [The meaning of 'investment' is conveyed as follows: 'Because some of a man's background characteristics increase in value with the time and ability he "put in" in various groups and jobs, we speak of them for the purposes of distributive justice as *investments*' [p. 236].] The 'third rule of justice [is] . . . what a member of a group gets in the way of reward should be directly proportional to what he gives up, his costs, provided that the costs are of a kind that others, his inferiors, are in no position to incur—costs of the kind we call congruent. For there are costs and costs: there are the costs that imply superiority, such as the cost of facing danger, and there are costs that imply nothing of the sort, such as the cost of doing work that is dull and dirty but safe' [Homans, 1961: 241]. The 'costs' here then are really different from the meaning of costs defined from the point of view of the actor alone. We shall call them *leadership costs*. So rewards, in the theory, are distributed according to three different criteria: contributions or efforts, investments, and leadership costs. Profits, or reward less costs, are distributed according to a single criterion: 'Profits should be proportional to investments' [1961: 243].

Actually, then, Homans' distributive justice principle consists of four rules for the distribution of rewards and profits. He says little about which of these rules are expected to operate in particular situations. Perhaps the most visible weakness here is the fact that the items to be distributed are two, not one, and that one is defined in terms of the other. Profits are defined as rewards less costs [1961: 61, 241], and costs are one of the criteria in the distribution of rewards. Homans does not help in verbal clarity when he says that 'the problem of distributive justice [refers to the] justice in the distribution of rewards and costs between persons' [1961: 74]. If there are rules for the distribution of 'costs' they are not presented in Homans' exchange theory, unless as they are included in the distribution of profits.

So stated, Homans' distributive justice principle would appear to be an updated version of Spencer's conception of justice in his sociology:

Justice then, as here to be understood, means preservation of the normal connexions between acts and results—the obtainment by each of as much benefit as his efforts are equivalent to—no more no less. Living and working within the restraints imposed by one another's presence, justice requires that individuals shall severally take the consequences of their conduct, neither increased nor decreased. The superior shall have the good of his superiority; and the inferior the evil of his inferiority. A veto is therefore put on all public action which abstracts from some men part of the advantages they have earned, and awards to other men advantages they have not earned [Spencer, 1893: 610].

But any similarities between Homans' analysis of distributive justice and Spencer's conception of justice are more apparent than real. Actually, the three criteria for the distribution of rewards and profits in Homans' theory, namely, efforts, investments (i.e., status characteristics), and leadership costs, fall under two moralities of distribution. When seen in a historical perspective, there is indeed a lively controversy about them. The nineteenth century emergence of the bourgeoisie in Europe—for whose ideals Spencer was a foremost spokesman in his sociology—was marked by the struggle to substitute a *bourgeois* criterion of ability and effort for the *aristocratic* traditional criterion of status in the distribution of rewards. Gouldner's modern statement of this matter is as good as any I know of:

The middle-class standard of utility developed in the course of its polemic against the feudal norms and aristocratic claims of the 'old regimes', in which the rights of men were held to be derived from and limited by their estate, class, birth, or lineage: in short, by what they 'were' rather than by what they *did*. In contrast, the new middle class held in highest esteem those talents, skills, and energies of individuals that contributed to their own individual accomplishments and achievements. The middle-class standard of utility implied that rewards should be proportioned to men's personal work and contribution. The usefulness of men, it was now held, should control the station to which they might rise or the work and authority they might have, rather than that their station should govern and admit them to employment and privileges.

Looked at in terms of how it appeared to those involved, the rising middle class's demand for usefulness was above all an attempt to revise the bases *on* which, and hence the groups *to* which, public rewards and opportunities would be open. 'Utility' took on meaning in a specific context involving a particular set of social relations, where it was used initially to dislodge the aristocracy from pre-eminence and to legitimate the claims and social identity of the rising middle class. In this regard the standard of utility entailed a claim that rewards should be allocated not on the basis of birth or of inherited social identity, but on the basis of talent and energy manifested in individual achievement. This was antitraditionalistic and antiascriptive, proachievement and proindividualistic. It entailed an emphasis on what the individual did, rather than on who he was or on what he was born [Gouldner, 1970: 62–63].

Seen in this light, Homans' distributive justice is not as straightforward as it appears at first sight. Two of his criteria for the distribution of rewards and profits—contributions and leadership costs—emphasize the bourgeois ideal of distributive justice, while his third criterion of 'investments' or 'background' characteristics emphasizes the aristocratic ideal of inequality of opportunities in distributive justice. In a revealing passage Homans indicates the potential contradiction in his theory of distributive justice, but his choice is obvious:

> Because some of a man's background characteristics increase in value with the time and ability he has 'put in' in various groups and jobs, we speak of them for the purposes of distributive justice as *investments*. Not all investments change: to be a Negro or a woman, as compared with being white or a man, are investments that in some groups never change in value yet are always weighed in the scales of distributive justice, and so some of us might say it was absurd to speak of justice here at all; but we must remember that we are talking about justice as seen by the members of a particular group and not about our own sense of justice, which is of course Olympian. No doubt, too, there are societies in which fewer investments increase in value with time and ability than do in our own, many societies in which more investments are ascribed and fewer achieved. Ascribed or achieved, the second rule of justice is this: the value of what a member of a group receives from other members should be proportioned to his investments [Homans, 1961: 236–237].

In other words where members of a society disregard the achievement or ability of certain individuals, as with Homans' 'Negroes' and women in U.S. society, the only valid criterion of distributive justice would appear to be the aristocratic criterion of status characteristics or 'investments'. We may therefore say that the bourgeois equalitarian criteria of 'effort' and 'leadership costs' are used only when that of the aristocratic inequalitarian criterion of 'status' (i.e. background) characteristics or investments are not clearly established or are effectively neutralized by the fact they are the same for all the actors.

The possibility of a conflict between equalitarian and in-equalitarian ideals of the distribution of rewards is not new in sociology. Pareto, the Italian sociologist whom Homans [1964b, as reprinted in Turk and Simpson, 1970: 378] calls his master, was confronted with it and his solution of the problem seems hidden behind Homans' theory of distributive justice. Pareto's solution was to assert, as Stark puts it, 'that underneath the power-distribution in society, and even under-neath the given income distribution, there lurks a more basic ability-distribution which is due to inborn and genetically transmitted features' [Stark, 1958: 52]. Hence current wealth distribution is only an outward manifestation of a greater and more permanent but hidden attribute of ability. Homans' position seems to agree with his master's: Homans seems to see a positive relationship between 'background characteristics' (i.e. a man's status in a group) and what his effort is able to fetch him. A man's status characteristics are an index of his ability. One could of course harass this position by considering the case of Georg Simmel, the man whose greatness Homans [1958] invoked to initiate his premier effort in social exchange theory. Was Georg Simmel's failure to acquire status—thus arresting the value of his background char-acteristics—in German universities an indication of his true abilities?

The characteristics of Homans' principle of distributive justice will become more visible if they are considered in the context of other attempts to formulate the rules of distributive justice. Rescher's [1966: 73] excellent summary of these various attempts is as follows:

> In the course of the long history of discussions on the subject, distributive justice has been held to consist, wholly or primarily, in the treatment of all people:
> (1) as equals (except possibly in the case of certain 'negative' distributions such as punishments).

(2) according to their needs.

(3) according to their ability or merit or achievements.

(4) according to their efforts and sacrifices.

(5) according to their actual productive contribution.

(6) according to the requirements of the common good, or the public interest, or the welfare of mankind, or the greater good of a greater number.

(7) according to a valuation of their socially useful services in terms of their scarcity in the essentially economic terms of supply and demand.

Correspondingly, seven 'canons' of distributive justice result, depending upon which of these factors is taken as the ultimate or primary determinant of individual claims, namely, the canons of equality, need, ability, effort, productivity, public utility, and supply and demand.

When assessed against this 'long history of distributive justice' Homans' emphasis becomes visible: ability, effort, and productivity are the canons for 'fair' distribution of rewards and profits in the group. But the greater significance of Rescher's catalog of the canons of distributive justice for Homans' theory of justice lies in what is missing from it. There is no reference in it to Homans' 'background' or status characteristics. It does not take a great deal of ingenuity to detect that Rescher is dealing with the liberal—not the aristocratic or conservative—literature on the theory of distributive justice. Homans'—indeed sociology's —theory of distributive justice is manifestly different in that it leads to a justification of status inequalities in the distribution of rewards.

It could be argued, of course, that the motivation for a theory of justice is different for the philosopher and the sociologist. The philosopher is typically involved in an exercise intended to establish ethical rules of conduct along which people *ought* to behave. On the other hand the sociologist may be more interested in studying *actual* behavior. In doing so, however, the sociologist may have either one of two motivations underlying his intellectual commitments. He may study a social phenomenon because it is morally undesirable and his study will help him to master its laws of operation with a view to controlling it. Thus the sociologist who studies crime and delinquency or suicide assumes these social maladies to be undesirable in society and, to the extent that his motivations are beyond pure academic pursuits, his studies will lead to their control by way of negation. Similarly, an American social scientist, like Gabriel Almond, who studies the social basis of communism assumes that it is a morally wrong system, in the same way that a Russian sociologist who studies capitalism assumes the Western system of distribution to be morally inappropriate. On the other hand, a sociologist may study a phenomenon which he considers morally appropriate, with a view to consolidating its laws of operation. Seymour Lipset studies democracy with such a view at the back of his mind— one can safely presume, at least. Now, there is hardly any subject where the nature of the moral preference of the social scientist affects the direction of his conclusions more readily than in the conception of the justice of inequalitarian arrangements.

Is the sociologist interested in studying inequality because it is morally undesirable? It is at this point that we come upon the significance of the distinction between collectivistic sociology and individualistic sociology. Both emphasize inequality—but in different directions. The collectivistic sociologist assumes that inequality before the totality of the social structure is justifiable. That is, there is justice in the superiority of society or more concrete groups over individuals who will have to consider their interests as unequal to the demands of the wider society. This may mean that inequalities between individuals, which interfere with the superiority of the total social structure, may become defined as unjustifiable. On the other hand, individualistic sociologists generally see individual attainments as evidence of ability differentials and hence see inequality as justifiable. These differing moral stances necessarily lead to different conclusions about the significance of existing inequalities in society.

Homans insists that he is not advocating his rules of distributive justice; rather they are patterns he interprets members of groups, particularly American groups, to establish in their interactions with others. 'We must remember,' Homans contends, 'that we are talking about justice as seen by members of a particular group and not about our own sense of justice, which is of course Olympian' [1961: 236]. Are Homans' rules of distributive justice, then, the norms of behavior? I think so—at least according to Homans' definitions. These rules are more than the implications of behavior as Homans [1961: 233] seems to indicate.

Sometimes the actors state these rules explicitly [e.g., 1961: 237–242] except that they use words like 'responsibility' and 'autonomy' instead of Homans' 'rewards', 'costs', and 'investments'. If we grant Homans' definition of a norm 'as a statement made by a number of members of a group, not necessarily by all of them, that the members ought to behave in a certain way in certain circumstances' [1961: 46], then these rules represent norms.[1] Homans [1961: 116] does give empirical content to the meaning of norms: 'we shall say that a *norm* is a statement made by some members of a group that a particular kind or quantity of behavior is one they find it valuable for the actual behavior of themselves, and others whom they specify, to conform to'. In terms of methodology then, the difference between the liberal philosophical exposition of justice and Homans' approach to the subject is that Homans says that he is looking at the matter from the point of view of the folk logic of the actors; the philosophers do include the point of view of the actors, but their principal concern is to translate such individual reasoning into ethical standards that transcend individual definitions of normative patterns of behavior. To employ Abraham Kaplan's [1964: 3–11] distinction, one may say then that Homans is interested in the *logic-in-use* of justice while the philosopher evolves a *reconstructed logic* of justice. They do draw their conclusions from the same raw data, even though they approach the subject at different levels. That the philosopher's approach and Homans' approach cannot be thoroughly separated, that is, that Homans does deal with the *reconstructed logic* of justice and the philosopher with the *logic-in-use* of justice, can be seen in Homans' [1961: 245–246] use and interpretation of Aristotle's and Jouvenel's statements on the matter. Indeed, insofar as Homans' views on justice have any methodological significance it seems to me that his principles of justice are best treated, as I believe they are being treated by many, as expected rules of behavior in social exchange processes against which actual behaviors in groups are to be measured.

This point about the normative character of Homans' rules of

---

[1] Cf. Sabine [1956: 3]: ' "justice" is characteristically used in a context that is institutionalized, impersonalized or depersonalized; a context which demands that one should hold in abeyance his private inclinations and weigh the claims that other persons make on him by virtue of his position in a situation and their positions relative to him'.

distributive justice has an important bearing on his exchange theory as a whole. One of the delimitations of the subject-matter of his exchange theory is that 'the behavior [it studies] must be actual behavior and not a norm of behavior' [1961: 3]. These rules of distributive justice are clearly outside the scope of exchange theory insofar as exchange is barred from studying normative behavior. The rules of distributive justice fall outside exchange theory as conceived by Homans in a second way. The rules apply to two types of interaction: dyadic interpersonal face-to-face contacts and nonface-to-face, third party mediated, inter-actions.[1] These two types of interactions are embodied in two corollaries of distributive justice:

> [1] the general rule of distributive justice ... means that unless the investments of the two men are greatly different, each man will further expect the following condition to hold good: the more valuable to the other (and costly to himself) an activity he gives the other, the more valuable to him (and costly to the other) an activity the other gives him. [2] Finally, when each man is being rewarded by some third party, he will expect the third party to maintain this relationship between the two of them in the dis-tribution of rewards [Homans, 1961: 75].

But Homans had ruled out such third party mediated interactions as outside the scope of his social exchange theory: 'when a person acts in a certain way toward another person, he must at least be rewarded or punished by *that* person and not just by some third party, whether an individual or organization' [1961: 2]. Homans [1961: 245] did notice this discrepancy in his examples of dis-tributive justice but he evaded the issue by arguing that the two parties whose interactions were mediated by an organization 'did behave a little as if they were exchanging with each other'.

My reason for pointing out these two discrepancies is not to show that Homans' distributive justice is outside the scope of exchange theory but rather to advance my view that Homans has

---

[1] Cf. Rescher [1966: 5–6]: 'Aristotle divides justice construed as [fair justice] ... into two kinds: (1) *Distributive justice*, which "is exercised in the distribution of [public assets such as] honor, wealth, and the other divisible assets of the com-munity"; and (2) *corrective justice*, which "supplies a corrective principle in private transactions". .... Aristotle's *distributive justice* requires the state to act equitably in its distribution of goods (and presumably of evils) among its members. Aristotle's *corrective justice* requires the individual to act equitably in actions or transactions affecting the interests of his fellow.'

overly restricted the scope of his theory—so much so that his most important conception of distributive justice cannot be contained within it. A theory is different from an ideology in that in the face of firm evidence the assumptions of a theory could be changed to accommodate new insights. Since distributive justice is critical to the survival of Homans' exchange theory, it appears necessary that these two discrepancies be reconciled with the theory. It seems to me that Homans' [1961: 2–7] delimitations of the scope of his theory are too restrictive and should be liberalized to accommodate distributive justice without strain. In this regard the stricture that the theory is not intended to explain normative behavior or indirect relations (mediated by third parties) should be questioned seriously. Homans formulated these confining conditions with an immediate eye to the principles of animal behavioral psychology. But human or symbolic behavior, as revealed in the rules of distributive justice for instance, is both normative and mediational (in terms of third party interventions). Even elementary behavior, the subject-matter of Homans' theory, can include within itself normative behavior and mediated behavior and still be elementary. It seems to me that the first four behavioral psychological propositions of the theory [1961: 53–55] are not needed to explain such human interactions and are, in any case, in fundamental conflict with the human principle of distributive justice.

It is of interest, in this connection, to consider how Homans has handled the problem of order in his theory. In discussing this matter Turk and Simpson [1971: 7] noted that:

> Social behavior described as exchange might seem to resemble a Hobbesian jungle in which every man strives for himself alone. Much of Homans' analysis, however, especially his analysis of distributive justice, shows how groups develop and enforce norms that regulate and thereby civilize the market of exchange. Thus the concept of distributive justice is a major element in Homans' solution to the problem of order and constitutes a nonnegotiable element in exchange.

But Turk and Simpson are being soft in their view of Homans' theory with respect to the problem of social order. Where do the 'norms that regulate and thereby civilize the market of exchange' come from? The truth of the matter is that Homans' first four behavioral psychological propositions created the 'Hobbesian jungle' of disorder which the distributive justice principle is then called upon to clear in place of established order. The former deny the existence of norms but the distributive justice principle is predicated on the acceptance of a norm of inequality by actors in the social system. In other words, Homans' problem of order is an artificial one created by his employment of behavioral psychology and he had to come back to good old-fashioned sociology for a solution.

Contributive, Distributive, and Retributive Justice

Homans' conception of justice is really much broader than what is usually regarded as distributive justice. Homans' conception includes at once distributive justice, retributive justice, and what I can only call contributive justice. Distributive and contributive justice are implicit in

> the following rule of distributive justice that people practically seem to respond to: if one man is 'better' than another in his investments, he should also be 'better' than the other in the value of the contribution he makes and in the reward he gets for it; his cost in making it should be higher too, so long as it is the sort that a superior contribution necessarily incurs [Homans, 1961: 245].

Here the reference is to the contribution that justice requires that a man with great investments (i.e., status in Homans' theory) should make and to the rewards he should get for it. When Marx declared 'from each according to his ability, to each according to his need', he was combining the principles of justice of contribution to the economy and of the justice of the distribution of the products of the economy. What Homans has in mind of course only meets Marx half-way: from each according to his ability and experience and to each according to his contribution. Homans and Marx could never share the same platform.[1]

---

[1] Cf. Tsanoff [1956: 15]: 'We recognize the first clause or premise in the various proposed formulas of just distribution: "From everyone according to his abilities", according to what his capacities have produced. Now what is the right completion of this statement of justice: "to everyone equally", or "to everyone according to his needs", or "to everyone according to his services"? The comparison and the eventual choice among these alternative standards mark the contending programs of social order.'

More fundamental to Homans' exchange theory is the distinction between distributive justice and retributive justice. Homans [1961: 90] once declared, 'Revenge is a form of justice' by which he means distributive justice. His fifth *frustration-aggression* proposition of social exchange runs in this vein of revenge and it is predicated on the principle of distributive justice [Homans, 1961: 75; 1967a]. For reasons I shall make clear shortly, it seems important for Homans' exchange theory to differentiate retributive justice from distributive justice. As Piaget [1932: 316] once emphasized, 'Let us distinguish retributive justice from distributive justice: for the two go together only when reduced to their fundamental elements'. Retributive justice means punishment duly defined in relation to the misdeeds of an individual. On the other hand, distributive justice refers to rules for the proportionate sharing of rewards (or goods and services) among individuals in a social situation. Comparison is built into the operation of distributive justice; in retributive justice punishments may be administered to an individual with or without comparison with others.[1] 'Revenge' and Homans' fifth 'anger' proposition would, according to this distinction, fall into retributive justice.

Retributive justice, however, is not all of a piece. Revenge may serve as an impulsive response to frustration on the spur of the moment. It is such revenge that Homans apparently holds responsible for the disruption of social exchange processes: 'While the exchange of rewards tends toward stability and continued interaction, the exchange of punishment tends toward instability and eventual failure in escape and avoidance' [1961: 57]. However, some forms of revenge, or exchange of punishments, may provide a basis for stability which Homans [cf. 1961: 61] seems to regard as essential for continued interaction between exchange partners. Invariably such revenge patterns involve the actor as a representative of a group, not as an individual tending exclusively to his self-interests. He avenges wrongs against himself or members of his group on behalf of his group. He accepts punishments brought against him for acts performed by members of his group as legitimate. This pattern of revenge may help to build up a basis for social solidarity because such acts restrain

---

[1] For the distinction between distributive justice and retributive justice see Piaget [1932], Tsanoff [1955], and Raphael [1951–52: 171–173].

and proportion the exchange of punishment [cf. Gluckman, 1957].

Perhaps the most fascinating example of such negative exchange is that intriguing phenomenon, 'Samsonic suicide' or 'suicide of revenge'. As Jeffreys, who coined the term, discusses it:

> Durkheim's analysis of the suicides in European cultures showed that there were three types—the Egoistic, the Altruistic and the Anomic. These types are conditioned by the general pattern of European society. African societies are patterned differently and a different type of suicide becomes manifest, namely suicides of revenge or as I have called them, Samsonic suicides, because Samson's suicide was one of revenge where by killing himself, he killed his enemies also. However, African suicides of revenge do not necessarily involve the destruction of one's enemies with the destruction of oneself. Many African suicides occur because (a) the suicide believes his ghost will torment his enemies; or (b) because he knows that his society will inflict penalties upon his enemies [Jeffreys, 1952: 118].

The emphasis in this type of revenge is thus on the ties between the individual and his group and the bond of emotional relationships and mutual beliefs between him and the man who has wronged him [cf. Bohannan, 1960: 11–12]. The supporting evidence cited by Jeffreys [1952: 11–12] underlines the power of such Samsonic suicides to restrain the excessive use of power:

> Cases of aggression turned against the self are apt not to be simple, since a certain amount of more or less direct aggression against others is likely to be involved. The hysteric with an ambivalent attitude of love and hate toward members of his family may have symptoms which injure them as well as himself. In American society suicide may harm others as well as the self. Among the Tikopia suicide is, according to Firth [1936: 177], the son's method of revenge, a threat which constantly serves to prevent tyrannical fathers from becoming too unjust [Dollard *et al.*, 1939: 47–48].

In the same way, we may consider Piaget's [1932: 200, 228–232] differentiation of retributive justice into punishment by reciprocity and expiatory punishment in terms of the degree of interpersonal ties involved. In expiatory punishment the dose of punishment is unrelated in kind to the crime committed by the offender. Thus a child may be *spanked* for making a noise with his toys. In punishment by reciprocity, the dose of punishment is related in kind to the type of crime committed by the offender.

Thus, the toys may be *taken* and *hidden* away from the child if he makes a noise with them. Piaget [1932: 228] sees expiatory punishment as closely connected with the morality of adult constraint while punishment by reciprocity 'corresponds with cooperation and an autonomous ethic'. Their consequences for social conformity are also different: While expiatory punishment is coercive and disruptive of social interaction, punishment by reciprocity needs no overt coercion, induces self-discipline, and promotes self-regulating solidarity [Piaget, 1932: 205–206].[1] It will be seen that the latter form of punishment emphasizes bonds that transcend dyadic relations, while expiatory punishment may more easily be limited to the offender and offended. Thus, punishment by reciprocity, but not expiatory punishment, may provide a basis needed for continued social exchange interaction.

The point of these examples, of 'Samsonic suicide' and of Piagetian conception of punishment, is to emphasize our view that exclusive restricted exchange, limited to two individuals, may not accommodate punishment insofar as the stability of social relations is considered as a prerequisite of social exchange interaction. It is punishment that directly or indirectly involves more than two individuals—that transcends the here-and-now—that may be accommodated in social exchange theory, unless of course we become interested in the processes leading to the termination of social exchange. In this latter case, disruptive forms of punishment may be useful conceptual tools in social exchange theory.[2]

---

[1] Cf. 'Punishment by reciprocity is characterized by the notion, not that one must compensate for the offense by a proportionate suffering, but that one must make the offender realize by means appropriate to the fault itself, in what way he has broken the bond of solidarity' [Piaget, 1932: 231].

[2] In this connection Lamont's [1941] discussion of the relationship between distributive justice and retributive justice (for which he used the term corrective justice) may be of some importance for Homans' exchange theory: 'Distributive Justice is the creation of a system of rights (and consequently of duties and obligations) according to the principle of "equality of consideration" for all; and "rights" are protected fields for activity within which individuals or groups may pursue their interests. Corrective [i.e., Retributive] Justice comes into operation when the scheme created by distributive justice has been infringed; and it may take the form either of Reparation or of Punishment. The particular aim of reparation is to restore the enjoyment of the infringed right (or, if this is impossible, compensation) to the injured party; and the particular aim of punishment is to prevent rights from being infringed; hence the ultimate aim of both reparation and punishment is the maintenance of the system of rights. Thus, *Distributive Justice* is the

Justice and Equality and the Premises of Inequality in Sociology

George Sabine, in a rather well-known discussion of justice, declared that equality has generally been regarded as the salient characteristic of justice [1956: 3]. Equality has been central to all discussions of justice, as Homans' [1961: 245] only references to other authorities on the subject of justice should indicate to readers of *Social Behavior*.[1] But equality is a protean concept with several meanings. My point here is to argue that modern individualistic sociology has imparted to sociologists a specialized meaning and ideology of equality and that Homans' conception of distributive justice is biased in favor of this sociological meaning of equality. Since one's conception of justice is as good as the meaning of equality one is using, I am suggesting that the sociological conception of justice has taken up a specialized connotation as well.

An argument that says that all men are *equal* because they are born human, or because they are all Americans, is irrelevant in sociology. Sociologists are more likely to see justice in the claim that men are unequal because they have different capacities. Sociologists are by their trade more likely to detect inequalities than equality. What distinguishes the sociological conception of justice is not the existence of the notion of justice but the content of that notion or how it works in actual usage. As McCloskey [1966: 58-59) has expressed it:

---

creation of a system of rights according to the principle of "equality of consideration", and *Corrective Justice* is the effort to *maintain* this system' [Lamont, 1941: 3]. Let the reader note that this statement of distributive justice is more general and more inclusive than Homans'. Also noteworthy is the fact that the relationship between distributive justice and retributive justice is more clearly defined by Lamont. Homans' fifth 'anger' or 'frustration-aggression' proposition has a consummatory character while Lamont sees retributive justice as one instrument for realizing distributive justice.

[1] Homans' [1961: 245] only references are to Aristotle and B. de Jouvenel. Unhappily other sociologists, including Blau [1964, 1968], who have written on the subject have not done more and the conception of justice in sociology remains isolated from the rich sources on the subject of justice, distributive and retributive, in philosophy, welfare economics, and psychology. Those interested in exploring this field further may wish to consult the following sociologically-relevant discussions of justice: Piaget [1932], Ryan [1916], Rescher [1966], McCloskey [1966], Lamont [1941], Berlin [1955-56] and Runciman [1966].

S.E.T.-6*

There has been wide agreement that justice (in our dealings with other men) consists in treating equals equally and unequals unequally in the distribution of goods and evils . . . It is in the working-out of the implications of the principle that disagreement occurs. The egalitarian, arguing from an egalitarian theory of justice from the principle that 'equals should be treated equally', usually feels obliged, not surprisingly, to make a factual or quasifactual claim that all men are in fact equal. The anti-egalitarian stresses the differences between men.

Sociology is a science that studies differences, that specializes in the investigation of roles and status arranged in social hierarchies. If such hierarchies are not visible the sociologist tries to discover them; if they are absent he invents them. The basic assumption of individualistic sociology especially is that inequalities are essential to the social structure. The major premise of justice in sociology is that *unequals should be treated unequally* and sociologists only secondarily accept that equals should be treated equally. When McCloskey's formula is translated into sociology it reads as follows: unequals in any system of status hierarchies should be treated unequally and then equals within each of these hierarchies should be treated equally. This is ultimately the meaning of Homans' [1961: 244] aphorism: 'Justice is a curious mixture of equality within inequality'. The sociological theory of justice is inherently anti-egalitarian.

The matter is one of morality. If sociologists want to discover the basis of equality in any group, it is ready at hand: all the members are human; or all are men; or all are Americans; or all speak the English language, etc. They could then argue, if they wished, that since they are equal in all these attributes they ought to be equal in all other respects. But sociologists consider such attributes as irrelevant for their profession. They look for roles and status hierarchies. Ultimately, then, it is the profession that has handed to the sociologist a morality of inquiry that he considers his profession, a morality of inequalities. If a small group experimenter wanted, he could arrange matters in his experiments in such a way as to discover the conditions for reducing inequalities within the group and for creating egalitarian ideals. But that is not the nature of his profession. He would rather start with equals and discover or create conditions for the rise of status hierarchies.

This anti-egalitarian strain in sociology runs against the liberal conception of justice in relation to equality. The liberal conception of justice would turn Homans' aphorism around: 'Justice is a curious mixture of inequality within equality'. The difference is this: liberal thought treats equality in social relationships among men as the rule and inequality as the exception. Sociology, at least in the hands of Homans, treats inequality as the rule and equality as the exception. 'Equality,' declared Sabine [1956: 3], 'might be described as ethical likeness of kind, requiring like judgement and treatment unless there is a valid reason for making a distinction.' The assumption here is that people should be treated equally unless and until they prove themselves unequal. As Isaiah Berlin [1955–56: 326] has observed, 'Equality is one of the oldest and deepest elements in liberal thought, and is neither more nor less "natural" or "rational" than any other constituent in them. Like all human ends it cannot itself be defended or justified, for it is itself which justifies other act-means towards its realization.' When this liberal view is pursued further it leads to McCloskey's [1966] assumption that equality is an irreducible ideal or good and that equality is dictated by justice. All these strands in liberal thought are opposed by the sociological view, more or less strongly espoused by various types of individualistic sociologists, that status hierarchies are functionally necessary for the maintenance of the social order. Sociologists regard status hierarchies as an irreducible attribute of social groups. Homans' [1961: 236] contention that the sociologist is simply describing what groups regard as just should be viewed with caution. Moral preferences help the sociologist—as any other social scientist—to define the salience of his subject-matter. Inequality has a special moral appeal to the individualistic sociologist because it points up, for one thing, that individuals and individual efforts do matter.

It is at this point that one must distinguish the collectivistic sociologist's conception of the relationship between justice and equality from the individualistic sociologist's. While the individualist—as can be seen in the dominant American theory of stratification [cf. Davis and Moore, 1945; Parsons, 1940, 1953]— is led by his moral preference to postulate that inequalities are beneficial for society on the assumption that high status individuals embody society's morals to a greater extent than lower status individuals, the collectivistic sociologist promotes, or thinks he sees the need for, the equality of all individuals before the superiority of society. His moral premises for postulating such equality between individuals are, however, remarkably different from the liberal philosopher's. The latter sees an inherent benefit in equality as an ultimate end. But the collectivistic sociologist is far less interested in the welfare of the individual. He fears that inequalities may disrupt the normalcy of society in that it will not derive maximum benefit from all individuals in the face of such inequalities. Equality is promoted, is considered just, because it enhances social solidarity.

Such were the reasons given by Durkheim in his condemnation of inequalities as unjust. He bluntly stated that 'all external inequality [meaning approximately what Homans calls 'background characteristics' brought into the exchange situation] compromises organic solidarity' [Durkheim, 1933: 379]. It should not come as any surprise, therefore, that Durkheim's conception of the relevance of justice for social exchange processes are almost the opposite of Homans' and the individualistic sociologist's. Durkheim [1950: 219] makes a clear-cut distinction between 'distributive justice' (which relates the distribution of goods to 'office and rank allocated or shared out by the society among its members') and 'commutative justice' which regulates the relationship between what the individual gives and receives in return for his activities in society. Durkheim [1950: 219] reasons that 'If exchanges are to be equitable, they [these types of justice] have to be justly balanced, and of course the distribution of things, even if it had followed all the rules of equity to begin with, would still remain unjust, if exchanges could be contracted on unjust terms'. Ultimately, Durkheim [1950: 219] asserts, justice dictates that 'there shall be no social inequalities as between one man and another, except those that reflect their own unequal value to society'. It is society then that shall determine what terms of exchange are just, irrespective of prior background characteristics brought into the social exchange situation: 'It is society, we find that is coming to exercise complete dominion over nature, to lay down the law for it and to set this moral equality over physical inequality which in fact is inherent in things' [Durkheim, 1950: 220].

It may be claimed that in talking thus Durkheim is leaning

over into moral philosophy. I would agree. But I would add that all sociologists who discuss justice have at least a hidden moral philosophical premise. Durkheim has made clear his rationale for establishing conditions of equality between individuals. I have sought to expose the rationale for the individualistic sociologist's theory of justice emphasizing the value of inequalities between individuals. As Runciman [1966] has recognized, any social scientific study of justice necessarily implies a philosophical consideration of the relationship between justice and equality.

Durkheim [e.g. 1950: 220] was fully aware that his imagery of the relationship between justice and equality is an ideal that is often breached. But to the extent that such a breach reaches great proportions, he assumes that the result for society will in part be anomic social solidarity. It is nearly in the same sense that Lévi-Strauss [1969: 266] argues that equality between partners in generalized exchange should lead to greater social solidarity and that inequality leads to a breach of the conditions of stable generalized exchange and therefore to its downfall. An alternative way of assessing the value of the collectivistic sociologist's concerns here may be to treat them as referring to an ideological norm of equality that provides individuals with an opportunity to see others on a common basis in spite of existing inequalities. That is the way that T. H. Marshall, for instance, has conceived of citizenship. Citizenship may be seen as an ideological equalizing element in the face of actual social class inequalities [1949: e.g., 77, 91ff].

Perhaps, a short note here concerning the relationship between the moral preferences of sociologists and their scientific engagements is in order. Some may argue that sociologists' conceptions of social justice with respect to social exchange processes should not be subjected to the same treatment as the philosopher's concern with justice. On the contrary, I see the subject of justice as providing the appropriate forum for underlining, not to say exposing, the ethical and moral givens of the academic pursuits of sociologists. Very often in his scientific investigations, the *ought* is hidden behind the *is*. At any rate, when the *is* comes out of data as the *ought* dictates there is no occasion for surprise.

Science and Ideology in Homans' Sociology

Taken by itself, Homans' social exchange theory is weak. It is when we impose, or somehow accept, his theory of justice as part of his social exchange theory that his overall presentation gains strength. Yet his theory of justice shows a bias in the direction of conservative thought. We are led to ask, then: why is Homans' theory of justice so much at variance with the liberal philosophical theory of justice or indeed the collectivistic sociological conception of justice? Is there any way we can shed light on this matter beyond what we have said above?

Perhaps it needs full investigation at some future time. At the moment I wish to suggest that we may obtain a partial answer— from Homans' 'autobiographical' accounts of his academic interests. Surely this style of investigation will be resisted by many sociologists. After all, sociologists are not especially known for writing autobiographies. The whole exercise may seem unusual, if not unfair. But Homans is an extraordinary sociologist: He is bold enough to set forth his views about his motivations for adopting sociology and for pursuing it in his own particular way. Perhaps it is not reckless to meet him half-way and engage in these speculations with him. But then, there would be two further points of resistance. First: we have just completed a detailed examination of what Homans says about social exchange and justice. Much of it is in disagreement with Homans. Is it fair then to accept Homans' autobiographical accounts of his work, including in fact friendly self-revelations and self-analysis, as correct when we rejected his views on many other points? This is a difficult question for me to answer: my assumption will be that in this case it is not unfair to accept Homans' accounts and self-evaluation of his work as legitimate raw data for reaching conclusions, no matter how speculative they may be, in order to shed light on a matter of interest to sociology. Secondly, however, if we probe Homans' unconscious motivation for his work, was it not important to do the same thing in the case of Lévi-Strauss, the collectivistic theorist of social exchange? My plea would be, first, that we are at this point dealing more with the theory of justice, which has far greater relevance for Homans' social exchange theory than Lévi-Strauss'. Besides, anthropologists have been rather more enterprising in probing the motivations of fellow anthropologists than sociologists have been—and such material may be found in Edmund Leach's [1970] intellectual biography of Lévi-Strauss. Some sociologists may still urge that it is naïve to accept Homans' self-revelations and self-analysis at their face value, that a serious approach should address itself to a more complete biographical study of Homans'— perhaps paralleling Gouldner's [1970] dissection of Parsons' background. Needless to say, such an enterprise is beyond the scope of this monograph. And I trust that I will not be doing violence to Chinese wisdom by saying that one honest autobiography is worth a thousand good biographies. If it seems unfair to Homans to exploit his honesty as follows, one gains comfort from the fact that sociology may be benefited by Homans' self-revelations and self-analysis. Greater still will be the benefits to sociology if the reader recognizes that Homans is revealing a background that many prominent sociologists share with him, but about which many of them are reticent in their public pronouncements. Perhaps it is in the very style of Homans' scholarship that we seek the forces that shape sociology by peering through his social background.

I am of course referring to Homans' forty-nine page 'Autobiographical Introduction' to his *Sentiments and Activities*. In his frank way, Homans starts that account by revealing the forces that drew him to sociology. We can gain a great deal of insight into the motive forces that shaped Homans and his conception of justice from his account of his confrontation with Great Depression politics. My experience has been that many sociologists, to their loss, have not bothered to read that long 'Introduction'. Let me therefore cite the relevant passage in full. Homans was writing about his choice of sociology for a profession:

> I took to Pareto because he made clear to me what I was already prepared to believe. I do not know all the reasons why I was ready for him, but I can give one. Someone has said that much modern sociology is an effort to answer the arguments of the revolutionaries. As a Republican Bostonian who had not rejected his comparatively wealthy family, I felt during the thirties that I was under personal attack, above all from the Marxists. I was ready to

believe Pareto because he provided me with a defense. His was an answer to Marx because an amplification of him. Marx had taught that the economic and political theories of the bourgeoisie —and I was clearly a bourgeois—were rationalizations of their interests. Pareto amplified Marx by showing that this was true of most theories of human behavior, Marx' included. In the *Sociologie* and *Les systèmes socialistes*, Pareto was careful to point out that Marx was not *mere* rationalization, and that when he talked about class warfare he was talking about something real. But in showing that some of Marx, like the famous theory of surplus value, was certainly rationalization Pareto provided a kind of answer to him. At least the proletariat had no more intellectual justification in demanding my money or my life—and it looked as if they were demanding both, and my liberties to boot—than I had for defending myself. Emotional justification was something else again. As a beneficiary of inherited capital I was a good emotional target, and I was fond of quoting the lisping Bostonian who said: 'Someday the pwoletariat is going to wise up and take away my pwopetty.' But it was some comfort to realize that the proletariat did not have reason as well as emotion on its side. If we could only meet as honest men—or honest rationalizers—we might divide up the take without fighting. It was the intellectual guff talked by the alleged leaders of the proletariat that put one's back up and got in the way of a settlement. Whatever one did, one was not going to yield to men like that [Homans, 1962: 4].

To those who say that such *ad hominem* factors have no place in the history of the development of sociology, I can only repeat that sociology's theory of justice has come from a man who volunteered into sociology, in part at least, to fight the *unjust* demands of the egalitarians of the Great Depression for his family's wealth. No matter however partial evidence it provides, this passage tells us, or should tell us, a lot about why Homans was interested in the theory of justice in the first place and why his sociological theory of justice is so anti-egalitarian in the second place. My more general point, of course, is that Homans is not different from the mainstream elements of sociology in this regard. In sociology the theory of justice is the theory of inequalities. Even Homans may admit that his theory of distributive justice may well be a case of Paretean rationalization of 'bourgeois' interests.

On the face of it Homans' conception of justice would appear to be a theory of inequalities that has very little to do with his exchange theory. At least he could have formulated a theory of distributive justice outside his theory of social exchange behavior. The reverse, however, would not be true. Homans' distributive justice rules represent an important unit idea of social exchange, namely, the exploitation of social exchange relations to maintain the *status quo*. Unlike Frazer, whose exchange theory we have examined, and unlike Blau, whose exchange theory we shall examine soon, Homans makes use of distributive justice to maintain the social order rather than as a means of attaining new power structures as in these other two utilitarian theorists. Whatever the case, Homans' distributive justice rules represent the first sophisticated intellectual argument and justification for the exploitation of social exchange transactions to maintain the power structure in society.

This then leads us to a wider problem: how much has Homans' well-known and well-earned reputation as an advocate of scientific rigor in theory and research [cf., e.g., Homans, 1968] been influenced or tainted by ideological biases introduced into his investigations by the fortune of a good family background? As the last passage cited above indicates, indeed as the foremost follower of Pareto, Homans is not unaware that men do make use of science to defend their position in life; that their intellectual life work may represent what Werner Stark [1958] has characterized as 'interest-begotten theories' or ideologies. Marx and Pareto may be old-fashioned enough to probe the ideological content of other theorists' work and ignore theirs; Homans is modern and introspective enough to raise serious questions about the ideological content of his own work. I pay attention to the matter here because it could provide the key to unmasking the riddles in Homans' theories.

In his 'Autobiographical Introduction' to *Sentiments and Activities* Homans valiantly wrestled with the problem of *why* he carried out his studies. With respect to his excursus into English history, resulting in his *The English Villagers of the Thirteenth Century*, Homans adumbrates his possible 'unconscious motives' [pp. 11–12] for his work:

I am sure there was another and deeper reason for my interest in medieval England. I was a New Englander and, as a New Englander, preoccupied with my ancestry. I was, moreover, in the language of New England, a Yankee, that is, a descendant of Englishmen who had come to America in colonial times; and we Yankees were being numerically and politically overwhelmed by what we were pleased to call the 'newer races'. Whether we liked it or not, they, 'ethnic groups' themselves, were making *us* into just another ethnic group. They called in question what we English-Americans stood for, what we meant, what indeed we *were*. The answers might be sought in English history, not just its political history to which the United States owed its freedom, but in its underlying social and economic history, especially in the centuries before the Englishmen came to America, for it was obviously not the modern Englishmen who were our ancestors. The study of medieval English countrymen was a search for what the Nazis called *blut und boden*, though I was slow to recognize the similarity. And I still deny the implied prejudice: I was not looking for my superiority, to the Irish, for instance; I was looking for my own identity [Homans, 1962: 11].

Homans' search for scientific generalizations was at least partially guided by what he unconsciously felt called upon to defend, what (the poet would call) his mind's eye told him was important. Science can easily become the handmaid of ideology. As Werner Stark has warned, 'Nowhere are [ideological influences] more dangerous than where they make use of, and abuse, undeniable scientific truths':

A good example is Social Darwinism. The Malthusian-Darwinian doctrine of the survival of the fittest in the natural war of all against all reflects a demonstrably occurrent process in the animal world and is the appropriate explanation of many factual phenomena. And there are also societies in which the law of the jungle reigns supreme, and which can truthfully be described in terms of it. But if those with the strongest elbows in a society, those who have been most successful in the struggle for the trough, proclaim that the elimination or exploitation of the weak by the strong is necessary, natural, or at least desirable, then we are confronted with a distortion of thinking in those who believe this pseudo-science which it is all-important to rectify. For a human society is not under the laws of nature but under its own laws, and it can in freedom decide to what degree it wishes to admit or suspend the principle, operative in the lower creation, of the war of all against all. To expose the selfish roots of Social Darwinism in some of its representatives, to prove that it is a piece of propaganda and self-justification, and not a scientific truth, is a task of the doctrine of ideology which nobody should belittle [Stark, 1958: 50–51].

Just how much Homans has used science to shore up his ancestry and his privileged position in American society is a topic that may profitably be explored by an enterprising sociologist of the future, not blinded by current fads and passions in sociology. At the very least, however, I am suggesting here that there is an ideological side to Homans' theory of distributive justice—in its emphasis on 'background characteristics' as the principal criterion for the distribution of rewards and profits and in its justification of inequality in society. If Homans could react with so much intellectual vigor to the encroachment of other lesser white 'ethnics' into his 'English-American' heritage in the thirties when he wrote *The English Villagers*, how much unconscious motivation is there in Homans' theories of social exchange formulated in the fifties and sixties, at a time when Black and other non-white 'minorities' were being admitted into the mainstream of American society? We may never know, unless of course Homans has the insight to write up another self-analysis.

At least one theme is ever present in Homans' theories of social exchange and distributive justice: *the past completely dominates the present*. In spite of Gouldner's [1970: 395–396] characterization of Homans' exchange theory as 'tough-minded', it remains a theory about the subordination of the present to the past: Social exchange processes depend on what one has actually learned by experience; distributive justice is dominated by 'background characteristics' of individuals—what they bring from the past to the present. Indeed in no other theorist in sociology have I seen so much of the past brought to bear on and to dominate the present —except in Pareto!

Is it any wonder that Homans has never lent his intellectual weight to the study of social change? Again Homans has benefited us with the results of his self-analysis: Homans tells us that his desertion of his clinical work at the Boston Dispensary and the Boston City Hospital during his career as a student

> fell into a pattern. Given the chance, I have always deserted anything that had contemporary practical importance or that might lead to reforms. I have deserted the twentieth century for the thirteenth, social pathology for primitive kinship, industrial

sociology for the study of small groups. It may have been mere escapism; my nerves may have been too weak for the modern world. More likely I was reluctant to change a world that, on the whole, was behaving so well toward me. But I have found a description of the syndrome that is more flattering to me and that may well be true. I have come to think now—I did not see it then —that what never failed to interest me was not sociology as an agency of change or as a means of understanding my immediate environment but sociology as a generalizing science. What were the best possibilities for establishing generalizations? What were the main intellectual issues? What was the subject really about? By what handle should we lay hold on it? A science may naturally turn out to have practical applications, but it certainly does not grow just through its practical applications. The modern world offers plenty of material for generalizations about social behavior, but it is not the only world that does. Thus the briefest look at primitive kinship showed plenty of generalizations lying embedded in the matrix of fact and crying for formulation. So did industrial sociology if one forgot about reforming industry and thought only of the opportunities its captive groups provided for studying social behavior at first hand. If the emphasis was on science, what made a particular subject matter 'important' was simply the chance of exploiting it intellectually [Homans, 1962: 9–10].

For those who are interested in this intellectual 'syndrome' as part of a larger whole and as a topic in the sociological understanding of the ideological use of science to maintain the *status quo* I offer Werner Stark's excellent pronouncement on the matter:

Throughout history, we find philosophies which assert that permanence is real and change a delusion—philosophies whose detail is vastly different, but whose kernel is simple and can be formulated in a very few words such as those just used. There is, near the beginning of the story, Plato with the assertion that rest is the perfection of being and movement only an impoverished form of it; there is, towards the end, Pareto with his 'scientific' 'proof' that social life is the same at all times and places since it is controlled by the unchanging 'residues' while only the surface seems to show development—a development which is not really development at all because it consists only in the replacement of one kind of idle talk (or 'derivation') by another. Now both Plato and Pareto were aristocrats who lived in an age which was very unkind to aristocracy. Both saw an upsurge of egalitarianism; both disliked what they saw and turned away from contemporary reality in disgust and dismay. Both fled from the real world with its changes into an unreal world of permanencies: their theories are ideological in origin and content. At their (subconscious) inception stood a practical and political preoccupation and prejudice. Underneath the threshold of consciousness there worked the anguished sentiment and desire that the world *should* not change; above the threshold of consciousness there formed—nourished from its subterranean root—the conviction, the delusive conviction, that the world *does* not change, does not *really* change, that change is only a ripple on the surface of the ocean which leaves the deeper layers of the water calm and unmoved [Stark, 1958: 51].

Plato and Pareto lived in the past. Homans lives in the present—but it is not rash to suggest that the American aristocrat, associated with the 'Harvard Pareto Circle', may not be unlike Plato and Pareto in their unconscious search for theories that would restore or at least consolidate the respectability of their embattled class.

7
Blau's Elaboration of Individualistic Social Exchange Theory

Much has been written on social exchange theory in the U.S. following Homans' *Social Behavior: Its Elementary Forms*. Of the attempts aimed at strengthening and elaborating the social exchange perspective two stand out. In the lesser of these two attempts Emmerson [1969; 1972] goes behind Homans to Skinner's behavioral psychology to derive, in a pure exercise in logico-deductive reasoning, a large number of propositions mostly ungrounded in empirical data. Emmerson seems to out-Homans Homans in his faith in the ability of operant psychology to perform the function of the fountain-head of all behavioral sciences. In concluding his major treatise on the topic, he says:

> We have taken [operant] psychological material as a *given* base to build upon. But the direction taken in the building process was partly predetermined, and it was not contained within that base. Conceptual distinctions were selectively introduced, guiding the analysis toward sociology. From that same base we could have moved into economics (we did in part) or into animal ecology [Emmerson, 1972: 87].

This is more than Homans ever claimed for behavioral psychology. Clearly if what Emmerson has written is only a 'preliminary effort' and if he lives up to his promise to build all subfields of sociology and all the other behavioral sciences on operant psychology, Homans' social exchange theory will have been changed beyond recognition—with its economic base destroyed. This pessimistic assessment of Emmerson's exchange theory on my part is not intended to belittle his brilliant insights on social phenomena, particularly his rich analysis of social power [e.g., Emmerson, 1962]. The purpose of this monograph will not, however, be advanced appreciably if we were to review Emmerson's exchange theory at any length.

Blau's [1964a, 1968] exchange theory has a different kind of relationship to Homans' social exchange theory. While ignoring Homans' overwhelming emphasis on the primacy of operant behavioral psychology in social exchange theory, he goes further than Homans to strengthen the economic basis of social exchange behavior. Blau does have some intuitive conception of psychology, but it is totally different from behavioral psychology. From the point of view of this monograph, Blau's theory of social exchange behavior is provocative for the important reason that it purports to stand at the cross-roads of the individualistic and collectivistic orientations in sociology—or in Blau's [1964a: 3] own words between 'the Scylla of abstract conceptions too remote from empirical reality and the Charybdis of reductionism that ignores emergent social and structural properties'.

My purpose here is to examine Blau's self-imposed attempt to achieve a compromise between the collectivistic and the individualistic orientations in sociology. Like most compromisers, Blau is characteristically non-polemical in his social exchange theory and sometimes appears embarrassingly eclectic. Apart from deliberately formulating some hypotheses which, as Glaser and Strauss [1966: 11n] have charged, Blau knew to be incorrect but which he nevertheless wished to be proved wrong to the long-run benefits of his theory [cf. Blau, 1964a: 9], he has widely cited apparently supportive evidence from diverse authors, with the notable exception of Spencer and Frazer, even when the contexts of these citations contradict Blau's theses.[1] My central point is that, in spite of his attempt to achieve a compromise between the individualistic and the collectivistic orientations in sociology, Blau's social exchange theory is eminently individualistic—indeed it is nearer Spencerian and Frazerian individualism in its emphasis on economic self-interest as the motive force for social action than Homans' conditioned behavioral individualism.

---

[1] I have earlier pointed out one such contradiction between Blau's claim that Lévi-Strauss supports his superordination function of social exchange hypothesis and Lévi-Strauss' own position that postulates equality between social exchange partners as an attribute of stable social exchange.

The Elements of Blau's Social Exchange Theory

Blau [1964a: 4] conceives of social exchange 'as a social process of central significance in social life, which is derived from simpler processes and from which more complex processes are in turn derived'. There are thus three distinct elements in Blau's social exchange theory: (a) the basic premises of the theory; (b) the social exchange processes derived from the basic premises; and (c) the more complex structural and emergent properties that are derived from the social exchange processes. The obvious task in the evaluation of Blau's social exchange theory consists in understanding what each of these steps means and the nature of the relationships between the more elementary processes and the more involved and complex processes derived from them. Blau [1964a: vii] believes that the first half of his *Exchange and Power in Social Life* deals with the first two processes and that his treatment of these themes owes a lot to Homans' *Social Behavior: Its Elementary Forms* 'despite some fundamental differences in approach'. The second part of *Exchange and Power in Social Life*, Blau says, deals with the more complex structural and emergent properties of social exchange. Furthermore Blau [cf. 1964b; 1969: 50] believes that Homans did not deal with these latter structural and emergent properties of social exchange; at most he assumed them as given. In a sense then Blau seems to see his major contribution to social exchange theory in his attempt to point up the relevance of these derived social structures for social life.

In treating these various themes in Blau's social exchange theory, I believe our grasp of social exchange processes will be enhanced if we juxtapose Homans' own conceptions, especially what he says in connection with Blau's efforts, with Blau's own attempts at promoting the social exchange perspective. In doing so we may be able to highlight in what ways Blau builds on, and in what ways he modifies, Homans' social exchange theory.

The Basic Premises of Social Exchange

According to Blau [1964a: 19], 'The basic social processes that govern associations among men have their roots in primitive psychological processes, such as the underlying feeling of attraction between individuals and their desires for various kinds of rewards'. On closer examination, these primitive processes turn out to be two, the chief of which can hardly be termed psychological. For Blau argues that 'An individual is attracted to another if he expects associating with him to be in some way rewarding for himself, and his interest in the expected social rewards draws him to the other' [1964a: 20]. In other words, the primary basis of association is the *calculated gain* that the actor expects to derive from the association. This hope of gain is the sort of thing that Frazer, Malinowski, and Lévi-Strauss had referred to as *economic motives* in social exchange—with Frazer of course approving and the latter two discouraging their inclusion in social exchange theory. The fact that Blau uses psychological terminology does not alter the crucial importance of economic motivation in his social exchange theory. These economic motives are so strong in his theory that Blau [1964a: 6] limits social exchange relations 'to actions that are contingent on rewarding reactions from others and that cease when these expected reactions are not forthcoming'.[1] To vulgarize Blau's exchange theory: in social relationships between individuals nothing goes for nothing. In the final analysis, social exchange processes flow from the anticipated and calculated gains that individuals expect from associations. One does not go into associations from altruistic motives—ultimately altruism is reducible to egoism [cf. Blau, 1964a: 17]—or for the sake of building up a stable social structure *per se*, but entirely for individual self-interest profits. One's evaluation of the attractiveness of others is governed by such economic motives: 'The reason a person is an

---

[1] This sentence is the direct contradiction of Malinowski's position in the characterization of social exchange relations: 'it is important to realize that in all forms of [social] exchange in the Trobriands, there is not even a trace of gain, nor is there any reason for looking at it from the purely utilitarian economic standpoint, since there is no enhancement of mutual utility through the exchange' [Malinowski, 1922: 175]. It is distressing to read so many citations from Malinowski's *Argonauts of the Western Pacific* in Blau's [1964a, 1968] theory that seem to favor his position without any mention of Malinowski's central position that 'economic motives' have no place in social exchange theory—a position that so blatantly contradicts Blau's. There is no doubt but that the central thesis of Malinowski's exchange theory is the direct opposite of the central thesis of Blau's, as it is of Frazer's, theory of exchange behavior.

attractive associate is that he has impressed others as someone
with whom it would be rewarding to associate' [Blau, 1964a: 35].
Blau does not deny that other non-self-interest motives exist in
social life; however, he sternly rules them out of the motivating
factors of social exchange behavior:

> To be sure, not all needs or interests are satisfied directly in social
> interaction, as hunger illustrates, and not all social interaction is
> primarily governed by an interest in rewards, since irrational
> forces and moral values also influence it. But many aspects of
> social life do reflect an interest in profiting from social interaction,
> and these are the focus of the theory of social exchange [Blau,
> 1968: 452].

The keynote in Blau's social exchange theory is *profiting* from
social interaction. This means that he emphasizes the maximization of gains. In spite of occasional, usually incongruous, references to psychological needs, economic motives activate social
interaction. In effect, Blau [e.g., 1964a: 20] implies that these
economic motives are determined, partially at least, by the
psychological state of the individual: 'The psychological needs
and dispositions of individuals determine which rewards are
particularly salient for them and thus to whom they will be
attracted'.

But at this level of the conceptualization of 'psychological
needs and dispositions' Blau becomes extremely vague. Probably
because he assumes them to be given, not problematic for his
theory [1964a: 19], their meaning remains buried in his theory.
However, they seem to refer to only human behavior; that is,
these 'psychological needs and dispositions' that partially determine the economic motives for social exchange interaction refer
to human behavior as distinct from animal behavior. That is
another way of saying, of course, that they are different from
Homans' meaning of psychology as used in his social exchange
theory. Blau's model of social exchange is the behavior of the
economic man; Homans' is the behavior of the economic pigeon.
This difference is not likely to be impressive because Homans
elaborates his model of animal behavior while Blau, characteristically non-polemical in his social exchange theory, does not
take issue with Homans' assumptions but only implies that his
model of exchange behavior is distinctively human.

Economic Exchange and Social Exchange in Blau's Theory

Having predicated his social exchange transactions on underlying economic motives, Blau's image of social exchange is
essentially that of economic exchange. This is so once it is understood that the meaning of economic goods is not restricted to
material goods. Nearly ninety years ago, an early American
sociologist pleaded for the expansion of the meaning of economic
goods in sociology to include non-material goods:

> In working out the principles which ought to control the exchange
> of society, Adam Smith and his followers have only taken in con-
> sideration things of a material nature, their object being to show
> that the popular belief that gold and silver alone constitute wealth
> is wrong, and that it really consists of all the material products
> which contribute to the welfare of mankind.
>
>   But if Political Economy treats of material production only,
> Sociology cannot stop there, for its fundamental tenet is that
> happiness and not wealth, is the real aim of the actions of men,
> and that all things which help to increase happiness, whether they
> minister to our physical, emotional, or intellectual faculties, are
> fit subjects for exchange [Chavannes, 1884: 57–58].

Although Knox' [1963] attempt to draw parallels between
Chavannes' [1884] and Homans' [1961] sociological expansions of
the meaning of economic goods has considerable merit, especially
from an historical point of view, Homans' effort in this direction
is vitiated by underlying behavioral psychological emphasis on
the here-and-now, robbing the Economic Man of his only virtue,
namely, to save for the morrow:

> Indeed we are out to rehabilitate the 'economic man'. The trouble
> with him was not that he was economic, that he used his resources
> to some advantage, but that he was antisocial and materialistic,
> interested only in money and material goods and ready to sacrifice
> even his old mother to get them. What was wrong with him were
> his values: he was only allowed a limited range of values; but the
> new economic man is not so limited. He may have any values
> whatever, from altruism to hedonism, but so long as he does not
> utterly squander his resources in achieving these values, his
> behavior is still economic. Indeed if he has learned to find reward

in *not* husbanding his resources, if he values *not* taking any thought for the morrow, and acts accordingly, his behavior is still economic. In fact, the new economic man is plain man [Homans, 1961: 79–80].

Having ignored Homans' behavioral psychology with its 'fun morality' emphasis on the here-and-now, Blau is able at once to expand the meaning of economics to include sociological goods and at the same time to let the Economic Man maintain his virtue of hard-work and of future anticipations. The excision of psychological pleasure from social exchange theory as a prime mover of social behavior and the restriction of social exchange processes to economic self-interests solves for Blau a major dilemma in Homans' exchange theory: the difficulty of reconciling hedonistic here-and-now pleasure-seeking and total avoidance of pain *with* the economic principle of maximization of profit in the future, including in this latter case the deliberate inclusion of costs for the moment for the benefit of greater gains in the future.

The similarities that Blau [1968: 454] sees between economic exchange and social exchange are very strong indeed. For one thing he seems to indicate, without elaboration, that both are part of a general phenomenon of exchange: 'Economic exchange may be considered a special case of the general phenomenon of exchange, with social exchange being the excluded residual category' [1968: 455]. But he does spell out in more detail the similarities between the two:

> The very term 'social exchange' is designed to indicate that social interaction outside the economic sphere has important similarities with economic transactions. Above all, the expectation that benefits rendered will yield returns characterizes not only economic transactions but also social ones in which gifts and services appear to be freely bestowed. Moreover, the economic principle of eventually declining marginal utility applies to social exchange as well [Blau, 1968: 454].[1]

In spite of these strong similarities which he indicates, Blau bends over backwards to draw a distinction between them. To start from the least important: First, 'Only social exchange tends

---

[1] For a knowledgeable critique of Blau's employment of economic concepts in his theory, including marginal utility and indifference curves, see Heath [1968].

to engender feelings of personal obligation, gratitude, and trust; purely economic exchange as such does not' [Blau, 1964a: 94]. It should be clear that Blau's characterization of pure economic life, even pure American economic life, is ideal-typical. The distrust of the salesman is proverbial; the proliferation of consumer groups is a fact of life that attests to the importance of trust or distrust in economic life. Does one not feel obligated to a used car dealer who has been honest in his recommendations of his product? It is even doubtful that Wall Street, the model of the economic marketplace, is immune from the need for trust or distrust in economic activities.

Secondly, 'Social benefits [from social exchange] are less detachable from the source that supplies them than are economic commodities [from economic exchange]' [1968: 455]. In other words, social exchange is more personalized than economic exchange, with impersonal relations dominating 'pure' economic transactions. Blau [1968: 455] is quick to see that this difference is of degree only, since 'most social benefits are intermediate between these extremes, having a value that is extrinsic to the exchange relations in which they are supplied but having this value modified by the significance of these relations'. If there is any clear-cut difference between economic exchange and social exchange, it is clearly not in this area.

Thirdly, economic exchanges are transacted through a well defined single medium of exchange, viz., money. On the other hand, social exchange transactions lack such single media of exchange [Blau, 1968: 455]. This difference is clearly the most unrealistic of those indicated by Blau, since it would exclude trade by barter reported in many parts of the world [cf. Malinowski, 1922; Bohannan, 1955; Belshaw, 1965] from economic exchange.

The most substantive and the most problematic distinction drawn between economic exchange and social exchange is in terms of contractual obligation in economic exchange transactions and moral obligations in social exchange transactions:

> The most basic difference is that the obligations incurred in social transactions are not clearly specified in advance. In economic transactions the exact obligations of both parties are simultaneously agreed upon: . . . a contract is made that stipulates precisely the obligations either party has to discharge in the future. In social exchange, by contrast, one party supplies benefits to another, and

although there is a general expectation of reciprocation, the exact nature of the return is left unspecified . . .

[S]ocial exchange requires trusting others, whereas the immediate transfer of goods or the formal contract that can be enforced obviates such trust in economic exchange. *Typically, however, social exchange relations evolve in a slow process, starting with minor transactions in which little trust is required because little risk is involved and in which both partners can prove their trustworthiness, enabling them to expand their relation and engage in major transactions. Thus, the process of social exchange leads to the trust required for it in a self-generating fashion.* Indeed, creating trust seems to be a major function of social exchange, and special mechanisms exist that prolong the period of being under obligation and thereby strengthen bonds of indebtedness and trust [Blau, 1968: 454; my italics].

Reduced to its fundamentals, the difference that Blau sees between social exchange and economic exchange may be stated as follows: Economic exchanges are made possible by *contractual obligations*, social exchanges by *moral obligations*. The distinction that Blau draws here between economic exchange and social exchange raises the spectre of classical intellectual differences between individualistic and collectivistic sociologists—more pointedly between Spencer and Durkheim.

Blau's image of economic exchange is of course Spencerian. While there are no contractual obligations involved in social exchange, Blau clearly sees moral obligations in them; but these moral obligations are not to be assumed as given by the social exchange actors. The individual social exchange actor is never sure until he is convinced of his partner's trustworthiness—through a slow process of trial-and-error.[1] On the other hand, Blau's picture of economic exchange seems to be devoid of morality. The reason for this should be clear: Blau does not assume any generalized morality in society that governs all forms of exchange. 'The prototype of an economic transaction rests on formal contract that stipulates the exact quantities to be exchanged

---

[1] True to his eclectic style, Blau [1964a: 255] does not later hesitate to recognize the existence of cultural values that protect social exchange: 'Without social norms prohibiting force and fraud, the trust required for social exchange would be jeopardized.' Since, however, he recognizes the value of such societal norms only in the context of 'indirect exchange', one must assume that his theory of the more basic processes of direct exchange requires individual effort to build up whatever morality makes it possible.

. . . whether the entire transaction is consummated at a given time, in which case the contract may never be written, or not, all the transactions to be made now or in the future are agreed upon at the time of sale' [Blau, 1964a: 93]. Social exchange, on the other hand, merely requires trusting others [1968: 454].

In divorcing economic exchange from societal morality, Blau has resurrected Spencer without paying attention to Durkheim's objections. It is Durkheim's central argument that even legal contracts, which Spencer emphasized as providing the basis for social action and social solidarity in industrialized societies, are made possible only by underlying societal generalized morality:

> In sum, a contract is not sufficient unto itself, but is possible only thanks to a regulation of the contract which is originally social. It is implied, first, because it has for its function much less the creation of new rules than the diversification in particular cases of pre-established rules; then, because it has and can have the power to bind only under certain conditions [Durkheim, 1933: 215].

When seen in the light provided by Durkheim, the difference between social exchange and economic exchange in terms of contractual and moral obligations pales away. My point here, of course, is that Blau has overpainted the differences between economic exchange and social exchange—at least as far as contractual and moral obligations are concerned. More generally, it is my point that once one premises social exchange relations on economic motives, as Frazer and Blau have done, it is a vain attempt to try to separate economic exchange from social exchange.

There is an area of Blau's theory that bears close resemblance to Mauss' and Lévi-Strauss' collectivistic social exchange theories, but which nevertheless illustrates the individualistic nature of Blau's theory of social exchange. Both Blau [1964a: 94, 107; 1968: 454] and Lévi-Strauss [1969: 265] emphasize trust as an attribute of social exchange. And as we have seen, Mauss' central point in social exchange theory is that social exchange relations generate social trust which becomes generalized to the social system. But there is a fundamental difference between the French social exchange theorists' and Blau's conceptions of trust in social exchange. In Lévi-Strauss and Mauss, social exchange transactions take place within the matrix of social trust—which exist before individual social exchange acts and which therefore individual actors assume as given. In Blau, on the other hand, every exchange actor must move with caution: trust is an attribute of the individuals engaged in exchange. Part of the social exchange process is for the social exchange actors to build up a framework of trust. To repeat a memorable sentence, 'Typically, social exchange relations evolve in a slow process, starting with minor transactions in which little trust is required because little risk is involved and in which both partners can prove their trustworthiness, enabling them to expand their relation and engage in major transactions' [Blau, 1968: 454].

This difference has important consequences for the meaning of Blau's social exchange theory. Blau's trial-and-error exchange process must imply three things. First, social exchange has to be direct; that is, his has to be a theory of restricted exchange featuring mutual reciprocities. Secondly, it implies that the completion of a successful social exchange transaction takes time. At least time should be an important parameter in the theory. Thirdly, the exchange actor tries out each new actor. Instead of giving the benefit of the doubt to a new exchange partner, he goes by steps until he learns by experience to trust him. This same intellectual *ad hoc* posture in social exchange processes has led Blau to deny Gouldner's postulate that the norm of reciprocity is generalized to the social system and that it provides the context for social action. Instead Blau contends that 'When people are thrown together, and before common norms or goals or role expectations have crystallized among them . . . group norms to regulate and limit the exchange transactions emerge, including the fundamental and ubiquitous norm of reciprocity' [Blau, 1964a: 92].

In effect, Blau's intellectual posture dictates that human exchange involves *ad hoc* arrangements and that past experiences with other partners, even of a given status group or of religious or ethnic affiliation, need not be relied on for present social exchange transactions. It further implies that the exchange actor does not have the moral mandates of society to fall upon.

Restricted Exchange and Indirect Exchange in Blau's Theory

One of the deeper insights in Blau's social exchange theory is his recognition that Simmel saw a qualitative difference between the operation of dyads and that of larger groups: As Blau has correctly observed, Simmel's 'discussion of the triad is explicitly concerned with the significance of a multiplicity of social relations in social life, and his use of the triad for this purpose is apparently intended to emphasize [*sic*] the crucial distinction between a pair and any group more than two' [Blau, 1964a: 32]. Blau says, quite correctly in my opinion, that Simmel's principles of *divide et impera* and of *tertius gaudens* imply that the 'distinctive processes of the dynamics of power cannot be manifest in a dyad' [1964a: 32]. Since Blau's exchange theory is centrally concerned with power relations, should we assume that his social exchange theory rules out dyadic relations or, as we have termed it following Lévi-Strauss, restricted exchange?

Unfortunately, in spite of his recognition of the qualitative difference between the relationships in dyads and those in larger groups, Blau reverted to restricted—dyadic—exchange theory. This is probably because of his specialized and rather distorted interpretation of Simmel's meaning of the dyad as only referring to *isolated* pairs, instead also of extending its meaning to pairs included in larger wholes. Blau's conclusion is that

> It is essential, in the light of these considerations, to conceptualize processes of social association between individuals realistically as finding expression in networks of social relations in groups and not to abstract artificially isolated pairs from this group context. Crusoe and Friday were a dyad that existed in isolation, but most associations are part of a broad matrix of social relations [Blau, 1964a: 32].

In effect, Blau's is a theory of *inclusive restricted exchange*, as we have called it. Pairs of individuals interrelated—not isolated like Crusoe and Friday—are the exchange actors in Blau's theory. Thus the individual has a choice of breaking up his dyadic exchange relations with his exchange partners and forming new dyadic relationships with others. This is made possible because Blau's dyadic exchange relationships are implicated in larger social relationships. On the face of it at least, the theory does not preclude the possibility of one person engaging in several inclusive restricted exchange transactions. What it does preclude is any generalized exchange transactions in which one exchange

S.E.T.–7

actor, A, is not directly reciprocated for his rewarding activity to another actor, B—an exchange process involving at least three individuals implicated in what we have called, following Lévi-Strauss, univocal reciprocity. The mutual reciprocity and the restricted exchange nature of Blau's theory is implied in his definition of social exchange: 'the concept of exchange refers to voluntary social actions that are contingent on rewarding activities from others and that cease when these expected reactions are not forthcoming' [Blau, 1968: 454; 1964a: 6].[1] It is noteworthy that Homans' conception of restricted exchange cannot be so sharply characterized: for the most part Homans' exchange actors are isolated pairs—probably the isolated pairs that Blau [1964a: 32] complains about; at other times the impression is given that his conception of social exchange is that of inclusive restricted exchange [cf. Homans, 1967a: 55]. But there is little doubt that the caricature of exclusive restricted exchange transactions dominates Homans' theory.

To say that Blau's is a theory of restricted exchange is to arouse the curiosity of those used to Blau's concept of 'indirect exchange'. By 'indirect exchange' Blau meant something totally different from what Lévi-Strauss and Malinowski meant by that term or, as these social exchange theorists also call it, generalized exchange and circular exchange. As we have stressed before, in generalized exchange or circular exchange, at least three exchange actors engage in the unit exchange activity but none of them gives directly to the one he receives from. On the other hand by indirect exchange Blau ultimately means that mediating norms, social values, or organizations replace the role of individual exchange actors:

> Social norms substitute indirect exchange for direct exchange transactions between individuals. The members of the group receive group approval in exchange for conformity and the contribution to the group their conformity to social expectation

---

[1] This interpretation of Blau's exchange theory runs counter to Mulkay's [1971: 187] view 'that the basic unit [in Blau's theory] is the triad rather than the dyad'. Blau [1964a: 32] does not see the triad as the unique opposite of the dyad; rather, following Simmel, he sees the triad as prototypic of groups larger than dyads. In any case, it would not be in the spirit of Simmel's seminal distinction between the dyad and larger groups to treat the triad as the basic unit of multi-person social interaction.

makes. Conformity to normative standards often requires that group members refrain from engaging in certain direct exchange transactions with outsiders or among themselves . . . Conformity frequently entails sacrificing rewards that could be attained through direct exchange, but it brings other rewards indirectly [Blau, 1964a: 259].

In other words indirect exchange is mediated by impersonalized rules—thus limiting the part played by individuals. The nearest Blau comes to a conception of generalized exchange is individual-focused generalized exchange: 'Exchange transactions between the collectivity and its individual members replace some of the transactions between individuals as the result of conformity to normative obligations. There is no direct exchange of favors, but the group norms assure that each friend receives assistance when he needs it' [Blau, 1964a: 259].

In the final analysis, however, unlike Lévi-Strauss and Malinowski, Blau sees indirect exchange as complex behavior, well beyond the reach of individual actors. In Malinowski and Lévi-Strauss, indirect exchange—that is, circular exchange or generalized exchange—is elementary behavior, an attribute of individual behavior within the context of societal norms. In Blau, indirect exchange is the attribute of organizations, an impersonalized assemblage of rules.

Macro-Structures and Social Exchange Processes: Homans and Blau

Up to this point, I have indicated some areas in which I believe Homans and Blau differ in their social exchange theories. They may or may not agree with me in my interpretations of their theories in these areas. However, there is one outstanding region in which both men refuse to agree and they say so. This is the relationship between social exchange processes and the larger social structures built on them. Blau's first comment on Homans' theory shows the nature of the disagreement. According to Blau [1964b: 193], '[Homans'] insistence that all social processes can be reduced to underlying psychological phenomena—even though the focus of social exchange on emergent properties that inhere in social interaction would seem to belie such psychological reductionism—prevents him from [apparently among other things] drawing the fruitful implications his rule of justice has for an understanding of social structure and its dynamics.'

What Blau is complaining about here is not merely that Homans' theory does not deal with derived complex social structures. The point is more fundamental: do the laws that explain elementary social exchange processes also explain derived complex social structures? Homans [1968: 5–6] has readily confessed that his social exchange theory is an unfinished work and eventually he would extend it to handle, apparently more efficiently than Blau, the more complex social structures by explaining them in terms of the same primitive behavioral psychological principles in his social exchange theory. In this connection, Homans (1964b: 225–228; 1968: 5–6] has praised 'Coleman's [1964] recognition of the power of a simple rationality assumption to account for the development of certain norms' [1968: 6] as an example of what he means by the psychological explanation of complex social structures.

My purpose here is to make clear at what point the two foremost names in American social exchange theory refuse to agree. Both agree that complex social structures may be derived from basic social exchange processes. But Homans says decidedly that in the realm of functioning, these derived social structures have no autonomous laws of their own. On the other hand Blau terms them emergent, suggesting and saying thereby that once they emerge from the basic social exchange processes, they attain an autonomy of their own with their own laws of operation independent of the primitive processes from which they emerge.

On closer examination, however, the 'disagreement' between Homans and Blau in this matter is not as resounding as the two of them make it. Homans' exchange theory, we have said, is built at least partially on psychological principles. He says, to repeat, that these primitive psychological principles can explain more complex social structures. Blau's exchange theory, we have said, is built on economic motives—in spite of Blau's insistence that the underlying needs are psychological. It seems to me that Blau's explanation of the more complex social structures, e.g., of power and status, is also in terms of these economic motives. The difference between Homans and Blau, in their exchange theories at least, is not the calculus of explanation but the basic principles they separately assume to be primitive to their theories: psychological needs for Homans and economic motives for Blau.

Once this point is understood, then I see no substantial difference between Coleman's [1964] attempt to account for higher-order norms in terms of economic rationality assumption, so extravagantly lauded by Homans [1968: 6], and Blau's attempt to explain 'emergent properties' in terms of economic motives. In this connection it is worth pointing out that Coleman's [1964] article was a partial attack on Homans for retreating from economic motives to behavioral psychological needs as the motive force for social action: 'This paper [Coleman introduces his article] constitutes an attempt to extend a style of theoretical activity which is quite new to our domain. It is theory which rests upon the central postulate of economic theory. The introduction of this approach into sociological theorizing was carried out by Homans. Homans has since then by degrees led himself away from such an approach into that of operant conditioning' [Coleman, 1964: 166].

Thus the problem seems to be one of misplaced names. Blau, without saying it, has shed B. F. Skinner's conditional behavioral psychology from Homans' social exchange theory and has come to predicate his own social exchange theory entirely on economic motives. Yet he insists, apparently in conformity to Homans' original suggestions in his theory, that the underlying conditions of his theory are supplied by unspecified psychological processes. On the other hand, although he makes the assumption of economic motives as a basis of social exchange interaction, Homans has, as Coleman points out, become more attached to the principles of behavioral psychology in his social exchange theory. Of course both Homans and Blau are writing about social exchange theory; but their premises are different.

There is, however, a rather subtle difference of emphasis between Homans and Blau in their treatment of the relationship between basic social processes and the more complex social structures based on them. In his reformulation of his social exchange theory, Homans [1967a] included some added emphasis on the relationship between the basic social processes and higher-order phenomena, especially power and status, which were not so thoroughly examined in *Social Behavior* [cf. Homans, 1968: 5]. What seems to be the case is that Homans treats social exchange processes as providing the forum for the validation of power and status, not the grounds where they are developed. For instance, he concludes that 'Power, then, depends on the ability to provide rewards that are valuable because they are scarce' [Homans, 1967a: 55]. The assumption Homans makes is that the powerful individual has already acquired the ability and experience needed by the powerful and demanded by high status [cf. 1967a: 54] and all that the social exchange processes provide him is a forum for their validation. To put the matter in a style not altogether appealing to sociologists, we may say that Homans has a *status quo* social exchange theory of power.

Blau's emphasis is different. In Blau's social exchange theory the individual acquires status and power from the social exchange processes. It is within the context of social exchange that power and status develop. Where Homans talks of the *dependence* of power on social exchange, Blau emphasizes the *derivation* of power from social exchange processes. The difference here may have something to do with their treatment of time as a parameter in their social exchange theories. The duration of social exchange processes is not emphasized in Homans' theory and they are presumably only of short duration. Hence power and status are brought into the social exchange situation—there is not enough time to develop them in the duration of the social exchange processes, anyway. In Blau the duration of social exchange processes is emphasized [cf. Blau, 1964a: 277; 1968: 454], although it has not received systematic attention in his work. At the very least, Blau indicates that there is enough time to acquire power and status in the social exchange process.

The Origin and Functions of Social Institutions: Durkheim, Frazer, and Blau

Coleman [1964: 166] clearly overstated his case when he says that the assumption of the central postulate of economic theory, namely, individual self-interest rationality, is new to sociology or that it was introduced into sociology by Homans. Spencer's sociology was violently attacked by Durkheim precisely because of such self-interest rationality assumption. But within the sphere of social exchange theory, the name that is foremost in this matter of rationality assumption is Sir James G. Frazer. It would not be a misnomer to term his social exchange theory an iron law of economic motives.

My concern here is to point out the rather striking similarities between Frazer and Blau in their social exchange theories. There is little doubt that Blau's social exchange theory is closer to Frazer's than to that of anyone else.[1] Basic to both is the fundamental assumption that economic motives act as the springboard of social exchange processes. Beyond this basic assumption, Frazer and Blau converge, more or less strongly, on three fronts of social exchange theory. First, they both assume that social structures are arranged in such a way as to conform to the principles of economic motives. Frazer has stated this case most strongly, but the thrust of Blau's theory would seem to follow the same direction: once social exchange processes are established, 'macrostructures' (to use Blau's terminology) that conform to the social exchange processes tend to be encouraged while those that do not conform to them are discouraged.

More profound is their common emphasis on the phenomenon of power in social exchange relations. For both, power is derived from social exchange processes. Those who have valued social exchange items buy power, so to speak, by benefiting those who lack such exchange items. Of course the exchange items in Frazer are limited since his social exchange theory did not include the expansion of the meaning of economic goods to non-material items, as in Blau. But their strategies are the same. Perhaps of central significance for social theory is the common implication in Frazer and Blau that power in any social context is highly limited and that if one man acquires power the other loses it. In other words, both Frazer and Blau have a zero-sum conception of power and status in society. Problematic for sociological theory, in this connection, is the question whether the phenomenon of the zero-sum conception of power is not inherent in any theoretical perspective that is predicated on the assumption of economic motives as the springboard for social action. To some extent, of course, any theory that emphasizes dyadic relations is more likely to show a sensitivity to power imbalances

---

[1] There is no reference to Frazer in any of Blau's writings on social exchange and I assume that he has never read Frazer's *Folklore in the Old Testament Vol. II* in which the British anthropologist put forward his social exchange theory.

than a theory of multi-person interaction. This is perhaps why power and status imbalances are minimized in Lévi-Strauss' theory of generalized social exchange, while they gain maximum attention in Blau's inclusive restricted exchange theory.

A third area of convergence between Frazer and Blau in their social exchange theories flow from their common emphasis on power relations. Built into their theories is a common legitimation of the exploitation of social exchange relations. The aim of participating in social exchange relations is not just the hedonistic need of enjoying oneself, but more importantly, in Blau's words, 'of profiting from social interaction'. Exploiting one's social exchange partner for maximum benefit is integral to social exchange relationships, as defined by Blau and Frazer. This makes inequality a normal phenomenon in social exchange relations.

The bracketing of Frazer and Blau in their social exchange theories leads to a question of some relevance for contemporary American sociology. For some time now, Blau [e.g., 1960, 1969) has boldly introduced himself as representing a Durkheimian point of view in sociology. Since Homans' development as a sociologist has been largely tied up with his objections and opposition to Durkheim's sociology, it is not surprising that he has also frowned upon Blau's attempt to be Durkheimian [cf. Homans, 1964c: 971]. Now, Frazer's assumptions in his social exchange theory, which we say parallel Blau's, are pre-eminently individualistic and anti-Durkheimian. The question may therefore be raised as to where Blau stands in the distance between Durkheim's (and Lévi-Strauss') collectivistic social theory and Frazer's (and Spencer's) individualistic social theory.

There are two areas in Durkheim's sociology that can only be confused at theoretical peril [cf. Cohen, 1968: 35-36]. The first covers the *development* or *origin* of social institutions, norms, and values. *The Elementary Forms of the Religious Life* stands out as the prototype of a work that inquires into origins of social beliefs and institutions. The second area of central concern in Durkheim's theoretical interests is the *functioning* of these social institutions and the societal norms and values, once they have been developed. *Suicide* and, to a lesser extent, *The Rules of Sociological Method* most prominently represent this side of Durkheim's sociology. Now, when the issue of concern in sociological theory is the origin or development of institutions, Blau is as far apart from Durkheim or Lévi-Strauss as any individualistic sociologist—be he Spencer or Homans. For Durkheim, social institutions, norms, and values grow out of the moral mandates of society. For Spencer, Frazer, Homans, and Blau, the origin of social institutions and of societal norms and values is to be traced to either the psychological needs or the economic motives of individuals in society. At this level of the origins or development of institutions and societal norms, beliefs and values, Blau—if we are to judge by his social exchange theory—is anti-Durkheimian and eminently individualistic.

Let me illustrate the point here with Blau's [1964a: 92] treatment of the norm of reciprocity. As against Gouldner and definitely against the spirit of Durkheim's sociology, Blau sees the origin of the norm of reciprocity in individual needs. It is not, that is, developed phylogenetically—as an attribute of society into which individual actors are socialized and which they assume as given in their everyday activities—but rather it is developed situationally 'when people are thrown together'. This runs against the grain in Durkheim's sociology. Religious beliefs and symbolisms, for example, emerge as a result of the moral needs of society, as separate from individuals [cf. Durkheim, 1915: Chapter 6]. As Durkheim has said repeatedly, social institutions exist *sui generis*. It would be wrong to apply the same phrase to characterize Blau's conception of social institutions. For him they develop out of individual needs, and especially from individual economic needs. Blau fully conforms to Lévi-Strauss' [1969: 140] spiteful charge that [*sic*] 'This false interpretation of the origin of exchange [in terms of economic motives] comes, as we have said, from the fact that Frazer sees exchange itself as a derivative phenomenon, arising from calculation and reflection'. Lévi-Strauss' [1969: 140ff] further charge that Frazer was misled to derive dual organizations from social exchange could easily be made by any collectivistic Durkheimian sociologist against Blau's attempt to derive social institutions from social exchange processes [cf. Blau, 1964a: 25, 273].

But when Blau [e.g., 1960, 1969: 52–53] holds Durkheim as a pioneer in postulating 'structural effects' in sociology, he is referring to the second major area of interest in Durkheim's sociology, the functioning of social institutions and their effects on individual behavior. That is, he is referring essentially to Durkheim the author of *Suicide*. In effect, Blau says that the institutions in society, whatever their origins, have their own effects on individual behavior independent of variable psychological dispositions of individuals in the group. In saying so he is not far removed from Durkheim. The difference, though, is that Blau attaches significance to psychological factors in the explanation of social phenomena, whereas Durkheim tended to disregard them. Durkheim of course knew that individual psychological factors had some effect on men's behavior, but he thought they were irrelevant in explaining aggregate social patterns. Thus, with respect to suicide he plays down the role of individual psychological factors as follows:

> Of course, not all the peculiarities which suicide may present can be deduced in this [sociological] fashion; for some may exist which depend solely on the person's own nature. Each victim of suicide gives his act a personal stamp which expresses his temperament, the special conditions in which he is involved, and which, consequently, cannot be explained by the social and general causes of the phenomenon. But these causes in turn must stamp the suicides they determine with a shade of their own, a special mark expressive of them. This collective mark we must find [Durkheim, 1951: 277–78].

In the language of multi-variate analysis, Durkheim was not interested in explaining the total variance of suicide or of any other phenomena. Rather he was only interested in accounting for that part of the total variance of the phenomenon which owes to social forces. In stressing 'structural effects' in his analysis of data, Blau includes Durkheim's strategy of highlighting the distinctive effects of social factors in explaining social phenomena, but he does not play down the need for detecting individual variable psychological factors as Durkheim so clearly does.

Whether one regards Blau as Durkheimian or not depends largely, therefore, on whether one is emphasizing Durkheim's pioneering work in the explanation of the origins or development of institutions and societal norms and beliefs—as in *The Elementary Forms*—or whether one is identifying Durkheim, as many tend to do, exclusively with his work in *Suicide* in which the emphasis is on the functions of social institutions. It seems to me that in his social exchange theory, Blau was more interested in the origin or development of social institutions and norms. In this area, Blau has written his theory like an individualistic sociologist and he is directly anti-Durkheimian in doing so. He was less interested in underscoring the functions of the social institutions that derive from the social exchange processes. If he were more interested in this area, he might have been more Durkheimian in his social exchange theory. Obviously, it will not be difficult to detect stains of Durkheimianism—and collectivistic sociology —in *Exchange and Power in Social Life*. Such stains, I maintain, are left there by Blau's attempt to be a compromiser between individualistic and collectivistic sociology. My point, of course, is that in spite of his claims his social exchange theory furthers individualistic sociology along a particular route—the economic motives route. Whatever collectivistic sociology appears to exist in his theory consists of stains, not well designed trade marks.

Part Four

CONCLUSIONS

Introduction

In the course of writing this book I have had to read, more or less thoroughly, several books and articles on social exchange. Of these various sources of information and insight, two stand out: Lévi-Strauss' *The Elementary Structures of Kinship* and Homans' *Social Behavior: Its Elementary Forms*. Without knowing it, a writer may be influenced or repulsed by such books. I want to state here the way in which these books will affect the style of this last section of my book. The two books are vastly different, of course. But there are two remarkable similarities between them. The first concerns the common word in their titles: 'elementary'.[1] Both Lévi-Strauss and Homans claim to be writing about 'elementary' social structures and behaviors. Of course their levels of 'elementarism', to use Parsons' [1968] felicitous term, varies greatly. What Lévi-Strauss treats as elementary, Homans would consider complex. I cannot be like the two social exchange theorists in their common quest to deal with elementary principles of social exchange, since I am not creating my own theory *de novo*, as they claim to have done. But I want to look at another way in which their books are remarkably similar, in spite of their vastly different subject-matters and disparate contents: this concerns

---

[1] The use of this term by Homans has led Parsons [1964b: 208] to wonder 'whether Homans' use of the phrase "elementary forms" as his subtitle is meant to suggest a desire to be associated with the Durkheim–Levy–Strauss tradition' of emphasizing 'Those features characteristic of what in a developmental or evolutionary sense are the most "primitive" or underdeveloped systems of social behavior' as in *The Elementary Forms of the Religious Life* and in *The Elementary Structures of Kinship*. Homans [1964b: 224] has scoffed at Parsons' 'speculation', insisting that the 'fact' was that the title of the book was 'a compromise [between him and his publisher], reached in thirty seconds over the telephone, and without any thought for the Durkheimian tradition except that I certainly knew the titles of his and Lévi-Strauss' books'. It would seem that the matter may be a better topic for an investigation on a Freudian slip of the tongue rather than for the sociology of knowledge.

their last chapters.[1] In contradistinction to the 'elementary'
structures and behaviors with which they were principally concerned, Lévi-Strauss and Homans both claim of their last chapters
to be dealing with complex structures: Lévi-Strauss deals with
'The Transition to Complex Structures' and Homans [1961: 378]
examines 'the relations between the elementary and the more
complex forms of social behavior, between the informal and the
formal, between the subinstitutional and the institutional'. It is
not that I wish to deal specifically and extraordinarily with 'complex' structures and behaviors. Rather I wish to follow the
examples of their common *style* in dealing with the last chapters
of their books. For both of them claim to be only exploring a
frontier area with the audacity and even rashness of great ex-
plorers. What Homans says of his last chapter is equally true of
Lévi-Strauss' uninhibited and uncontrolled application of his
distinction between restricted exchange and generalized exchange
to modern social structures in his last chapter. As Homans has
most explicitly put it:

> According to my lights, a last chapter should resemble a primitive
> orgy after harvest. The work may have come to an end, but the
> worker cannot let go all at once. He is still full of energy that will
> fester if it cannot find an outlet. Accordingly he is allowed a time
> of license, when he may say all sorts of things he would think
> twice before saying in more sober moments, when he is no longer
> bound by logic and evidence but free to speculate about what he
> has done [Homans, 1961: 378].

But, of course, Claude Lévi-Strauss and George Caspar Homans
are the names of giants who bestride the Atlantic. They have high
status credit and can get away with whatever they say more easily
than smaller men. I must be more cautious in using my license
in this last part, lest I risk its revocation. I want, therefore, to
spell out the limited ways in which I will use my license: First,

---

[1] Again the extent to which Homans owes the style of his last chapter to his
acquaintance with the two French social scientists can only be wondered about.
It is noteworthy that in arrangements Lévi-Strauss' *The Elementary Structures of
Kinship* is remarkably similar to Durkheim's *The Elementary Forms of the Religious
Life* in that their 'Conclusions' seek to generalize from primitive structures
to more complex structures. If in nothing else, Homans' book bears a striking
resemblance to the French social scientists' books in this matter of having a last
part of a book that attempts to generalize beyond the scope of the book.

in this part of the book I shall more freely relate social exchange processes to general sociological theory. I want to be insightful rather than systematic. Therefore, I shall be free to make suggestions concerning possible relationships that I would be more hesitant to assert in more guarded moments. To do that is not to be reckless, but to suggest new possibilities that cannot be immediately explored. Secondly, I shall refrain from crowding this last part with citations of sources that have appeared in the first seven chapters of this book. My citations will refer mainly to new source materials, introduced here for the first time. Thirdly, I shall more freely speculate about the intentions, and discuss the weaknesses or even apparent limitations, of some of the exchange theorists discussed in this book, especially those of them who are sociologists.

One unstated assumption in this book so far is that the study of the two types of social exchange theories will point up the main outlines of sociological theory in general. It cannot be said that this assumption has been fully borne out in the first seven chapters of this book. In this last 'licensed' Part I cannot claim to show conclusively that the assumption has validity. But I want to emphasize that the central problems of social exchange theory are broadly representative of the general problems of sociology. To say this is not to accept the contention by Homans and Blau that social exchange processes supply a general theory of social behavior or a prolegomenon to such theory. Rather, to say so is to point out that the study of social exchange processes occupies a significant, if limited, area in sociological theory.

8

Social Exchange Processes and Sociological Theory

The history of the development of social exchange theory in sociology is a curious one. When Homans wrote his 1958 article, 'Social Behavior as Exchange', he made the puzzling claim that 'so far as I know, the only theoretical work that makes explicit use of it [exchange] is Marcel Mauss's *Essai sur le don*, published in 1925, which is as ancient as social science goes' [Homans, 1958: 598]. This claim is made in spite of the fact that three years earlier Homans and Schneider [1955] had published a book totally dedicated to the refutation of Lévi-Strauss' [1949] *explicit* social exchange theory of cross-cousin marriage. Even if Mauss was the first theorist known to Homans to have written about social exchange, his is hardly as theoretical or as explicit as Lévi-Strauss' *Les Structures élémentaires de la Parenté*, a book on social exchange with which Homans was thoroughly familiar. Nor is it out of place to note—at least for the historical record—that Homans' [1958] article, 'Social Behavior as Exchange', important as it is, is not the first of Homans' own writings on the subject of social exchange. His first thoughts on social exchange are contained in *Marriage, Authority, and Final Causes: A Study in Unilateral Cross-Cousin Marriage.*

Two years after the publication of *Social Behavior: Its Elementary Forms*, Knox [1963] took the significant step of dusting up an earlier attempt at the formulation of a social exchange perspective by an amateur American sociologist, Albert Chavannes [1884]. Knox' point was to demonstrate, with considerable justice, that Chavannes' writings on social exchange bore remarkable resemblances to Homans' social exchange theory. The apparent fact that Homans was unaware of this work should make that document all the more impressive—for when two minds independently converge on a topic there is good reason to suspect that there is an underlying substance to what they are saying. Of special significance in Chavennes' interesting work is his plea that the meaning of economic goods be given a sociological orientation by broadening them to include non-material goods—a definition that is central to Homans' and Blau's social exchange theories. This plea has the markings of a pioneer in that Chavannes' better known contemporary sociologist, Herbert Spencer, was still unable to accept the inclusion of such non-material goods in exchange transactions [cf. Spencer, 1896: 390–391].

Ten years after Homans' [1958] article on social exchange, and four years after his own lengthy book on the subject, Blau [1968: 453], writing in *The International Encyclopaedia of the Social Sciences*, was able to make the claim that 'Homans developed the first systematic theory that focuses on social behavior "as an exchange of activity, tangible or intangible, and more or less rewarding or costly, between at least two persons"'. Blau, of course, mentioned Mauss [1925] as one of the earlier writers to call attention to the significance of social exchange. This claim, in 1968, concerning the first systematic theorizing on social exchange, perhaps more than anything else, illustrates the gap in our knowledge of social exchange theory. Surely, if Blau had gained more acquaintance with Lévi-Strauss' work on social exchange in ways other than through Lévi-Strauss' heavily edited 'The Principle of Reciprocity' in Coser and Rosenberg, *Sociological Theory: A Book of Readings* [see Blau, 1964: 98, 108; 1968: 457], he would not have made such a misleading claim—even if one concedes that there is some justice in the mention of 'activity' in relationship to Homans' work. Blau apparently was not aware that as far back as 1949 Lévi-Strauss had developed a 'systematic theory of social exchange' of cross-cousin marriage with a claim to recognition as any later work on the subject of social exchange. Indeed, if Blau had read Lévi-Strauss' book, as Homans did, he might have chanced on the important fact that Lévi-Strauss' [1949] social exchange theory was a major attack on an earlier 'systematic social exchange theory' of cross-cousin marriage by Sir James G. Frazer, a theory very much like the one that Blau has independently developed. Again convergences in thought, as between Blau [1964a] and Frazer [1919], should be suspected for indicating important underlying intellectual concerns.

All of this is a way of indicating simply that 'systematic social exchange theory' is not as young as 1958 nor is it an invention of two past Presidents of the American Sociological Association.[1] Two factors have conspired to hide away the substance of social exchange theory from academic sociologists. The first of these is the fact that the theory originated in the hands of social anthropologists—in the hands of Frazer, Malinowski, and Lévi-Strauss, not to mention later anthropologists like Bohannan [1955]. The only man who was early involved in its development to bear a sociologist's trade mark was Marcel Mauss. In my view sociologists have given him extravagant credit, while limiting the recognition of the more substantial contributions of anthropologists to adventitious citations from their works. In his conception of social exchange processes, Marcel Mauss was neither as systematic nor as comprehensive as Frazer, Malinowski, or Lévi-Strauss. My prediction is that if sociologists eventually disregard trade marks and pay full attention to social exchange theory in all its dimensions, including its historical development, then social exchange theory will turn out to have a similar history with that of the development of functionalism. In both functionalism and social exchange theory, the early developers were mostly anthropologists, not sociologists.

The second factor that has contributed to hide away the origin of social exchange theory from academic sociologists may well be the fact of language. Homans is a rare sociologist, rare enough to be able to understand Lévi-Strauss' cumbersome book in its original French. The fact that *Les Structures élémentaires de la Parenté* was not translated into English for twenty years after its appearance in French has clearly retarded the English-reading sociologists' acquaintance with Lévi-Strauss' social exchange theory.[2] Its translation into English should be a source of

---

[1] As late as August 1972, in the most prestigious journal in American sociology, one writer still advises its readers: 'For original formulations of exchange theory, see Homans [1961, 1958], Blau [1964a], and Thibaut and Kelley [1959]' [Singelmann, 1972: 415n].

[2] My first effort to read the book in French was an exhausting and not altogether rewarding experience. If one is to judge from Lévi-Strauss' admission that 'On reading it today, the documentation seems tedious and the expression old-fashioned' [1969: xxvii] and his complaint that his 'critics have been quick to seize upon

stimulation to those interested in social exchange theory, provided they can tolerate its anthropological kinship terminology.

What I have written so far in this chapter does not constitute the central concern of this book. References to 'the social exchange perspective' are to be found in any graduate course syllabus in sociological theory nowadays. Yet what is available represents one version of what social exchange theory is all about. My main contention is that social exchange theory typifies sociological theory in its two broad divisions. The 'collectivistic' and the 'individualistic' orientations in sociology are still very much alive in sociology—in spite of Parsons' [1961b: 87) belief that their separate existences were bargained away in 'a special type of marriage between the individualistic and the collectivistic strands'. Each of these independent strands has received more attention at some periods than at others. More importantly, perhaps less acceptable to some sociologists, is my view that, as Parsons indicated originally, the collectivistic strand in sociology has been broadly more French in origin, while the individualistic orientation has been broadly British in origin; furthermore the British tradition has largely infused American sociological theory. Equally central to the argument of this book is my view that the two strands are polemically interrelated: the fortunes of one have affected those of the other. Reactions against each other's tradition of thought have been a key factor in the development of these two strands of sociological theory.

The divisions in social exchange theory conform to this broad division into the individualistic and collectivistic orientations in sociology and the development of social exchange theory has largely been in the context of the polemical interrelationships between the two orientations. In my research on the subject of social exchange, I became convinced that Sir James G. Frazer, a man hardly ever credited with systematic theorizing, nevertheless wrote the first body of literature that can be styled social exchange theory. His theory is entirely individualistic, with much of it predicated on individual economic motives. Lévi-Strauss' strong reaction to this individualistic theory of social exchange led to his own collectivistic theory of social exchange, which included

passages which they have not fully understood through lack of familiarity with the French language' [1969: xxviii], then I suspect that my experiences with the book in its original French were not unique.

a major development in social theory, namely, the conception of univocal reciprocity and generalized exchange. Homans' reaction to Lévi-Strauss' work—one would have liked to call it counter-reaction if Homans had recognized Frazer's exchange theory—led him to an individualistic theory of social exchange. But Homans' conception of individualism has plunged individualistic social exchange theory into intellectual confusion. For Homans had been independently exposed to two strains of individualism: to economic individualism (as in Pareto and Spencer) and psychological individualism (as in Malinowski). Rather than accept one and leave the other out of his theory, Homans decided and attempted to 'mesh' them together in his social exchange theory.

Here lies the unfortunate crisis in individualistic social exchange theory. For individualistic social thought has never had the unity of orientation that collectivistic social thought has enjoyed. On the one hand, there is psychological individualism that emphasizes the here-and-now, an emphasis on untarnished pleasure with total avoidance of pain. On the other hand, there is economic individualism that is built on a self-interest calculation of gain, with the deliberate toleration of present costs and pains for greater benefits in the future. These are incompatible strands in individualism. To my knowledge, in modern social science only one man has boldly claimed that the two can be reconciled with ease. The cardinal error in Homans' social exchange theory is to seek to achieve maximum individualistic sociology by combining two inherently incompatible strands in individualism: psychological needs and economic motives. Except for Homans, all other individualistic social exchange theorists have tended to adopt one of these rather than the other. Malinowski's social exchange theory is predicated on social psychological needs (in which individual psychological needs and the needs of society are blended together); Frazer's social exchange theory on economic motives; and, in spite of his eclectic claims, Blau's on economic motives.

To say that social exchange theory is differentiated is not to imply that it does not represent a perspective. That it does so is attested to by the fact that in spite of particular sociological suasions and orientations of the social exchange theorists we have considered, certain central ideas are common to them. These 'unit-ideas' represent an emergent 'synthesis' of the social exchange perspective in spite of internal divisions. Needless to say, there are differences in the way the 'unit-ideas' are regarded by each of the social exchange theorists considered in this book. But there is a system to this diversity: there is a broad division between collectivistic social exchange theorists and individualistic social exchange theorists in the way they see these unit-ideas. There is one point, however, where such consistency breaks down. In his conception of social exchange processes, Malinowski emphasizes both psychological needs and social needs and he is consistently against the assumption of economic motives in social exchange processes. In many respects, indeed, he seems closer to the collectivistic social exchange theorists than to the individualistic social exchange theorists. However, Malinowski's concomitant emphasis on individual psychological needs places him at odds with the collectivists, just as his denial of economic motives in social exchange processes pitches him against Frazer, Homans, and Blau.

I have freely applied Professor Nisbet's introduction of the strategy of consolidating unit-ideas into sociology to the narrow province of social exchange theory. Professor Nisbet [1966: 5] sees unit-ideas in sociology as providing 'fundamental, constitutive substance to sociology amid the manifest differences among its authors, ideas which persist throughout the classical age of modern sociology, extending indeed to the present moment'. In spite of the considerable differences between the different traditions in social exchange theory, with authors separated by more than six decades, certain unit-ideas of social exchange processes persist. It seems to me that these provide whatever distinctive perspective may be claimed for social exchange theory. Needless to add, these unit ideas receive varying degrees of emphasis and of approval or disapproval from the various social exchange theorists. The following five unit-ideas seem to me to be central to social exchange theory: (a) the relationship between economic exchange and social exchange; (b) the structure of reciprocity; (c) restricted exchange and generalized exchange; (d) exploitation and power; and (e) the contribution of social exchange processes to social solidarity. The relationships of these unit-ideas to sociological theory in general constitutes the sociological significance of social exchange theory.

Economic Exchange and Social Exchange

The most popular unit-idea, mentioned by all the social exchange theorists, is the relationship between social exchange behavior and economic exchange behavior. In many instances, the discussions on this topic take the form of commentary on the Economic Man. The Economic Man, be it remembered, is a cold, calculating, self-seeking individualist whose only objective is the endless acquisition of material goods with a minimum of moral inhibitions. Broadly speaking, the tenets of the Economic Man are accepted and adopted by social exchange theorists who regard economic motives as the springboard of social action, while social exchange theorists who deny that economic motives are important in social exchange tend to reject the values of the Economic Man. So it is that Malinowski and Lévi-Strauss regard economic motives as unimportant in social exchange and both of them reject the assumptions of the Economic Man in social exchange theory. On the other hand Frazer and Blau accept, implicitly at least, the Economic Man and Homans [1961: 79–80] embraces him provided he would only stop worrying about the future and have a little more of fun morality. In Homans and Blau, the meaning of economic goods is expanded to include non-material, intangible, 'goods'—to include, that is, all things that contribute to man's happiness or that would deprive him of it. In Frazer, Malinowski, and Lévi-Strauss the exchange items are specialized: women, necklaces and armshells. Of course only Frazer of the three considers exchange items, women in his case, as economic goods.

We are led, at this point, to the issue of the valuation of social exchange items. In general, those social exchange theorists who build their conceptions of social exchange processes on economic motives see the social exchange items as economic goods and therefore amenable to the laws of supply and demand. Social exchange items are valued for their own *economic* worth—for what they fetch the man who acquires them or who gives them up. In direct opposition to this view, those who reject economic motives as providing the incentive for social exchange action only attach *symbolic* value to the social exchange items. They are sought for, not for what they are worth in themselves, but rather for what they represent between the giver and the receiver of the exchange items. Thus Malinowski and Lévi-Strauss and, less explicitly, Mauss—all hostile to the premises of economic motives in social exchange—see the exchange items as having only symbolic value, the function of which is to build up a framework of social solidarity between the individuals or groups that participate in social exchange processes.

Usually unspelt out, but of crucial significance for social exchange theory, is the issue of the scarcity of the social exchange items. In the economically motivated social exchange theories, the value of the exchange items depends very much on their physical supplies and alternative sources for the exchange items. This is why Frazer emphasized the scarcity of women in his theory and that is why Homans and Blau rely so heavily on laws of supply and demand in classical economics and on the law of marginal diminishing returns. The issue of scarcity does not receive a great deal of attention in Malinowski, but since his social exchange items have no economic value they are *ipso facto* robbed of any economic scarcity value. Lévi-Strauss is more forthright in discussing the matter. As I have restated it, the issue for him is one of *social scarcity*, not economic scarcity. That is, social exchange items have social scarcity value as defined by society—not by natural laws of physical availability. Even when some exchange items are physically available society may endow them with a scarcity value by defining rules of exclusion that bar certain actors from possessing certain categories of them or else society may define rules that limit the occasions for exchanging gifts. The classical example is of course women—a bad example nowadays, but it is a classical example anyway. The laws of incest —which vary notoriously from society to society—define the social scarcity value of women by excluding certain males from marrying certain categories of women. Even though women may be available in physical abundance, society may use exclusion rules to prohibit the individual from marrying his maternal or paternal cousins—thus creating a social scarcity value for women. The same principle holds for the exchange of gifts. Annual, say Christmas, gifts have a social scarcity value because society creates special occasions for them: it is not the physical availability of Christmas gifts that give them their scarcity value, but

rather the societal definitions of special occasions on which they
are given. In other words, according to Lévi-Strauss' social
exchange theory, society renders exchange items scarce—not the
economic laws of supply and demand.

Malinowski and Lévi-Strauss do not deny that economic
motives govern economic exchange. But they do see a qualitative
difference between the motives underlying economic exchange
and social exchange. For Lévi-Strauss, as for Mauss, the motives
for participating in social exchange transactions can only be
termed *social*: the motive behind social exchange transactions is
to build up social networks interlinking the social exchange
actors. This is of course the assumption that led to Homans and
Schneider's [1955] attack on Lévi-Strauss' social exchange theory
of cross-cousin marriage. For Malinowski the motivation for
engaging in social exchange transactions is two-fold: *psychological*,
to satisfy the psychological needs of the individual and, secondly,
social, to build up an interlocking network of social relationships.
On the other hand, Frazer, Homans, and Blau[1] deny that social
motives *per se* underlie social exchange processes; rather, economic
motives constitute the salient factors. But Homans adds, as we
have said, a second underlying motive for social exchange transactions: psychological needs for immediate gratification.

There is an important difference between Frazer, on the one
hand, and Homans and Blau, on the other, in the matter of
valuation in social exchange theory. It owes to the fact that
Frazer limits his exchange items to one type, women, whereas
Homans and Blau expand their exchange items to a whole range
of 'tangible and intangible' objects. The result is that in Frazer's
theory one knows at least that one woman is the equivalent of
another. In Homans and Blau, on the other hand, effective transvaluation of one exchange item in terms of others, particularly
if they are intangible 'sentiments', would require a common unit

---

[1] It is significant that those theorists who draw distinctions between economic
motives in economic exchange and social or social-psychological motives in social
exchange have been mostly ethnographers as well, including in this case Bohannan
[1955]. Indeed Malinowski, Lévi-Strauss, and Bohannan attribute the distinction
between social exchange and economic exchange—and between the underlying
social motives and economic motives—to native thought. On the other hand those
who see no differences in the motives underlying economic exchange and social
exchange, i.e., Frazer, Homans, and Blau, tend to be 'armchair theorists'—at least
as far as social exchange behavior is concerned.

of measurement or currency. This is a point that Deutsch and Krauss [1965: 114–115] have made in a telling manner about Homans' theory—and the same criticism applies to Blau's:

> [Homans'] theory implies that there is a common *currency* or a single dimension to which the value of different experiences ('getting a B+ on an exam', 'being kissed by one's sweetheart', 'hearing a Beethoven quartet', 'being served a cold beer') can be coordinated so that the value of a 'unit' of one such activity received can be compared with the value of another unit. If there is such a common currency of 'value', it has not yet been identified nor have methods of unitizing activity been worked out (is the kiss or the date the unit? the symphony or the movement?).

The broader problem posed for sociological theory by the distinction between social exchange theories predicated on economic motives and those that deny economic motives concerns the motive for social action. In postulating an iron law of economic, and in the case of Homans also hedonistic, motivation in social exchange behavior, Frazer, Homans, and Blau more or less deny that social actors have variable motivations, depending on circumstances and situations, for social action. They cling to Weber's *zweckrational* as the sole basis of social action, while denying the importance of what Weber has termed *wertrational*, 'involving a conscious belief in the absolute value of some ethical, aesthetic, religious, or other form of behavior, *entirely for its own sake and independently of any prospects of external success*' for the individual actor [Weber, 1947: 115, my italics].[1] On the other hand, Mauss, Lévi-Strauss, and Malinowski pay maximum attention to Weber's *wertrational* in their social exchange theories. While they concomitantly deny that *zweckrational* conduct has a place in social exchange behavior, they do not disregard its significance in economic exchange behavior.

---

[1] My conclusion here runs against Blau's [1964a: 5] own claim that 'a wide range of behavior is pertinent for a study of exchange . . . including particularly "wertrational" as well as "zweckrational" conduct, in Weber's terms'. The inclusion in social exchange processes of *wertrational* social action is clearly incompatible with Blau's own conception of social exchange as 'limited to actions that are contingent on rewarding reactions from others and that cease when these expected reactions are not forthcoming' [Blau, 1964a: 6].

The Structure of Reciprocity

Some of the most incisive analyses of social exchange processes, albeit under the guise of a critique of functionalist theory, are contained in Gouldner's [1959, 1960] two articles on reciprocity. His discussion of reciprocity is important not only because of its depth of theoretical suggestiveness, but even more importantly, at least from my own point of view, because it points up the inadequacies of the central conception of reciprocity in socio-logical theory. Sociological theory has remained stunted, thanks in part to a common commitment by Parsons and Homans to a two-person interaction model, at the level of mutual reciprocity. Indeed when used by itself, the term 'reciprocity' has come to be understood in sociology to mean 'mutual reciprocity' between Ego and Alter, to use Parsons' terms, or Person and Other, to use Homans'. In spite of himself, and apparently sensitive to the inadequacies of a two-person interaction model, Homans several times smuggled Third Man into his social exchange theory, but Homans made it clear to his readers that Third Man had no permanent place in his theory.

It is Gouldner who seemed to have recognized the limitations of a two-person inter-action model, resulting in mutual reciprocity, but he balked at condemning them. His own favorite model was one of a two-person 'A-B' mutual reciprocal interaction. It is a matter for regret, nevertheless, that Gouldner's deepest insight into the structure of reciprocity has not been developed any further. (It is only a small point, but it is true that Gouldner did misrepresent Lévi-Strauss' [*sic*] 'generalized interchange' as a uniquely three-person model, instead of being more inclusively a multi-party interaction model.)

As I see it, the significance of Lévi-Strauss' social exchange theory for social theory in general consists in his recognition that a two-party interaction model is highly limited in its explanatory power and in his provision of an alternative model that would handle extra-dyadic social exchange relations. The classical mutual reciprocity model, which has governed Parsons' and Homans' models of social analysis, could only explain a small part of the kinship social exchange behavior he wished to explain. The introduction of a multi-party inter-action model helped him to explain much more than he could ever explain with the aid of the classical mutual reciprocity model.

The distinction he introduced into social analysis in this area is that between *mutual reciprocity* and *univocal reciprocity*. By univocal reciprocation Lévi-Strauss meant that system of social interaction in which, say, A does not expect a direct rewarding activity from B to whom A does benefit, but rather from another individual, say, C or Z. Perhaps it is worth emphasizing that those involved in any given univocal reciprocation process must be at least three in number but the number could be higher. Univocal reciprocity means first and foremost that an actor does benefit to another actor for which he does not expect immediate or direct reciproca-tion. This implies, above all, that there is enough trust that the giver will be reciprocated from someone and somewhere else in the future. This means that univocal reciprocity can only operate in an atmosphere of generalized morality and trust that the system will work.

Let me employ the distinction between mutual reciprocity and univocal reciprocity to analyze two themes brought out by Gouldner [1960] in his discussion of reciprocity. Of course, in spite of his implicit recognition of the possibility of univocal reciprocity in functional analysis [1959: 249–251], Gouldner's is a model of mutual reciprocity between A and B. It is on this basis that he defined reciprocity: 'Reciprocity connotes that *each* party has rights and duties' and 'there can be stable patterns of reciprocity *qua* exchange only insofar as *each* party has both rights and duties' [Gouldner, 1960: 169]. But the matter is much more complicated in the case of univocal reciprocity. If A has a duty to give to B, A does not have a right to receive from B but from someone else, say, N. That is, the relationship between rights and duties in univocal reciprocity does not conform to Gouldner's conception of rights and duties in mutual reciprocity. As Gouldner [1960: 168] sees it, mutual reciprocity 'may mean that a right (x) of Alter against Ego implies a duty ($-y$) of Alter to Ego . . . [or it] may mean that a duty ($-x$) of Ego to Alter implies a right (y) of Ego against Alter'.

On the contrary, univocal reciprocity implies generalized duties to others (Y_i) from whom one (X_i) cannot expect the fulfilment of one's (X_i) rights, although eventually the rights (of X_i) will be forthcoming from some other source (Z_i). If I see burglars in my neighbor's house, I have the duty of doing something about it (e.g., calling the police), not because I expect any reciprocation—of whatever type from my unfortunate neighbor —but perhaps because I expect *any* neighbor of mine to do the same thing if he sees burglars in my own house. Thus the concept of univocal reciprocity leads directly to the conception of *generalized duties* and *rights*.

It is the concept of univocal reciprocity that can only lead the sociologist from Gouldner's analysis of mutual reciprocity to such higher-order conceptions as citizenship. T. H. Marshall [1949: Chap. V] and Bendix [1964: 74–101] have defined citizenship as a relationship—more or less mediated by social groups— between the individual and the state in which the individual has certain duties (e.g., to pay taxes, perform military duties) and certain rights (e.g., be protected from illegitimate violence, to vote) in terms of this relationship. What is involved in such a complicated process is of course univocal reciprocity. When I pay my taxes to the government, I do not always expect direct benefits from the government. With them roads may be constructed which will facilitate the growth of industry, which will give members of my family employment. In general, the application of mutual reciprocity in the analysis of duties and rights is liable to limit sociologists to face-to-face relations. The analysis of duties and rights in terms of univocal reciprocity leads to such higher-order conceptions as citizenship.

The same shortcoming is apparent in Gouldner's [1960: 171–172] conception of the norm of reciprocity: 'Specifically, I suggest that a norm of reciprocity, in its universal form, makes two interrelated, minimal demands: (1) people should help those who have helped them, and (2) people should not injure those who have helped them' [Gouldner, 1960: 171]. Praiseworthy for its seminal conception, this statement of the norm of mutual reciprocity is nevertheless limiting. It suggests that the norm of reciprocity operates in face-to-face interactions and that it compels reciprocation only for what has actually been given or received. In its wider form, however, the norm of *univocal reciprocity*, as a universal phenomenon, requires that people (X_i) should help others (Y_i) who now need the type of help they (X_i) themselves may need from some others (Z_i) in the future. Similarly, it also requires that people (X_i) should help others (Y_i) who now need help for which they (X_i) were provided by some others (Z_i) in the past. The second part of Gouldner's statement of the norm of mutual reciprocity can also be generalized into a univocal reciprocity form. It might require, though, that the matter be looked at not entirely in negative terms. For instance, the norm of revenge—an eye for an eye—may well be made part of the second part of the norm of reciprocity. However, I shall leave that task alone at this point—after all, the second part of Gouldner's statement is less important for social exchange processes.

So far, I have attempted to point up the crucial significance of Lévi-Strauss' distinction between mutual reciprocity and univocal reciprocity for general sociological theory. I have not dealt with what conceptions of reciprocity other social exchange theorists employed in characterizing social exchange processes. Although Lévi-Strauss was the first, at least in the domain of social exchange theory, to see the need to draw a distinction between mutual and univocal reciprocities, the conception of univocal reciprocity was already implied in Malinowski's social exchange theory. His may not be very visible because he tended to combine mutual reciprocity and univocal reciprocity in the same social exchange transaction.

As the reader may have suspected, Homans' and Blau's social exchange theories remain stunted at the level of mutual reciprocity. This is hardly a specific criticism directed against them. In relying on mutual reciprocity for their analysis, they were being true to modern sociological theory in its emphasis on mutual reciprocity as providing the dominant basis for social interaction. But both Homans and Blau did see the disadvantages of the two-person interaction model. Homans rationalized them away; Blau interpreted the problem as one limited to isolated pairs and took comfort in broadening the meaning of mutual reciprocity to two-person interactions implicated in larger wholes.

As Gouldner [1960: 169] has indicated, one's conception of social exchange is as good as one's conception or reciprocity. From this consideration of the structure of reciprocity we now move over to examine social exchange processes more directly.

Restricted Exchange and Generalized Exchange

It is dissatisfaction with the two-party model of mutual reciprocity and two-party exchange theoretical formulations that led Lévi-Strauss [cf. 1969: 144, 220] to generalized exchange:

> A formal study of the notion of exchange, such as sociologists have so far employed, has shown us that it did not succeed in embracing the facts in their integrity. Rather than deciding to lend a sterile discontinuity to phenomena which are, after all, of the same type, we have preferred to seek a wider and modified conception of exchange in an attempt to arrive at a systematic typology and an exhaustive explanation [Lévi-Strauss, 1969: 220].

'Generalized exchange' is the term introduced by Lévi-Strauss to account for what restricted exchange, limited to two parties, could not explain or could only explain at the cost of distorting social reality. Restricted exchange operates on the principle of mutual reciprocity—and its companion moral principle is the norm of mutual reciprocity as stated by Gouldner. Generalized exchange operates on the principle of univocal reciprocity—and its companion moral principle is the norm of univocal reciprocity.

Lévi-Strauss' distinction between restricted exchange and generalized exchange is by far the most important development in social exchange theory. As he has stressed, he introduced the concept of generalized exchange into social theory for the important reason that the explanatory power of restricted exchange was limited. Ironically, Homans' distaste for the conception of generalized exchange led him back to an ever greater emphasis on restricted exchange in his social exchange theory and although he saw its limitations he was satisfied to live with them and sometimes to rationalize them. Blau has closely followed the footpaths of Homans in this matter, although he did complain about (apparently Homans') artificially abstracted isolated pairs of social exchange actors. Both Homans and Blau of course have a concept of 'indirect exchange', but it is totally different from generalized exchange. By indirect exchange Homans and Blau ultimately mean institutionalized behavior in which social roles, norms, and institutions replace the part played by individuals in social exchange.

I have sought to show that Lévi-Strauss' seminal distinction between restricted exchange and generalized exchange needs further elaboration to enrich its value for social theory. Briefly I have argued that there are two forms of restricted exchange: *exclusive restricted exchange*, in which the dyadic relationships are totally isolated; and *inclusive restricted exchange*, in which the dyadic relationships are implicated in a network with other dyadic exchange relationships. [Thus A↔B represents an exclusive restricted exchange. A↔B; C↔D; E↔F; represent inclusive restricted exchanges.] Similarly, I have argued that there are two main types of generalized exchange: *chain generalized exchange* and *net generalized exchange*. In chain generalized exchange [represented as A→B→C→Z→A] each unit of the social exchange process is equal. In net generalized exchange each unit acts in relationship with the group as a whole. There are two sub-types of this: *group-focused generalized exchange* [represented as A→BCDE; B→ACDE; C→ABDE; D→ABCE; and E→ABCD] and *individual-focused generalized exchange* [ABCD→E; ABCE→D; ABDE→C; ACDE→B; and BCDE→A]. On the whole the distinction between restricted exchange and generalized exchange represents a phenotypically qualitative difference in the operation of social exchange mechanisms in pairs and larger groups—analogous to Simmel's and Bales and Borgatta's [1955] qualitative distinction between the operation of dyads and of larger groups.

Malinowski also has a conception of circular exchange which is remarkably similar to Lévi-Strauss' generalized exchange. What is unique in Malinowski's social exchange theory, though, is that he interpreted Kula exchange in the Trobriands as simultaneously operating generalized exchange and restricted exchange—and thus working to combine the strength in the two types of exchange. While restricted exchange emphasizes the psychological needs of the individual exchange actors, generalized exchange strengthens the bonds of solidarity in society. This interpretation enables Malinowski to work out an isomorphism between individual psychological needs and the social needs of the wider society— a social theoretical strategy now well developed by Erich Fromm in his theory of social character. I believe, thus, that it is a mistaken interpretation to see Malinowski as opposing individual needs against societal needs or as implying that societal needs do not exist of their own—as Homans seems to suggest in his various comments on Malinowski's work.

Given his collectivistic orientation in sociology, Lévi-Strauss is antagonistic to the strategy of deriving higher-order phenomena from the more elementary processes of social exchange. But individualistic sociologists, notably Homans and Blau, have been enthusiastic in seeking to derive such higher-order processes from more basic social exchange processes. I suggest that their efforts would have been more successful and more realistic were they to seek to derive these higher-order processes from generalized exchange rather than, as they have sought to do, from restricted exchange. The theoretical potential, that is, of generalized exchange seems to me to open up new vistas for the adventurous social exchange theorist. By contrast, we may note that sociologists who have been limited to work within the framework of restricted exchange, as of the model of mutual reciprocity, are bound to strain the strength of their theoretical models very easily. We see this result in Homans' *Social Behavior: Its Elementary Forms* when he forces an interpretation of multiperson interactions into his theoretical model of restricted exchange.

Exploitation and Power

One of the unexplored potentials in Gouldner's [1960] essay on reciprocity is his conception of exploitation. He has predicted that the concept of exploitation would be difficult to salvage in sociology because of its anti-establishment ideological connotations. But Gouldner has failed to see another important reason why sociology has systematically neglected the analysis of exploitation: it is the fact that *exploitation* is predicated on the value obverse of the *legitimation of power*. As long as sociology concerns itself with discovering the mechanisms for the legitimation of power and status differentiations, so long will exploitation be brushed aside in sociology. The reason behind this inverse relationship between legitimation of power and focus on the problem of exploitation will be my central concern at this point.

In fearing that sociologists would demur at the notion of exploitation, Gouldner coined a substitute term 'reciprocity imbalance'. Blau has adopted the term into his social exchange theory. Curiously, however, the adoption was made by Blau in the analysis of social power, not in the analysis of exploitation. In effect, Blau's analysis of social power denies that there is anything like 'unequal exchange' (another of Gouldner's substitute terms for 'exploitation'). Blau's theory of social power implies that the social exchange equation always balances between the two sides to the exchange. If A does not have enough to reciprocate B for services rendered, A compensates B by recognizing B's power over A.

There is a hidden assumption in Blau's social exchange theory of power. It assumes that inequality is a legitimate value premise in social exchange relations. Such an assumption is directly opposite that implied in the conception of exploitation. Social exploitation results in situations in which there are certain normative expectations about the equality or inequality of those engaged in an interaction. If, as Lévi-Strauss emphasizes, equality of status between partners is expected in social exchange relations, then inequality is viewed in the context of exploitation. If, on the other hand, as Frazer, Homans, and Blau assume, inequality between the parties to social exchange is expected in social exchange relations (partly because, anyway, the exchange items have differential economic values), then power replaces exploitation in the view of the social exchange theorist. That is why what Blau calls power could readily be termed exploitation by Durkheim, Lévi-Strauss, or Marx. For in this matter the collectivistic sociologists and the Marxists agree: individuals in social relations are expected to be equal. This is the 'latent convergence' between the Marxist tradition and the 'Comtcian' (i.e., collectivistic) tradition in sociology that Gouldner [1960: 167] has emphasized.

In effect, the theory of power becomes the theory of exploitation once the *value assumptions* about the legitimacy of equality or of inequality of the social exchange partners are reversed. Exploitation, thus, can be defined into existence in any society by a new sensitivity to the need for equality or by changes in the value premises of the society concerning inequality. Blau's social exchange theory of power can similarly be reversed by, say a Marxist, into a social exchange theory of exploitation by making the opposite assumptions on the justice of inequality that Blau makes. Exploitation and power are the opposite results of value assumptions concerning the justice or injustice of inequality in a social system.

It is in terms of such value premises concerning the equality of social exchange partners that we must assess the sociological meaning of Homans' conception of distributive justice. As I emphasized previously, Homans' distributive justice rules are premised on the value expectations that inequalities are just in society. On the other hand, liberal thought, let alone Marxist radical thought, makes the assumption [e.g., McCloskey, 1966] that equality is a desideratum in social relations and, indeed, that equality is an irreducible value in society. Homans' posture leads to an emphasis on the legitimacy of power and status differentiations; the liberal assumption directs attention to the injustice of inequality and exploitation between social exchange actors.

Gouldner's [1960] conception of exploitation is thus tacitly based on the legitimacy of equality (or, perhaps more powerfully, the illegitimacy of inequality) between the parties to the exchange. (It should be remembered that Gouldner's concern was with functional reciprocity between the parts of the social system.) Blau's conception of power, on the other hand, is premised on the legitimacy of inequality in social exchange relations. But both of these conceptions of exploitation and power are predicated on restricted exchange relations and mutual reciprocity (with their companion moral principle of the norm of mutual reciprocity). As such their meanings of exploitation and power are circumscribed by the limited potentials of restricted exchange and mutual reciprocity in social analysis. The meanings of these terms become immeasurably expanded, however, if we seek to predicate them on the broader conceptions of generalized exchange and univocal reciprocity. In particular, the application of these conceptions in the analysis of social power in social exchange relations would lead to some important results. For one thing, it opens up the possibility that social power can be exercised simultaneously by several persons in the same unit time and space, rather than be concentrated in the hands of one man. As such the cost of power to subordinates may be appreciably reduced. Perhaps more importantly, the conception of power in terms of univocal reciprocity and generalized exchange would seem to lead to a conception of plenitude of power, rather than to a sterile zero-sum conception of power. For another thing, univocal reciprocity and generalized exchange operate much more on societal moral mandates than mutual reciprocity and restricted exchange; accordingly power derived from generalized exchange and univocal reciprocity may be more sanctioned by societal norms—especially those justifying inequality—than the market-place definition of power that flows from restricted exchange as an economically expendable quantity.

The analysis of exploitation in terms of univocal reciprocity and generalized exchange may lead to similar expansions of meaning. Exploitation in mutual reciprocity, as in monogamous marriages, is readily visible. Imbalances in restricted social exchange, as Homans [1961: 61] was quick to see, can lead to a break-up of the social exchange transactions because, although Homans would not of course use that term given his value assumptions, they make the relations exploitative. But exploitation in univocal reciprocity and generalized exchange situations is much more subtle: the source of exploitation is less easily detectable and exploitation therein will contribute to social disruption less readily. This appears to be the meaning of exploitation in Marx. As Gouldner [1970: 181] puts it elsewhere, Marx saw that 'the fault of capitalist exploitation . . . rests not with the individual capitalist but with the social system that constrains him to exploit or be ruined'. Exploitation in generalized exchange situations is attributable to the system rather than to individuals. By making the imbalanced exchanges less visible, univocal reciprocity and generalized exchange make the exploitation more thorough-going and more effective.

Social Exchange and Social Solidarity

One of the signal inadequacies in Homans' social exchange theory is his impotent recognition that imbalanced exchanges, in which one party is making a profit but the other is not, are inherently unstable [Homans, 1961: 61]. It is impotent because he does nothing to solve the problem of maintaining social order by avoiding such instabilities except through the stealth of his distributive justice rules, the regulative normative basis of which he denies anyway. The truth is that by itself restricted social exchange based on economic motives poses a dilemma that Gouldner [1970]

detects in Parsons' sociology. Once economic motives determine
our actions it is important that we maximize our resources and
seek the best sources for striking the most profitable bargain. Yet
restricted exchanges involve visible comparisons. The individual
can find out without difficulty that his efforts are either more or
less productive than his partner's and if he gains less from the
interaction his self-interest dictates that he should break up the
relationship and seek new partners. Instabilities would thus be
the rule rather than the exception in social exchange interactions.

Homans sought to solve this problem by deadening the hedonist
urge and the potency of the economic motives in the social
exchange actor through the introduction of his theory of distributive justice. The theory, based on the legitimacy of inequalities in social relations, supports stable social relations in
spite of differential rewards because it conditions rewards on
inequalities of status, ability, and contributions to the group. Yet
inequalities in restricted exchange situations are very costly
because they are very visible. That is to say, inequalities based
on distributive justice may be difficult to justify in mutual
reciprocity. On the whole then the dilemma of social instabilities
(created by hedonist urges and the drive of economic motives)
cannot be fully solved in terms of the theory of distributive
justice in dyadic relationships to which Homans limited his social
exchange theory. It does not seem unfair to say that Homans did
not solve the problem of social disorder which his theory leads to.

Homans could of course object that there is nothing like
social order apart from what individuals in the group judge to
be desirable for them. Maybe, then, we should say that Homans'
social exchange theory may lead to the expectation of a high
turnover in social relations, hardly an appetizing way of describing
what is desirable for individuals in a group. If Homans had
attempted a social exchange theory of social solidarity, beyond
his theory of distributive justice, his would have to be a contractual theory of social solidarity. Actors would individually
seek to maximize their private interests by agreeing to what is
mutually beneficial to everybody in the group. There are two
reasons, however, why Homans could not maintain such a contractual theory of social solidarity within the framework of his
social exchange theory. First, the emphasis on conditioned
psychological behavior is antithetical to any emphasis on future

and voluntarily planned actions which are implied in contractual theories of social solidarity. Secondly, mutual reciprocity and restricted exchange transactions emphasize the cost of social action as well as its rewards and would expose agreements to emotional reactions that are hardly conducive to mutually contracted social solidarity. As we have stated the matter, restricted exchanges encourage interpersonal comparisons rather than intrapersonal comparisons. It is univocal reciprocal relationships that could eliminate such interpersonal comparisons and make possible contractual social solidarity by leading the individual to evaluate his acts independently—in terms of his rewards as compared to his costs.

My point here is that it is difficult to derive social solidarity from mutual reciprocity and restricted exchange processes. It would be much easier for individualistic sociologists to attempt to derive contractual social solidarity from univocal reciprocity and generalized exchange and from the morality of social exchange generalized to the society, including the norm of univocal reciprocity. The difficulty here can be illustrated from Blau's [1964a] attempt to account for social solidarity in society. In effect he offered two independent sources for social solidarity. Blau at first sees social solidarity in terms of mutual reciprocal relations between high and low status sections in groups in restricted exchange terms:

> Associations have to be intrinsically attractive for large-scale participation to occur, and integrative bonds of fellowship make them so. Some group members must compete for superior status to furnish a screening device for effective leadership, but to maintain social integration there must be many who do not participate in this competition. The members who cease to compete for superior status win social acceptance in the group in exchange for the contribution they make to group solidarity [Blau, 1964a: 50].

In other words, group solidarity is the result of individual decisions and actions or inactions. But Blau would be at a loss were he to give reasons why some individuals must give up competition for leadership for the sheer joy of 'social acceptance' in the group. Such *ad hoc*, apparently unplanned, contractual relations between high status and low status individuals in a mutual reciprocity fashion would be inherently unstable given the premises of the maximization of one's resources implied in his economically motivated social exchange theory. In the long run Blau had to beg the question by freely accepting Durkheim's theory of social solidarity, without however mentioning Durkheim's criticisms of his first position, that of Spencerian contractual theory of social solidarity. By freely swinging from one level to another, Blau was able to slip from an untenable micro-self-interest theory of social solidarity, in terms of his restricted exchange theory, to a more acceptable macro-group-attribute theory of social solidarity:

> Particularistic social values . . . are media of social integration and solidarity. The distinctive values they share unite the members of a collectivity in common social solidarity and extend the scope of integrative bonds far beyond the limits of personal feelings of attraction. These cultural or subcultural beliefs become symbols of group identity that define the boundary between the ingroup and the outgroup. The particular shared values that distinguish a collectivity from others constitute the medium through which its members are bound together into a cohesive community. They serve in this way as functional substitutes for the sentiments of personal attraction that integrate the members of a face-to-face group into a cohesive unit [Blau, 1964a: 267].

Blau's acceptance of Durkheim's theory of mechanical solidarity must be seen outside the context of his social exchange theory. His social exchange theory can only result in contractual social solidarity. But such contractual social solidarity would be fragile were it to be based on mutual reciprocity and restricted exchange. Blau, thanks to the freedom of easy escape from one level of analysis to another, had to look for his theory of social solidarity in the realm of constraining social values. Generalized exchange might have provided Blau with a consistent social exchange theory of social solidarity and spared him the embarrassment of introducing social values *sui generis*, which implicitly deny the potency of individual economic motivations in social exchange situations.

Lévi-Strauss and Mauss were able to indicate, more or less clearly, the possibility of a consistent social exchange theory of social solidarity by denying individual economic motivations in social exchange processes. Lévi-Strauss' conception of restricted exchange and generalized exchange parallels Durkheim's distinction between mechanical solidarity and organic solidarity. Emotion-laden restricted exchanges are not a powerful basis for erecting lasting social solidarity; it is generalized exchanges that provide such a basis. By denying economic motivations in social exchange processes, Lévi-Strauss' social exchange theory complements Durkheim's theory of social solidarity in basing stable social relations on shared values and in thus rejecting Spencerian contractual social solidarity implied in Homans' and Blau's characterizations of social exchange processes.

The most intriguing possibility, still largely unexplored, in the area of social solidarity with respect to social exchange processes is contained in Malinowski's discussion of Kula social exchange processes. Social solidarity emerges as a result of the interaction between restricted exchange and generalized exchange. For Malinowski, these two processes are not mutually exclusive; rather the highest and the finest in social relations is achieved when they converge. Thus in Kula exchange the individual actor simultaneously satisfies his psychological needs by direct or restricted exchange transactions, and helps to build up a framework for social solidarity by engaging at the same time in generalized exchange. Again, it is noteworthy that Malinowski sees such social solidarity as possible only in the absence of economic motivations in social exchange transactions.

Concluding Remarks

One of the enduring differences between the natural sciences and the social sciences may be seen in terms of the nature of progress in these fields. In the natural sciences, progress renders past achievements smaller and past great names become matters of historical curiosity. It is a rare physicist who goes back to read Newton! On the other hand, in sociology new discoveries and new insights only serve to deepen past achievements and the significance of early thinkers. Our examination of social exchange theory may provide a clue to this attribute of progress in sociological theory: development is hardly ever in a linear form. Social exchange theory has been developed in the midst of reactions to other theorists' positions on the subject of social exchange behaviors. Hence a theorist's position on the subject of social exchange has usually enhanced other positions.

Discourse and debate deepen and give stability to any sociological theoretical perspective. Unlike functionalism and social conflict—both of them prominent theoretical perspectives that benefited from this aspect of the sociological enterprise—social exchange theory has so far seen very little of such debate and discourse. If this monograph is able to provoke any meaningful debate on this subject, it will have contributed something to the sociological profession. Neither the theorists discussed in this book nor the unit-ideas analyzed in the last chapter are likely to disappear from serious sociological thinking as a result of such debate and discourse. On the contrary, any deepening of the social exchange perspective is bound to enhance the significance of these theorists and to lead to a richer analysis of these unit-ideas. Try as they may, sociologists cannot brush aside their intellectual forefathers. This is partly because the forefathers in sociology do not belong to all of us. Homans is likely to remain a forefather for some, while Lévi-Strauss will remain the authentic forefather for other exchange theorists. Such diversity will benefit the social exchange perspective—as it has brought richness and insight to other perspectives in our discipline.

References

Aberle, D. F., A. K. Cohen, A. K. Davis, M. J. Levy, Jr., and F. X. Sutton
   1950 'The Functional Prerequisites of a Society.' *Ethics*, 60 (Jan.):
         100–111.
Abrahamson, Bengt
   1970 'Homans on Exchange: Hedonism Revisited.' *American Journal of
         Sociology*, 76 (Sept.): 273–285.
Bales, Robert F. and Philip E. Slater
   1953 'Role Differentiation in Small Decision-Making Groups,' in Talcott
         Parsons, Robert F. Bales, and Edward A. Shils, *Working Papers in the
         Theory of Action*. Glencoe, Illinois: The Free Press.
Bales, Robert F. and Edgar F. Borgatta
   1955 'Size of Group as a Factor in the Interaction Profile.' Pp. 396–413
         in A. Paul Hare, E. F. Borgatta, and R. F. Bales, eds., *Small Groups:
         Studies in Social Interaction*. New York: Alfred A. Knopf. First
         Edition.
   1965 'Size of Group as a Factor in the Interaction Profile.' Pp. 495–512
         in A. Paul Hare, Edgar F. Borgatta, and Robert F. Bales, eds.,
         Small Groups: Studies in Social Interaction. New York: Alfred A.
         Knopf. Revised Edition.
Banfield, Edward C.
   1958 *The Moral Basis of a Backward Society*. New York: The Free Press.
Barnett, S. A.
   1967 *Instinct and Intelligence: Behavior of Animals and Man*. Englewood
         Cliffs, N.J.: Prentice-Hall.
Bavelas, Alex
   1950 'Communication Patterns in Task-oriented Groups.' *The Journal of
         the Acoustical Society of America*, 22 (Nov.): 725–730.
Belshaw, Cyril S.
   1965 *Traditional Exchange and Modern Markets*. Englewood Cliffs, N.J.:
         Prentice-Hall.
Bendix, Reinhard
   1964 *Nation-Building and Citizenship*. New York: John Wiley & Sons.
Berlin, I.
   1955–56 'Equality.' *Proceedings of the Aristotelian Society*, 56: 281–326.
Bertalanffy, Ludwig von
   1969 'Chance or Law.' Pp. 56–76 in Koestler & Smythies (1969).

Bertling, J. and H. Philipsen
    1960 'Solidarity, Stratification and Sentiments: the Unilateral Cross-Cousin Marriage According to the Theories of Lévi-Strauss, Leach, and Homans and Schneider.' *Bijdragen tot de Taal-, Land- en Volkenkunde*, 116: 55–80.

Blain, Robert R.
    1971a 'An Alternative to Parsons' Four-Function Paradigm as a Basis for Developing General Sociological Theory.' *American Sociological Review*, 36 (August): 678–692.
    1971b 'On Homans' Psychological Reductionism.' *Sociological Inquiry*, 41 (Winter), 3–25.

Blau, Peter M.
    1960 'Structural Effects.' *American Sociological Review*, 25: 178–193.
    1964a *Exchange and Power in Social Life*. New York: John Wiley & Sons.
    1964b 'Justice in Social Exchange.' *Sociological Inquiry*, 34: 193–206.
    1968 'Interaction: Social Exchange.' Pp. 452–458 in David L. Sills, ed., *International Encyclopedia of the Social Sciences, Volume 7*. New York: Macmillan and The Free Press.
    1969 'Objectives of Sociology.' Pp. 43–71 in Robert Bierstedt, ed., *A Design for Sociology: Scope, Objectives, and Methods*. Philadelphia: The American Academy of Political and Social Science.

Blumer, Herbert
    1937 'Social Psychology' in Emerson P. Schmidt, ed., *Man and Society*. New York: Prentice-Hall.
    1969 *Symbolic Interactionism: Perspective and Method*. Englewood Cliffs, N.J.: Prentice-Hall.

Bohannan, Paul
    1955 'Some Principles of Exchange and Investment Among the Tiv.' *American Anthropologist*, 57: 60–70.
    1960 (ed.), *African Homicide and Suicide*. Princeton, N.J.: Princeton University Press.

Burgess, Robert L. and Don Bushell, Jr.
    1969 *Behavioral Sociology: The Experimental Analysis of Social Process*. New York: Columbia University Press.

Busia, A. K.
    1951 *The Position of the Chief in the Modern Political System of Ashanti*. London: International African Institute.

Chavannes, Albert
    1884 *Studies in Sociology* cited in Knox (1963).

Cohen, Percy S.
    1968 *Modern Social Theory*. New York: Basic Books. London: Heinemann Educational Books.

Coleman, James S.
    1964 'Collective Decisions.' *Sociological Inquiry*, 34: 166–181.

Comte, Auguste
    1848 *General View of Positivism*. [Academic Reprints, Stanford, California].

Cooley, Charles Horton
    1909 *Social Organization*. New York: Charles Scribner's Sons.

Coser, Lewis A. and Bernard Rosenberg, editors
   1957   *Sociological Theory: A Book of Readings.* New York: The Macmillan Company.
Davis, Kingsley and Judith Blake
   1964   'Norms, Values, and Sanctions.' Pp. 456–484 in Robert E. L. Faris, ed., *Handbook of Modern Sociology.* Chicago: Rand McNally & Company.
Davis, Kingsley and Wilbert E. Moore
   1945   'Some Principles of Stratification.' *American Sociological Review,* 10: 242–249.
Denzin, Norman K.
   1969   'Symbolic Interactionism and Ethnomethodology: A Proposed Synthesis.' *American Sociological Review,* 34: 922–934.
Deutsch, Morton
   1964   'Homans in the Skinner Box.' *Sociological Inquiry,* 34: 156–165.
Deutsch, Morton and Robert M. Krauss
   1965   *Theories in Social Psychology.* New York: Basic Books.
Dollard, John, Neal E. Miller, Leonard W. Doob, O. H. Mowrer, and Robert R. Sears
   1939   *Frustration and Aggression.* New Haven: Yale University Press.
Durkheim, Emile
   1915   *The Elementary Forms of the Religious Life.* New York: The Free Press Paperback Edition, 1965.
   1933   *The Division of Labor in Society.* New York: The Free Press. First published 1893.
   1938   *The Rules of Sociological Method.* New York: The Free Press.
   1950   *Professional Ethics and Civic Morals* translated by C. Brookfield. New York: The Free Press, 1958.
   1951   *Suicide.* New York: The Free Press. First published 1897.
Ekeh, Peter P.
   1968   'Issues in Social Exchange Theory.' *Berkeley Journal of Sociology,* 13: 42–58.
Emmerson, Richard M.
   1962   'Power-Dependence Relations.' *American Sociological Review,* 27: 31–41.
   1969   'Operant Psychology and Exchange Theory.' Pp. 379–405 in Robert L. Burgess and Don Bushell, Jr. *Behavioral Sociology.* New York: Columbia University Press.
   1972   'Exchange Theory, Part II; Exchange Relations, Exchange Networks and Groups as Exchange Systems' in Joseph Berger, Morris Zelditch, and Bo Anderson, editors, *Sociological Theories in Progress Vol II.* Boston: Houghton-Mifflin.
Etzioni, Amitai
   1963   'The Epigenesis of Political Communities at the International Level,' *American Journal of Sociology* [68: 407–421], as reprinted in Amitai Etzioni and Eva Etzioni, *Social Change.* New York: Basic Books, 1964.
   1966   *Studies in Social Change.* New York: Holt, Rinehart and Winston.

Firth, Raymond W.
  1936   *We the Tikopia.* London: Allen and Unwin.
  1957   'The Place of Malinowski in the History of Economic Anthro-
          pology.' Pp. 209–277 in R. Firth, ed., *Man and Culture, An Evaluation
          of the Work of Bronislaw Malinowski.* New York: The Humanities Press.
Fortes, M.
  1945   *The Dynamics of Clanship Among the Tallensi.* New York: Humanities
          Press.
  1949   *The Web of Kinship Among the Tallensi.* New York: Humanities Press.
  1960   'The Structure of Unilineal Descent Groups.' Pp. 163–189 in Simon
          and Phoebe Ottenberg, eds., *Cultures and Societies of Africa.* New
          York: Random House.
Frankl, Viktor E.
  1969   'Reductionism and Nihilism.' Pp. 396–416 in Arthur Koester and
          F. R. Smythies (1969).
Frazer, Sir James G.
  1910   *Totemism and Exogamy: A Treatise on Certain Early Forms of Super-
          stition and Society. Vol I.* London: Dawsons of Pall Mall, 1968.
  1919   *Folklore in the Old Testament Vol. II.* London: Macmillan & Co.
  1922   'Preface' to *Argonauts of the Western Pacific.* [Pp. vii–xiv.] London:
          Routledge & Kegan.
Freud, Sigmund
  1913   *Totem and Taboo.* New York: Vintage Books.
Fromm, Erich
  1944   'Individual and Social Origins of Neurosis.' *American Sociological
          Review,* 9: 380–384.
Gardner, Howard
  1973   *The Quest for Mind: Piaget, Lévi-Strauss and the Structuralist Movement.*
          New York: Alfred A. Knopf.
de George, Richard T. and Fernande M. de George, eds.,
  1972   *The Structuralists: From Marx to Lévi-Strauss.* New York: Doubleday
          & Company.
Glaser, Barney G. and Anselm L. Strauss
  1966   *The Discovery of Grounded Theory.* Chicago: Aldine Publishing
          Company.
Gluckman, Max
  1957   *Custom and Conflict in Africa.* Glencoe, Illinois: The Free Press.
Gouldner, Alvin W.
  1959   'Reciprocity and Autonomy in Functional Theory.' Pp. 241–270 in
          Llewellyn Gross, ed., *Synposium on Sociological Theory.* New York:
          Harper & Row.
  1960   'The Norm of Reciprocity: a preliminary statement.' *American
          Sociological Review,* 25: 161–179.
  1970   *The Coming Crisis of Western Sociology.* New York: Basic Books.
          London: Heinemann Educational Books.
Hagen, Everett E.
  1962   *On the Theory of Social Change: How Economic Growth Begins.* Home-
          wood, Illinois: The Dorsey Press.

Halévy, Elie
 1928　*The Growth of Philosophical Radicalism.* London: Faber & Faber.

Hartuung, Frank E.
 1960　'Behavior, Culture, and Symbolism.' Pp. 231–248 in Gertrude E. Dole and Robert L. Carneiro, eds., *Essays in the Science of Culture in Honor of Leslie A. White.* New York: Thomas Y. Crowell Co.

Heath, A.
 1968　'Economic Theory and Sociology: a Critique of P. M. Blau's *Exchange and Power in Social Life.*' *Sociology*, 2: 273–292.

Homans, George C.
 1941　*English Villagers of the Thirteenth Century.* Cambridge, Mass.: Harvard University Press.
 1947　'A Conceptual Scheme for the Study of Social Organization.' *American Sociological Review*, 12 (Feb.): 13–26.
 1950　*The Human Group.* New York: Harcourt, Brace & World.
 1958　'Social Behavior as Exchange.' *American Journal of Sociology*, 63 (May): 597–606.
 1961　*Social Behavior: Its Elementary Forms.* New York: Harcourt, Brace & World.
 1962　*Sentiments and Activities.* New York: The Free Press.
 1964a　'Bringing Men Back In.' *American Sociological Review*, 29: 809–818.
 1964b　'Commentary.' *Sociological Inquiry*, 34: 221–231.
 1964c　'Contemporary Theory in Sociology.' Pp. 951–977 in Robert F. L. Faris, ed., *Handbook of Modern Sociology.* Chicago: Rand McNally.
 1967a　'Fundamental Social Processes.' Pp. 27–78 in Neil J. Smelser, ed., *Sociology.* New York: Wiley & Sons.
 1967b　*The Nature of Social Science.* New York: Harcourt, Brace & World.
 1968　'A Life of Synthesis.' *American Behavioral Scientist*, 12 (Sept.–Oct.): 2–8.
 1969　'The Sociological Relevance of Behaviorism.' Pp. 1–24 in Robert L. Burgess and Don Bushell, Jr. *Behavioral Sociology.* New York: Columbia University Press.
 1971　'Reply to Blain.' *Sociological Inquiry*, 41: 19–24.

Homans, George C. and David M. Schneider
 1955　*Marriage, Authority, and Final Causes: A Study of Unilateral Cross-Cousin Marriage.* New York: The Free Press. Reprinted in Homans (1962).

Inkeles, Alex
 1959a　'Personality and Social Structure.' Pp. 249–276 in Robert Merton, Leonard Broom, and Leonard S. Cotterel, Jr., *Sociology Today.* New York: Basic Books.
 1959b　'Psychoanalysis and Sociology.' Pp. 117–129 in Sidney Hook, ed., *Psychoanalysis, Scientific Method, and Philosophy.* New York: New York University Press.
 1963　'Sociology and Psychology.' Pp. 317–387 in Sigmund Koch, ed., *Psychology: A Study of a Science, Vol 6.* New York: McGraw-Hill Book Co.

Janowitz, Morris
1967 'Review of *The Sociological Tradition*.' *American Sociological Review*, 32: 638–640.
Jeffreys, M. D. W.
1952 'Samsonic Suicide or Suicide of Revenge Among Africans.' *African Studies*, 11: 118–122.
Kaplan, Abraham
1964 *The Conduct of Inquiry*. San Francisco: Chandler Publishing Co.
Karpf, Fay Berger
1932 *American Social Psychology: Its Origins, Development, and European Background*. New York and London: McGraw-Hill Book Co.
Knox, John B.
1963 'The Concept of Exchange in Sociological Theory: 1884 and 1961.' *Social Forces*, 41: 341–346.
Koestler, Arthur and F. R. Smythies, eds.,
1969 *Beyond Reductionism: New Perspectives in the Life Sciences*. Boston: Beacon Press.
Lamont, W. D.
1941 'Justice: Distributive and Corrective.' *Philosophy: The Journal of the British Institute of Philosophy*, 16 (Jan.): 3–18.
Lane, Barbara
1961 'Structural Contrasts between Symmetric and Asymmetric Marriage Systems: A Fallacy.' *Southwestern Journal of Anthropology*, 17 (Spring): 49–55.
Lauer, Robert H.
1971 'The Scientific Legitimation of Fallacy: Neutralizing Social Change Theory.' *American Sociological Review*, 36 (October): 881–889.
de Lauwe, Paul-Henri Chambat
1966 'The Interaction of Person and Society.' *American Sociological Review*, 31 (April): 237–248.
Leach, Edmund
1970 *Claude Lévi-Strauss*. New York: The Viking Press.
Lemann, T. B. and R. L. Solomon
1952 'Group Characteristics as Revealed in Sociometric Patterns and Personality Ratings.' *Sociometry*, 15 (Feb.–May): 7–90.
Lévi-Strauss, Claude
1949 *Les Structures élémentaires de la Parenté*. Paris: Presses Universitaires de France.
1957 'The Principle of Reciprocity.' Pp. 84–94 in Lewis A. Coser and Bernard Rosenberg, eds., *Sociological Theory: A Book of Readings*. New York: The Macmillan Press.
1958 *Structural Anthropology*. New York: Basic Books, 1963.
1960 'On Manipulated Sociological Models.' *Bijdragen tot de Taal-, Land-en Volkenkunde*, 116: 45–54.
1962 *The Savage Mind*. Chicago: The University of Chicago Press, 1966.
1963 *Structural Anthropology*. New York: Doubleday & Company, 1967.
1964 *Mythologiques I: le cru et le cuit*. Paris: Plon.

1966a *Mythologiques II: du miel aux cendres.* Paris: Plon.
1966b 'The Scope of Anthropology.' *Current Anthropology,* 7: 112–123.
1968 *Mythologiques III: l' origine de manières de table.* Paris: Plon.
1969 *The Elementary Structures of Kinship.* Boston: Beacon Press. English translation of Claude Lévi-Strauss, *Les Structures élémentaires de la Parenté.* 1967 Revised Edition.
Linton, Ralph
1936 *The Study of Man.* New York: Appleton-Century.
Lloyd, P. C.
1962 *Yoruba Land Law.* London: Oxford University Press.
Lowenthal, Leo
1944 'Biographies in Popular Magazines.' Pp. 507–548 in Paul F. Lazersfeld and Frank N. Stanton, eds., *Radio Research 1942–43.* New York: Duell, Sloan and Pearce.
Malinowski, Bronislaw
1922 *Argonauts of the Western Pacific.* London: Routledge & Kegan Paul.
1926 *Crime and Custom in Savage Society.* London: Routledge & Kegan Paul.
1939 'The Group and the Individual in Functional Analysis.' *American Journal of Sociology,* 44 (May): 938–964.
1944 *A Scientific Theory of Culture and Other Essays.* Chapel Hill: The University of North Carolina Press.
Mannheim, Karl
1952 *Essays on the Sociology of Knowledge edited by Paul Kecskemeti.* London: Routledge & Kegan Paul.
Marshall, T. H.
1949 *Class, Citizenship, and Social Development.* New York: Doubleday & Company, 1964.
Mauss, Marcel
1925 *Essai sur le don in Sociologie et Anthropologie.* Paris: Presses Universitaires de France, 1950. Translated into English as *The Gift* (by Ian Cunnison). New York: The Free Press, 1954.
Mead, George Herbert
1934 *Mind, Self & Society From the Standpoint of a Social Behaviorist.* Chicago: The University of Chicago Press.
Miller, Daniel R. and Guy E. Swanson
1958 *The Changing American Parent.* New York: Wiley & Sons.
Mulkay, M. J.
1971 *Functionalism, Exchange, and Theoretical Strategy.* New York: Schocken Books.
McClelland, David C.
1955 'Some Social Consequences of Achievement Motivation.' Pp. 41–65 in M. R. Jones, ed., *Nebraska Symposium on Motivation.* Lincoln: University of Nebraska Press.
1961 *The Achieving Society.* Princeton, N.J.: D. Van Nostrand Company.
McClelland, David C. and David G. Winter
1969 *Motivating Economic Achievement.* New York: The Free Press.

McCloskey, H. J.
  1966 'Egalitarianism, Equality and Justice.' *Australasian Journal of Philosophy*, 44 (May): 50–69.
Needham, Rodney
  1962 *Structure and Sentiment.* Chicago: The University of Chicago Press.
Nisbet, Robert A.
  1966 *The Sociological Tradition.* New York: Basic Books. London: Heinemann Educational Books.
Park, R. E. and E. W. Burgess
  1922 *Introduction to the Science of Sociology.* Chicago: University of Chicago Press.
Parsons, Talcott
  1937 *The Structure of Social Action.* New York: McGraw-Hill Book Company.
  1940 'An Analytical Approach to the Theory of Social Stratification.' *American Journal of Sociology.* 45 (May): 841–862.
  1951 *The Social System.* New York: The Free Press.
  1953 'A Revised Analytical Approach to the Theory of Social Stratification' in R. Bendix and S. M. Lipset, eds., *Class, Status, and Power: A Reader in Social Stratification.* New York: The Free Press.
  1961a 'An Outline of the Social System.' Pp. 30–79 in Talcott Parsons, Edward Shils, Kaspar D. Naegele, and J. R. Pitts, eds., *The Theories of Society.* New York: The Free Press.
  1961b 'The General Interpretation of Action.' Pp. 85–97 in Talcott Parsons, Edward Shils, Kaspar D. Naegele, and J. R. Pitts, eds., *Theories of Society.* New York: The Free Press.
  1961c 'Some Considerations on the Theory of Social Change.' *Rural Sociology*, 26: 219–239.
  1964a 'Durkheim's Contribution to the Theory of Integration of Social Systems.' Pp. 118–153 in Kurt H. Wolff, ed., *Essays on Sociology and Philosophy by Emile Durkheim et al.* New York: Harper & Row.
  1964b 'Levels of Organization and the Mediation of Social Interaction.' *Sociological Inquiry*, 34: 207–220.
  1966 *Societies: Evolutionary and Comparative Perspectives.* Englewood Cliffs, N.J.: Prentice-Hall.
  1967 'Review of *The Sociological Tradition.*' *American Sociological Review*, 32 (Aug.): 640–643.
  1968 'Utilitarianism II: Sociological Thought.' Pp. 229–236 in David L. Sills, ed., *International Encyclopedia of the Social Sciences, Vol. 16.* New York: The Macmillan Company and The Free Press.
  1971 *The System of Modern Societies.* Englewood Cliffs, N.J.: Prentice-Hall.
Parsons, Talcott and Neil J. Smelser
  1956 *Economy and Society.* New York: The Free Press.
Piaget, Jean
  1932 *The Moral Judgement of the Child.* New York: The Free Press, 1955.
  1968 *Structuralism.* New York: Basic Books, 1970.
Radcliffe-Brown, A. R.
  1935 'On the Concept of Function in Social Science.' Reprinted in

A. R. Radcliffe-Brown, *Structure and Function in Primitive Society*. New York: The Free Press, 1952.

1940 'On Social Structure.' Reprinted in A. R. Radcliffe-Brown, *Structure and Function in Primitive Society*. New York: The Free Press, 1952.

Raphael, Daiches D.

1951–52 'Justice and Liberty.' *Proceedings of the Aristotelian Society*, 51: 167–196.

Redfield, Robert

1957 'The Universally Variable and the Culturally Variable.' *Journal of General Education*, 10 (July): 150–160. Also reprinted in *Human Nature and the Study of Society. The Papers of Robert Redfield, Vol. 1*, edited by Margaret Park Redfield, University of Chicago Press, 1962.

Rescher, Nicholas

1966 *Distributive Justice: A Constructive Critique of the Utilitarian Theory of Distribution*. Indianapolis: Bobbs-Merrill Company.

Rieken, Henry W. and George C. Homans

1954 'The Psychological Aspect of Social Structure.' Pp. 786–829 in Gardner Lindzey, ed., *Handbook of Social Psychology, Vol. 11*, Reading, Mass.: Addison-Wesley Publishing Company.

Riesman, David with Nathan Glazer and Reuel Denney

1950 *The Lonely Crowd, A Study of the Changing American Character*. New Haven: Yale University Press.

Ross, W. D.

1949 *Aristotle*. London: Methuen & Co.

Runciman, W. G.

1966 *Relative Deprivation and Social Justice, A Study of Attitudes to Social Inequality in Twentieth-Century England*. Berkeley and Los Angeles: University of California Press.

Ryan, John A.

1916 *Distributive Justice: The Right and Wrong of Our Present Distribution of Wealth*. New York: The Macmillan Company.

Sabine, George

1956 'Justice and Equality.' *Ethics*, 67 (October): 1–11.

Sahlins, Marshall D.

1965 'On the Sociology of Primitive Exchange.' Pp. 139–236 in *The Relevance of Models for Social Anthropology*. Associations of Social Anthropologists of the Commonwealth.

Scott, John Finley

1971 *Internalization of Norms: A Sociological Theory of Moral Commitment*. Englewood Cliffs, N.J.: Prentice-Hall.

Simmel, Georg

1950 *The Sociology of Georg Simmel. Translated, edited with an introduction by Kurt H. Wolff*. New York: The Free Press.

Singelmann, Peter

1972 'Exchange as Symbolic Interaction: Convergencies Between Two Theoretical Perspectives.' *American Sociological Review*, 37 (August): 414–424.

Skinner, B. F.
  1953 *Science and Human Behavior*, New York: The Free Press.
Smelser, Neil J.
  1959 *Social Change in the Industrial Revolution: An Application of Theory to the British Cotton Industry*. Chicago: The University of Chicago Press.
  1966 'Mechanisms of Change and Adjustment to Change.' Pp. 32–48 in Bert F. Hoselitz and Wilbert E. Moore, eds., *Industrialization and Society*, UNESCO, Paris: Mouton.
  1967 'Sociology and the Other Social Sciences.' Pp. 3–44 in Paul F. Lazersfeld, William H. Sewell, and Harold L. Wilensky, eds., *The Uses of Sociology*. New York: Basic Books.
Spencer, Herbert
  1864 *Reasons for Dissenting from the Philosophy of M. Comte and Other Essays*. Berkeley: The Glendessary Press, 1968.
  1893 *The Principles of Sociology. Vol. II-2*. New York and London: Appleton and Company.
  1896 *The Principles of Sociology. Vol. II-3*. New York and London: Appleton and Company.
Stark, Werner
  1958 *The Sociology of Knowledge: An Essay in Aid of a Deeper Understanding of the History of Ideas*. New York: The Free Press.
Stinchcombe, Arthur L.
  1968 *Constructing Social Theories*. New York: Harcourt, Brace & World.
Thibaut, John W. and Harold H. Kelley
  1959 *The Social Psychology of Groups*. New York: John Wiley & Sons.
Thompson, Clara, with the collaboration of Patrick Mullahy
  1950 *Psychoanalysis: Evolution and Development*. New York: Grove Press.
Thorpe, W. H.
  1969 'Retrospect.' Pp. 428–434 in Koestler and Smythies (1969).
Tsanoff, Radoslav A.
  1956 'Social Morality and the Principle of Justice.' *Ethics*, 67 (Oct.): 12–16.
Turk, Herman and Richard L. Simpson, eds.,
  1971 *Institutions and Social Exchange: The Sociologies of Talcott Parsons and George C. Homans*. Indianapolis: The Bobbs-Merrill Company.
Turner, Ralph H.
  1967 'Types of Solidarity in the Reconstituting of Groups.' *The Pacific Sociological Review*, 10: 60–68.
Uberoi, J. P. Singh
  1962 *Politics of the Kula Ring*. Manchester: Manchester University Press.
van den Berghe, Pierre L.
  1963 'Dialectic and Functionalism: Toward a Theoretical Synthesis.' *American Sociological Review*, 28: 695–705.
Veblen, Thorstein
  1954 *Imperial Germany and the Industrial Revolution*. New York: Viking Press.

Wallerstein, Robert S. and Neil J. Smelser
  1969 'Psychoanalysis and Sociology: Articulations and Applications.'
    International Journal of Psycho-Analysis, 50: 693–710.
Weber, Max
  1947 *The Theory of Social and Economic Organization*. New York: The Free
    Press.
White, Leslie A.
  1949 *The Science of Culture: A Study of Man and Civilization*. New York:
    Farrar, Strauss, and Giroux.
Whyte, William H., Jr.
  1956 *The Organization Man*. New York: Simon and Schuster.
Wolfenstein, Martha
  1951 'Fun Morality: An Analysis of Recent American Child-Training
    Literature.' *Journal of Social Issues*, 7: 15–25.
Wolin, Sheldon S.
  1960 *Politics and Vision: Continuity and Innovation in Western Political
    Thought*. Boston: Little, Brown, and Company.

Index

Aberle, D. F., and functional prerequisites, 70–1
American sociology, as individualistic sociology, 9
'Amoral familism', 59
Argonauts of the Western Pacific, 24–5, 31

Bales, R. F., group experiments of, 50, 52, 56
on reciprocity, 125, 126
Banfield, E. C., 59
Barnett, S. A., 102n
Bavelas, A., 55
Behavior, animal, 44–6, 98–102, 107, 108
conditioned, 98–102, 102–3, 107–110
human, 45, 46, 98–102, 107, 108
instinctual, 102–3
J. F. Scott on, 105, 106–7
natural, according to Lévi-Strauss, 45
social, 98–9, 101–2
symbolic, 102–3, 104, 105, 116
Behavior psychology, in social exchange theory, 166, 167, 172
and elementary economics, 111–19
and Homans, 90, 91, 95–7, 98–100, 120–21
extrapolation of, 112–13
Behaviorism, Watsonian, 104, 104n–105n
Belshaw, C. S., on economic exchange, 173
on Kula exchange, 60n

Bendix, R., on reciprocity, 206
Bertalanffy, Ludwig von, 93, 94
Blain, R. R., 72
Blake, J., *see* Davis, K.
Blau, Peter M., and logico-deduction tradition, 16
economic self interest, 167
on individualistic social exchange theory, 166–87
on reciprocity, 47, 109
on reductionism, 92
social exchange theory of, 20, 21, 23, 124, 167–87
basic premises of, 168–70
theory of power, 211
Blumer, H., on behaviorism, 108
Bohannan, Paul, 26n
on economic change, 173
on suicide, 151

Calvinism, 16–17, *see also* Protestantism
Ceremonial exchange, *see* Social exchange
Chavannes, Albert, on social exchange theory, 194–5
Circular exchange, of Malinowski, 30, 124, 125
Coleman, J. S., 180, 181, 182
Collective conscience, according to Durkheim, 40, 65–6
Collective unconscious, according to Lévi-Strauss, 40
Collectivistic sociology, 5–9
of Durkheim, 6–7, 8, 39, 40–2
of Lévi-Strauss, 39, 40–1

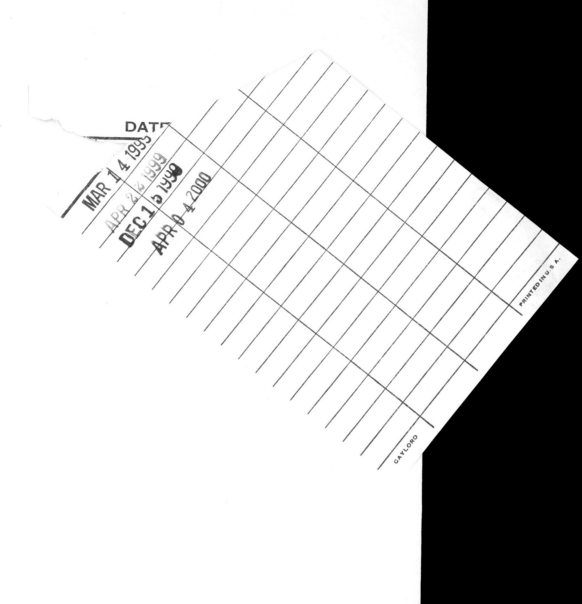